MEDALS OF THE BRITISH ARMY

THE INDIAN MUTINY MEDAL 1857–1858.

MEDALS OF THE BRITISH ARMY,
and how they were won

by
THOMAS CARTER
Author of "Curiosities of War, and Military Studies"

What is a ribbon worth to a soldier?
Everything! Glory is priceless!
Sir E.B. LYTTON, BART.

INDIA, CHINA, ETC.

dedicated by permission to
GENERAL LORD CLYDE, G.C.B.

First published **1861**

Lancer • New Delhi • Frankfort, IL
www.lancerpublishers.com

LANCER

Published in the United States by

The Lancer International Inc
19558 S. Harlem Ave., Suite 1,
Frankfort, IL. 60423.

First published in India by

Lancer Publishers & Distributors
2/42 (B) Sarvapriya Vihar,
New Delhi-110016

ISBN-13: 978-1-935501-25-1 • ISBN-10: 1-935501-25-9

Online Military Bookshop
www.lancerpublishers.com

IDR Net Edition
www.indiandefencereview.com

To

General Lord Clyde, G,C.B.,

Etc., Etc., Etc.,

The Accompanying Pages,

Forming The Third and Concluding Section of

The Medals of the British Army,

Are, with Permission,

Most Respectfully Dedicated,

By his Very Obedient Faithful Servant,

Thomas Carter.

CONTENTS

INDIA, CHINA, ETC.

PLATES

THE INDIAN WAR MEDAL
1799–1826

The Medal for the Peninsular War was shortly afterwards followed by a companion one for the several campaigns in India. On the 21st. of March, 1851, a General Order was issued, announcing that The Queen had been pleased to signify her assent to a measure that had been proposed by the Court of Directors of the East India Company, of granting a medal to the surviving officers and soldiers of the Crown, who were engaged in the following services in India:—Storm of Allighur, September 4th., 1803; Battle of Delhi, September 11th., 1803; Battle of Assye, September 23rd., 1803; Siege of Asseer Ghur, October 21st., 1803; Battle of Laswarree, November 1st., 1803; Battle of Argaum, November 29th., 1803; Siege and Storm of Gawilghur, December 15th., 1803; Defence of Delhi, October, 1804; Battle of Deig, November 13th., 1804; Capture of Deig, December 23rd., 1804; War in Nepaul in 1816; Battle of Kirkee, and Battle and Capture of Poona, November, 1817; Battle of Seetabuldee, and Battle and Capture of Nagpoor, November and December, 1817; Battle of Maheidpore,

December 21st., 1817; Defence of Corygaum, January 1st., 1818; War in Ava, 1824 to 1826; and Siege and Storm of Bhurtpore, January, 1826.

The mode of application was similar to that specified in the General Order granting the War Medal, (see page 14 of the Second Section of this work;) but the concluding paragraph announced that, "It having, moreover, been represented to Her Majesty, that the officers and soldiers of the Crown, who were engaged in the Mysore war, and at the Siege of Seringapatam have already received medals from the East India Company for those services, Her Majesty has further been graciously pleased to permit the same to be worn by them with their uniforms."

Following the order of date, the first service is

THE MYSORE WAR AND SIEGE OF SERINGAPATAM.
FEBRUARY TO MAY, 1799.

Although the reduction of the power and resources of Tippoo Saib, effected by the treaty of Seringapatam, which terminated the campaign of 1792, had weakened his influence, yet it had not extinguished the evils consequent on his intense hatred of the British. The Sultan had entered into a negotiation with the Governor of the Isle of France, in 1798, and sent an embassy to Zemaun Shah, Sovereign of Cabool, for the purpose of inducing him to attack the possessions of the Company. Having also derived encouragement from the successes of the French arms in Egypt, from which country the Directory intended to act against the British dominions in India, Tippoo commenced augmenting his military force, and his hostile designs became every day more apparent. The Governor-General the Earl of Mornington (afterwards Marquis of Wellesley) perceiving a rupture inevitable, resolved to anticipate the attack, and ordered the army to take the field, and march into the heart of Tippoo's territory.

Major-General George (afterwards Lord) Harris, who was serving with the local rank of Lieutenant-General, in conformity to these orders, advanced with the army under his command on the 11th. of February, 1799, and entered the Mysore territory on the 5th. of March. On the 27th. the troops arrived at Mallavelly, and on approaching the ground of encampment the forces of Tippoo were seen drawn up on a height a few miles off. The enemy attacked the advanced pickets, and a general action ensued, in which the 33rd. regiment highly distinguished itself. A body of two thousand men moved forward in the best order towards the regiment, which, firmly standing its ground, coolly reserved its fire until within a distance of about sixty yards, and then led by its Lieutenant-Colonel, the Honourable Arthur Wellesley, in person, boldly advanced, and charging with the bayonet, compelled the approaching column to give way. This movement being seconded by Major-General Floyd, who made a rapid charge with the cavalry, completed the disorder, and the enemy retreated before the whole of the British line, which immediately moved forward.

While this attack was being made by the left wing, under Lieutenant-Colonel the Honourable Arthur Wellesley, with the Nizam's contingent, the 33rd., and Major-General Floyd's cavalry, Lieutenant-General Harris with the troops, which formed the right wing, had been also engaged.*

In this affair Tippoo sustained a loss of nearly two thousand, including some of his most valuable officers; whilst the British casualties amounted to only sixty-six men.

---

* As the 12th. Foot moved forward, a large body of Mysorean cavalry formed in the shape of a wedge, having an elephant with a howdah on his back in front, appeared advancing to charge the regiment, and the British line halted to receive the attack. Immediately afterwards two other very large bodies of the enemy were discovered in two topes or woods, preparing to support the first charge. Lieutenant-General Harris, seeing the danger which menaced the regiment, placed himself in its rear, frequently repeating the words, 'Steady, Twelfth!' 'Steady, old Twelfth!' and when the wedge approached within a hundred yards of the line, the Mysoreans discharged their carbines and pistols, but without doing execution. The 12th. remained steady, with their muskets at the recover, until the enemy arrived within about thirty yards, when a well-directed volley, followed by a rapid file firing, carried destruction into the enemy's ranks; a rampart of killed and wounded men and horses lying along the front of the regiment. The rear of the wedge was embarrassed by the killed and wounded in front, and could not continue the charge. The elephant was severely wounded, his conductor killed, and the chiefs on his back had fallen, when, turning round, he directed all his fury upon the Mysoreans, overturning everything in his retrograde movement, and producing great havoc with a prodigious chain, which he swayed. A few Mysorean horsemen broke through the regiment, but they were instantly shot in its rear, and the British artillery arriving, and opening its fire, the enemy's cavalry fell back; at the same time the line advanced, and decided the fate of the day at that part of the field; a distant cannonade, however, indicated that the battle was raging elsewhere.

On the following morning the army advanced, and arrived before Seringapatam on the 5th. of April, when preparations for the siege were at once commenced.

An attack was made on an entrenchment of the enemy about six o'clock in the evening of the 20th. of April, in which the flank companies of the 12th. and the 73rd. regiments were employed. This was fully successful, and although the enemy had two hundred and fifty men killed and wounded, and the entrenchment was occupied by about eighteen hundred of Tippoo's infantry, the British had but one man wounded.

The siege was prosecuted with vigour, and a breach being reported practicable on the 3rd. of May, the assault was ordered to take place in the heat of the following day, as the besieged would then be the least prepared to oppose the attack. On this service were employed the ten flank companies of the European corps necessarily left to guard the camp and outposts, followed by the 12th., 33rd., 73rd., and 74th. regiments, three corps of grenadier Sepoys, two hundred of the Nizam's troops, a hundred of the artillery, and the corps of pioneers, the whole under the orders of Major-General (afterwards Sir David) Baird. The assault took place about half-past one o'clock in the afternoon of the 4th. of May, and in a short space of time the British colours waved over the fortress.* The Major-General had divided his force for the purpose of clearing the ramparts to the right and left; one division was commanded by Colonel Sherbrooke, and the other by Lieutenant-Colonel Dunlop; the latter was wounded, but both corps, although strongly opposed, were completely successful. The spirited attack, led by Lieutenant-Colonel Campbell, of the 74th. Highlanders, was particularly mentioned in general orders, in which all the officers and men were thanked for this memorable achievement. The body of Tippoo Sultan was found among heaps of slain, and was afterwards interred in the magnificent mausoleum which he had erected over the

---

* Eight stand of colours were captured by the 12th. Foot. A forlorn hope of each attack consisted of a sergeant and twelve Europeans, followed by two subaltern's parties; that of the right column, under Lieutenant Hill, of the 74th., and that of the left column, commanded by Lieutenant Lawrence, of the 77th., the father of sons subsequently memorable in Indian annals, and especially during the recent mutiny.

tomb of his father, the once powerful Hyder Ali, a portion of the victorious troops attending the ceremony.

In this manner terminated the siege of Seringapatam, and the fall of the capital placed the kingdom of Mysore at the disposal of the British government, and destroyed a power in India which had proved itself a formidable enemy.

During the siege the Anglo-Indian troops sustained the following casualties:—Europeans, twenty-two officers killed, and forty-five wounded; non-commissioned officers and men, one hundred and eighty-one killed, and one hundred and twenty-two wounded; native soldiers, one hundred and nineteen killed, and four hundred and twenty wounded: twenty-five of the above officers were killed and wounded in the assault.

The following regiments received the Royal permission to bear on their standards, colours, and appointments, the word "SERINGAPATAM," in commemoration of their gallantry in the storming and capture of that city and fortress on the 4th. of May, 1799; namely, the 19th. and 22nd. (late 25th.,) Light Dragoons, (both since disbanded;) the 12th., 33rd., 73rd., 74th., 75th., 77th. regiments, and the Scots Brigade, afterwards the 94th. regiment.*

---

* This was the old 94th., and not the present regiment, which was only ordered to be raised in December, 1823. The former was known for years, as the Scots Brigade before receiving its numerical title on the 25th. of December, 1802. This corps had been formed in 1568, for service in Holland against the oppression of Spain. Being a British corps, it was demanded from the United Provinces by King James II., on the rebellion of the Duke of Monmouth, in 1685, after the suppression of which it returned to Holland. It again embarked for England with the Prince of Orange, at the revolution of 1688, and remained there until the Protestant cause had been established, when it re-embarked for Flanders in 1691, and served in the campaigns of King William III. It remained in the service of Holland until 1793, until it was decided by King George III., upon the application of the British officers remaining in it, to require the corps to return to Great Britain. It was taken on the British establishment on the 5th. of July, 1793. It then consisted of three battalions; in 1795 it was reduced to two battalions, and embarked for Gibraltar. In 1796 it was formed into one battalion, and embarked for the Cape of Good Hope; it proceeded in 1798 to the East Indies, from whence it returned to England in 1808. It embarked for Cadiz and Lisbon, and served in the Peninsular War from January, 1810, to July, 1814. It was disbanded at Belfast on the 24th. of December, 1818.

THE SERINGAPATAM MEDAL,* 1799.

This medal was distributed to officers and soldiers—European and Native—on one side of it is represented the storming of the breach of Seringapatam, from an actual drawing on the spot, with the meridian sun, denoting the time of the storm, and the following inscription in Persian underneath:—"The Fort of Seringapatam, the gift of God, the 4th. May, 1799." On the reverse side is the BRITISH LION subduing the TIGER, the emblem of the late Tippoo Sultan's Government, with the period when it was effected, and the following words in Arabic on the banner:—"ASSUD OTTA-UL GHAULIB," signifying the Lion of God is the Conqueror, or the Conquering Lion of God.

---

* For the specimen of the ribbon of the Seringapatam medal I have to acknowledge my obligations to Albert Woods, Esq., Lancaster Herald, and Inspector of Regimental Colours, who has furnished me with much valuable information on this and other points. From a letter addressed to him by the gallant General Sir James L. Caldwell, G.C.B., now in his 91st. year, in reply to a query on this subject, the following interesting particulars have been afforded:– When the medal was issued no ribbon accompanied it, but the recipients were given to understand that it was to be of a deep yellow colour, and about an inch in width. This colour was adopted in reference to the tiger, selected by the Sultan Tippoo as his favourite insignia, the golden throne found in the palace being constructed on the back of that animal, and his chosen Sepoys being clothed in tiger jackets. The head of this animal of the throne is now at Windsor Castle, having been obtained by the Marquis of Wellesley from the prize agents, together with the ideal and fictitious bird termed the "Hume," supposed to ensure perpetual royalty to the person over whose head it is suspended, and being regarded as a bird of Mahomedan Paradise: it is shown to strangers under the misnomer of the Seringapatam Peacock. The above information was accompanied by a piece of the ribbon, the colour of which resembles the light fur of the tiger. It may be added that the name Tippoo signifies Tiger, and that the tiger-stripe was adopted in the uniform of the Sultan's infantry. In the United Service Museum, amongst other oriental curiosities, are two of Tippoo's pistols, having a tiger's head at the end, and also the dress he wore when killed. The famous organ of Tippoo representing a tiger tearing a prostrate British soldier is in the East Indian Museum, together with his suit of chain armour. When the handle of the organ is turned sounds are emitted similar to the shrieks of a human being and the growl of the animal.

A medal was also granted by the Indian Government for the Mysore campaign of 1791–1792, but its issue appears to have been limited to the Company's troops, the above being the first medal authorized to be worn by the Sovereign. Mr. Hudson, whose kindness I have already acknowledged, has a specimen in his valuable collection, and there is also one at the United Service Museum. It is of silver, and on the obverse is represented an English soldier holding the British standard half unfurled, with a distant view of the fortifications of Seringapatam. On the reverse is a Persian inscription, of which the following is a translation:—"Struck in the years 1791–1792," (corresponding with the Mahomedan era 1202.) "A memento of the self-sacrificing devotion of the servants of the British Government in Mysore."

THE SERINGAPATAM MEDAL 1799.

Of these medals gold ones were struck for His Majesty, the Right Honourable Lord Melville, the Governor-General of India at the time, the Marquis Cornwallis, the Nizam and his two ministers, the Peishwah and his minister, the Nabobs of Arcot and Oude, and the Rajahs of Tanjore, Travancore, Mysore, Coorga, and Berar, Dowlut Rao Scindiah, the Commander-in-Chief, general officers on the staff employed in the Service, and for the Oriental Museum.

Silver gilt medals were struck for the members of council at the three Presidencies, the Residents of Hydrabad and Poonah, the field officers, and the general staff on the service. Silver for the captains and subalterns, copper-bronzed for the non-commissioned officers, and pure grain tin for the privates. The European officers of the Company's service received permission in August, 1815, to wear the Seringapatam Medal. On the 16th. of that month the following representation was made to the Right Honourable the Earl of Buckinghamshire:—

"My Lord,

"Medals having been struck by the Court of Directors, with the approbation and concurrence of His Majesty's Ministers, in commemoration of the storming of Seringapatam, and of the other splendid successes of the British Army in Mysore, in 1799; to be executed by an eminent artist, and distributed to the officers and soldiers, both of His Majesty's and of the Company's troops, who served in that brilliant and decisive campaign.

"The European officers of the Company's Service have represented to us that highly as they have been gratified with the receipt of those honourable bestowments, they experienced considerable mortification in not feeling themselves at liberty to wear them on great public occasions, such as being presented at Court, and at the Military Levees of His Royal Highness the Commander-in-Chief.

"This sentiment necessarily strikes them with peculiar force at the present period, when all the officers of Europe, who have distinguished themselves in the service of their several Sovereigns, appear upon all public occasions, decorated with the honourable badges of their services and glory.

"We therefore intreat your Lordship to transmit these circumstances to His Royal Highness the Prince Regent, and to solicit his gracious permission, that the medals granted by the East India Company, upon the occasion of the capture of Seringapatam by storm on the 4th. of May, 1799, and the other splendid successes of the British Army in Mysore in that year, may be worn by the officers, who have received them, in such manner, and at such times as to His Highness may appear proper.

"We have, etc.,

"CHARLES GRANT.
"THOMAS READ."

This request was complied with in a letter, dated Whitehall, 29th. August, 1815, of which the accompanying is an extract:—

"Gentlemen,

"His Royal Highness has been pleased to grant his gracious permission that such officers may wear their medals in any part of His Majesty's dominions.

"I have, etc.,

"To the Chairman and   (Signed) BUCKINGHAMSHIRE."
Deputy-Chairman."

STORM OF ALLIGHUR.
4TH. SEPTEMBER, 1803.

This service occurred during the Mahratta war. The empire of the Mahrattas, of which Sevajee was the founder, had become a confederacy of five chieftains, the Peishwah, Scindiah, Holkar, the Rajah of Berar, and the Guicowar; each of whom, although acknowledging a kind of fealty to the descendant of Sevajee, was independent of the other. The Peishwah, who was regarded as the nominal head of the confederation, was considered only as an instrument in the hands of the strongest. Dowlut Rao Scindiah, who ruled over Malwa and Candeish, had acquired an absolute control in the councils of Bajee Rao, the Peishwah, and was regarded with great jealousy by his rival, Holkar. Both these chieftains had armies officered by Europeans, principally Frenchmen.

Holkar suddenly crossed the Nerbudda, marched on Poonah, and having defeated the united troops of Scindiah and the Peishwah, the latter placed himself under the protection of the British, and after his restoration, in May, 1803, it was ascertained that Scindiah was in negotiation with Holkar and the Berar Rajah, with a view to subvert the British alliance with the Peishwah. After the evasions and procrastinations inseparable from oriental diplomacy, hostilities commenced, Major-General the Honourable Arthur Wellesley being appointed to the chief command of the British and allied troops in the territories of the Peishwah, of the Nizam, and of any Mahratta state; subject alone to the orders of General Stuart and General Lake, the Commander-in-Chief in India.

General Lake was instructed to conquer the whole of Scindiah's territority between the Jumna and the Ganges, to seize upon Delhi and Agra, and to destroy the army commanded by General Perron, a French officer. On the 7th. of August, 1803, the troops advanced from Cawnpore, and entered the Mahratta territory on the morning of the 29th. of that month. Perron occupied a strong position, with about fifteen thousand men, in the vicinity of Coel. General Lake resolved to turn his left flank, against which he advanced, but the enemy retired after firing a few rounds, without venturing a regular engagement; the rapidity of his flight rendering the several attempts made to charge him quite ineffectual. After this affair, Perron took up a position between the town of Coel and the fortress of Allighur, and every effort to induce the governor to surrender proving unsuccessful, the necessary arangements were made for the assault of the fort.

Allighur was a place of considerable strength, the country being levelled around and open to its fire in every direction. It was provided with a broad ditch and a fine glacis, and had only one entrance, which was very intricate, and over a narrow causeway. On the 4th. of September, a storming party, consisting of four companies of the 76th., with two battalions and four companies of native infantry, was placed under the orders of the Honourable Lieutenant-Colonel Monson. At half-past four o'clock in the morning it had advanced within a few hundred yards of the place before being discovered;

when, a tremendous fire being opened, the colonel rushed forward with the flank companies of the regiment, in the hope of being able to enter the main gateway with a fugitive guard which had been stationed in a breastwork outside the place. In this he was disappointed, and, as the enemy's cross fire was very severe, Major Macleod, and two grenadiers of the regiment, endeavoured to scale the wall, but encountered each a powerful phalanx of pikemen that they were compelled to fall back. A gun was with some difficulty placed opposite to the gate, which, after a few discharges, was blown open. During these operations the party for twenty minutes was exposed to a raking fire of grape, wall-pieces, and matchlocks. Colonel Monson was severely wounded by a pike discharged from a gun, and the adjutant and four officers of grenadiers were killed.

After clearing the first gate, a long and intricate passage conducted the troops, in the midst of a heavy cross fire, through a second and third gateway, which were easily forced, to a fourth, that led immediately into the body of the place. With great difficulty the gun was brought up, but the gate could not be blown open. At last the grenadiers, with Major Macleod at their head, succeeded in pushing through the wicket, and mounted the ramparts, after which but little opposition was offered by the Mahrattas, who for the space of an hour had made a most vigorous defence. They lost about two thousand men, while the casualties of the assailants were likewise severe. Of the 76th., Captain Cameron, Lieutenants Fleming, Brown, Campbell, and St. Aubyn, with fifteen rank and file were killed; Lieutenant-Colonel Monson, Major Macleod, Lieutenant Sinclair, Ensign Fraser, and three sergeants, one drummer, and fifty-eight rank and file were wounded.

As Allighur was the chief residence and principal depot of General Perron, a large quantity of ordnance and military stores were captured, and several carriages were found laden with treasure, which the victors divided amongst themselves on the spot. A few days after the fall of this fortress, General Perron withdrew from the Mahratta service; his popularity amongst the natives had excited the jealousy of

Scindiah, whose conduct would have palliated a severe retaliation; but the high-minded Frenchman, disdaining an unworthy action, resigned the command under circumstances most honourable to his personal character. The 76th. may feel proud of the praise which was bestowed upon the regiment and its officers by the Governor-General for their gallantry.*

BATTLE OF DELHI.
11TH. SEPTEMBER, 1803.

Although General Perron had been permitted to enter the British territories, the troops which he had commanded still remained under other officers. Having left a sufficient force at Allighur, the British proceeded towards Delhi on the 7th. of September. After a fatiguing march of eighteen miles, and when, on the 11th. of that month, they had arrived within two leagues of the city, information was received that M. Louis Bourquein, another French officer in command of Scindiah's army, had crossed the Jumna with a numerous force, in order to attack General Lake. This intelligence was quickly confirmed by an attack upon the outlying pickets which had just been posted.

The British commander immediately proceeded with the whole of his cavalry to reconnoitre the enemy, and found them drawn up in order of battle on a rising ground, their flanks resting on a morass, while the front was defended by a line of entrenchments and a formidable artillery. As it was considered impossible to make any impression upon so excellent a position by a direct attack, stratagem was employed to induce them to quit it. The cavalry, which had proceeded considerably in advance, were directed to fall back before the Mahrattas, and afterwards to form behind the right

---

* "I think that General Lake's capture of Allighur is one of the most extraordinary feats that I have heard of in this country. I never attacked a fort that I did not attempt the same thing, namely, to blow open the gates; but I never succeeded. I have always taken them by escalade, which appears to have been impossible in this instance."—*The Wellington Dispatches.*

This practice of blowing open the gates has since, on more than one occasion, been successfully practised in India.

wing of the infantry. This manoeuvre was completely successful; the cavalry retired, while the infantry were quickly formed, and advanced in line, under a tremendous cannonade of round, grape, and chain shot. Nothing could exceed the steadiness of the troops; no man took his musket from his shoulder until arrived within a proper distance of the enemy. A volley was fired, and General Lake, placing himself at the head of the 76th., the whole line rushed forward to the charge with an impetuosity which it was impossible to withstand. Thrown into confusion, the Mahrattas fled in the utmost consternation, while the cavalry, dashing forward, completed the work which their irresistible companions had so well commenced.

By this splendid victory sixty-eight pieces of cannon, two tumbrils laden with treasure, and thirty-seven with ammunition, fell into the hands of the conquerors. The loss of the enemy was estimated at three thousand men out of thirteen thousand infantry, (nearly all regular troops,) and six thousand cavalry, which had been brought into the field. Of the British, who had four thousand engaged, four hundred and eighty-five were killed, wounded, and missing. The 76th., the only King's regiment at Allighur, Delhi, or at the subsequent battle at Laswarree, had two sergeants and thirty-one rank and file killed; Lieutenant Alexander Macdonald, one sergeant, and ninety-six rank and file were wounded.

Delhi was entered without opposition, and the venerable and blind emperor, Shah Aulum, the nominal sovereign of Hindostan, who had been for years in the hands of the Mahrattas, was restored to his throne.

In testimony of the gallantry of the troops under General Lake, the Governor-General in council ordered honorary colours, with a suitable device, commemorative of the reduction of Allighur and the battle of Delhi, to be presented to all. Those granted* to the 27th. Dragoons (since disbanded) and the 76th. regiment, were to be used by these corps while

---

* The 19th. Dragoons, (since disbanded,) the 74th. and 78th. regiments, had honorary colours for Assye conferred by the Governor-General of India. In consequence, however, of the inconvenience occasioned by taking a third officer from his duty to carry it, the 74th. received the orders of the Commander-in-Chief on the 81st. of August, 1830, to discontinue the use of the third colour in the field, and to carry it only at reviews, inspections, and on gala days.

they continued in India, or until His Majesty's pleasure should be signified.

BATTLE OF ASSYE.
23RD. SEPTEMBER, 1803.

This was the battle which gained a name for the illustrious Duke of Wellington, and it is commemorated on the colours of the 74th. and 78th. regiments. On the 21st. of September, Major-General the Honourable Arthur Wellesley had a conference with Colonel Stevenson, and a plan was concerted to attack the enemy's army with the divisions under their command on the 24th. This intention was not carried out, as circumstances occurred which determined the former to attack without waiting for the junction of the troops.

On the 23rd. of September, while on the march, it was discovered that the enemy was much nearer than was imagined; whereupon Major-General Wellesley immediately determined to move in advance to reconnoitre them, and if convenient bring them to action. He ordered the cavalry to mount, and went on with them for this purpose; the infantry, except the rear battalion, (1st. of the 2nd. Native Infantry,) received directions to follow by the right. The second of the 12th. to join the left brigade to equalize the two; the first of the second to cover the baggage on the ground marked for the camp, and to be joined by the rear-guard on its arrival, and the four brass light twelve-pounders of the park to be sent to the heads of the line.

These dispositions did not occasion ten minutes' halt to the column of infantry, but the cavalry moving in front with the Major-General, came first in sight of the enemy's position, from a rising ground to the left of the road, and within cannon-shot of the right of their encampment, which lay along one of the banks of the River Kaitna, a stream of no magnitude, but with steep sides and a very deep channel, so as not to be passable except in particular places, mostly near villages. Along their rear ran a similar stream, (the Jooee Nullah,) which fell into the Kaitna half a mile beyond their left. Scindiah's irregular cavalry formed their right, and the Berar troops their left. These were composed of seventeen battalions, amounting to about ten thousand five hundred men, formed into three brigades, each of which had a corps of cavalry of a better kind than the rest, and a body of skilled marksmen; and the artillery amounted to about one hundred and two pieces, or perhaps a few more.

The infantry were dressed, armed, and accoutred like the Sepoys; they were remarkably fine bodies of men, and in a high state of discipline. Although the English officers had left them, there was a number of French and other European officers both with the infantry and artillery. The guns were served by Golundaze, exactly like those of the Bengal service, which had been some time before disbanded, and were probably the same men. It was soon, however, found that they were extremely well trained, and that their fire was both as quick and as well-directed as could be produced by the Company's artillerymen. What the total number of the enemy was cannot be ascertained, or even guessed at with any degree of accuracy, but it is certainly calculated very low at thirty thousand men, including the light troops who were out on a plundering excursion, (and were those which had marched in the morning,) but they returned towards the close of the action.

In the field were the two Rajahs, attended by their principal ministers; and, it being the day of the Dusserah Feast, the Hindoos, of which their force was chiefly composed, had religious prejudices to make them fight with spirit, and to hope for victory.

The force of Major-General Wellesley's army in action was nearly four thousand seven hundred men, of whom about one thousand five hundred were Europeans, including artillery with twenty-six field-pieces, of which only four twelve and eight six-pounders were fired during the action; the remainder being the guns of the cavalry and of the second line, could not be used.

On the Major-General's approaching the enemy for the purpose of reconnoitring, they commenced a cannonade, the first gun of which was fired at twenty minutes past one, p.m., and killed one of his escort. He then resolved to attack their left, in order to turn it, and ordered the infantry column to move in that direction, while some of his staff looked out for a ford, to enable his troops to cross the Kaitna and execute this movement. All this march being performed considerably within the reach of the enemy's cannon, the fire increased fast, and by the time the head of the column reached the ford, about a short half-mile beyond their left flank, it was tremendously heavy, and had already destroyed numbers.

During this movement the first line of the enemy's infantry changed their front to the left, and formed with their left on Assye, or Assaye, a village on the Jooee, near the left of their second line, which did not change position, the right of their first line resting on the Kaitna, where the left had been. They brought up many guns from their reserve, and the second line to the first.

Being obliged to cross the ford in one column by sections, the British were long exposed to the cannonade. The first line formed nearly parallel to that of the enemy, at about five hundred yards distance, having marched down the alignment to its ground. The second line rather out-flanked the first to the right, as did the third (composed of the cavalry) the second. The left of the first line was opposite the right of the enemy's. During this formation their artillery fired round shot with great precision and rapidity, the same shot often striking the three lines. It was answered by the guns of the first line of the British with great spirit and coolness, but the number of gun bullocks killed soon put the advance of the artillery (except by men) out of the question.

The British lines were formed from right to left as follows:—First line; pickets, four twelve-pounders, one battalion of the 8th. and one of the 10th. Native Infantry, and the 78th. regiment. Second line; 74th. regiment, and the second battalion of the 12th. and the first of the 4th. Native Infantry. Third line; 4th. Native Cavalry, 19th. Light Dragoons, 5th. and 7th. Native Cavalry.

Orders were then given for each battalion to attach a

company to protect and assist the guns during the advance; this was immediately afterwards countermanded, but the order did not reach the 78th., consequently the 8th. battalion company, commanded by Lieutenant Cameron, remained attached to them. Major-General the Honourable Arthur Wellesley then named the picket as the battalion of direction, and ordered that the line should advance as quickly as possible, consistent with order, and charge with the bayonet, without firing a shot.

At fifteen minutes before three the word was given for the line to advance, and was received by Europeans and natives with a cheer. Almost immediately, however, it was discovered that the battalion of direction was not moving forward as intended, and the first line received the word to halt. This was a critical moment; the troops had reached the ridge of a little swell in the ground that had somewhat sheltered them, particularly on the left, and the enemy, supposing them staggered by the fire, redoubled their efforts, firing a number of chain shot with great effect. Dreading the consequences of this check to the ardour of the troops, the Major-General rode up to one of the native corps of the first line, and, taking off his hat, cheered them on in their own language, repeating the words "to march." Again the soldiers received the order with loud cheers, and the three left battalions of the first line, followed by the first battalion of the 4th., advanced in quick time, and with the greatest coolness, order, and determination upon their opponents.

On coming within about one hundred and fifty yards, the 78th. withdrew its advanced centre sergeant, and the men were cautioned to be ready to charge. Soon after the battalion opposed to them fired a volley, and about the same time some Europeans were observed to mount their horses and ride off. The 78th. instantly ported arms, cheered, and redoubled its pace, when the enemy's infantry, deserted by their officers, broke and ran. The 78th. pushed on and fired, the front rank to the charge, overtaking and bayonetting a few individuals. But Scindiah's gunners held firm by their guns; many were bayonetted in the acts of loading, priming, or pointing, and none quitted them until the bayonet was at the breast.

Almost at the same instant the first battalion of the 16th. closed with the enemy, and in the most gallant style. The smoke and the dust (which, aided by a brisk wind, in the faces of the British was very great,) prevented them seeing any further to the right.

The 78th. now halted for an instant to complete the files and restore exact order, and then moved forward on the enemy's second line, making a complete wheel to the right, whose pivot was the right of the army, near the village of Assye.

In consequence of the pickets having failed to advance the 74th. pushed up, in doing which they were very much cut down by grape, and at length charged by cavalry headed by Scindiah in person. They suffered severely, (as did the pickets and the second battalion of the 12th. Native Infantry,) and the remains were saved by the memorable charge of the cavalry, commanded by Lieutenant-Colonel Maxwell. This part of the British line, however, though it broke the enemy's first line, did not gain much ground; and the foe still continued in possession of several guns about the village of Assye, from which they flanked the British line when arrived opposite their second.

Several of the enemy also coming up from the beds of the river and other ways, attacked and killed a large proportion of the artillerymen, amongst whom were four officers. They also regained possession of many of the guns of their first line, which had been taken and passed, and from them opened a fire of grape on the British rear. The guns, with the escort of the 78th. Highlanders, before mentioned, escaped and joined the regiment when halted opposite the enemy's second line.

The British infantry was now in one line, the 78th. regiment still on the left of the whole, and as it had the longest sweep to make in the wheel, it came up last. When the dust cleared a body of the enemy's best cavalry was seen in front of the left flank, purposing to turn it, on which the left wing of the 78th. regiment was thrown back at a small angle, and preparations were made for opening the two guns, which at that moment came up.

It is impossible to praise too highly the behaviour of the infantry at this critical moment. Deprived of the assistance of their artillery, the enemy's second line being untouched and perfectly fresh in their front, firing steadily upon them, flanked by round shot from the right, grape pouring on the rear, and cavalry threatening the left. Not a word was heard or a shot fired, all waiting the orders of the general with the composure of a field day, amidst a scene of slaughter scarcely to be equalled. This, however, was not of long duration. The British cavalry came up and drove off the body that threatened the left, who did not wait to be charged, when Major-General Wellesley ordered the principal part of the line to attack the front, while the 78th. and 7th. Native Cavalry moved to the rear, and charged the guns which were firing from thence. The enemy's second line immediately retired; one brigade in perfect order, so much so that it repulsed a gallant charge of the 19th. Dragoons, at the head of which Colonel Maxwell was killed.

After being obliged to change front two or three times under the fire of grape, the 78th. succeeded in clearing the guns in the rear. The enemy's light troops, that had been out, now came on the ground, and were ordered to be attacked by the Mysore Horse, which they did not wait for, and the firing entirely ceased. About half-past four o'clock the enemy had set fire to all their tumbrils, which blew up in succession, many of them some time later; and the corps which had retired in such good order appear soon to have lost it, for they threw their guns into the river, four of which were afterwards found, exclusive of ninety-eight left on the field of battle.

Thus terminated the battle of Assye, or Assaye, the first victory gained by the Iron Duke in which he commanded in chief, and one of the most decisive as well as the most desperate at this period ever fought in India. The British loss was very great; of Europeans, killed and wounded, including artillery and officers, there were upwards of six hundred, and the natives were estimated at about nine hundred. ASSAYE is borne on the colours of the 74th. and 78th. regiments;* the

---

* The 19th. Light Dragoons, who had their commanding officer, Lientenant-Colonel

former had one hundred and twenty-four killed and two hundred and seventy wounded, and the latter had twenty-nine killed and seventy-six wounded. On the clasp of the medal it is spelt Assye.

Scindiah's first minister, who was considered the principal instigator of the war, and his principal French officer, Colonel Dorson, were killed, with about one thousand two hundred men, and three thousand wounded; such at least was under-stood afterwards to be their calculation, but as their army was so much dispersed it must have been an approximation. Their troops retired about ten miles along the Jooee, unpursued by the victors, and halted there about two hours, when they moved again towards Adjanta, proceeding down that ghaut into Candeish, at which time, from the reports of the people of the place, they had no guns, nor any body of men that looked like a regular battalion.

At sunset the British collected about the village of Assye, and lay on their arms all night, except the cavalry, which, after resting some hours, were sent back to assist in escorting the baggage; and about ten in the morning of the 24th. the troops were encamped on the left bank of the Kaitna, on the ground the column had moved over previous to crossing the ford into the field of battle. That evening at sunset the cavalry and one battalion of Native Infantry of Colonel Stevenson's division arrived, and the next morning (25th.) the remainder of his force, which a day or two afterwards were ordered to follow the enemy into Candeish, and to possess themselves of the city of Berhampore and the hill fort of Asseer Ghur.

Maxwell, killed, and the 74th. and 78th. regiments received honorary colours as stated in note at page 12. In the latter part of the action Major-General the Honourable Arthur Wellesley had a horse killed under him close to the 78th. Nearly all the mounted officers lost horses, some having two and even three killed. No part of the Mysore or Mahratta allies were engaged; their Infantry was left with the baggage, and the cavalry not being in uniform it was apprehended that mistakes might have arisen had they been brought into action.

SIEGE OF ASSEER GHUR.
21st. October, 1803.

Colonel Stevenson obtained possession of the city of Berhampore without opposition on the 15th. of October, 1803, and two days afterwards marched to Asseer Ghur, a strong fort in that vicinity. Having carried the pettah on the 18th., he opened a battery against the fort on the 20th.; about an hour afterwards a white flag was hoisted, which was the signal that had been agreed upon in case the terms of surrender, offered two days previously, should be accepted; hostages were sent down, and it was arranged that this important fortress should be delivered over on the following morning. This was the last of the possessions of Dowlut Rao Scindiah in the Deccan, and the operations of the troops were subsequently directed towards those of the Rajah of Berar. The casualties were trifling, and were confined to the native troops.

BATTLE OF LASWARREE.
1st. November, 1803.

On the 27th. of October, the British advanced against a division of the enemy, formed of two battalions which had escaped from the wreck at Delhi, and fifteen, which had been detached from the main army of Scindiah to support General Perron in the early part of the campaign. These troops amounting to nine thousand infantry and four thousand cavalry, and provided with a train of seventy-two pieces of cannon, had been directed to recover possession of Delhi. After great exertions the British cavalry came up with them about seven o'clock in the morning of the 1st. of November; they were discovered in an excellent position; their right resting on a rivulet, their left on the village of Laswarree, or Leswarree, and their whole front amply furnished with a powerful artillery. Being anxious to prevent their escape, General Lake immediately attacked them with the cavalry alone. The first brigade, under Colonel Thomas Pakenham Vandeleur,* of the 8th Dragoons, who fell mortally wounded, charged their lines, and dashed into the village; but finding that their attacks on the masses of infantry could make no sensible impression, the cavalry were withdrawn out of the range of the destructive fire of artillery which it encountered, in order to wait the arrival of the infantry and artillery. About eleven o'clock in the forenoon, the Anglo-Indian infantry arrived, but after so long a march, it was absolutely necessary to allow the men to refresh themselves, and during this interval Scindiah's forces offered to surrender their guns if certain terms were conceded.

After a fruitless negotiation, the infantry, which had been formed into two columns, were ordered to advance to the attack. The first of these headed by the 76th. regiment, under Major Macleod, was to turn the enemy's right, which since the morning had been thrown back from the rivulet, and to attack the village of Mohaulpoor, situated between his two lines; while the second and a brigade of cavalry were to support them in the execution of this movement. When the enemy perceived the direction of this attack he formed his right *en potence,* and opened a terrific fire upon the advancing columns. Having encountered several impediments, the rear divisions were so retarded in their march, that a considerable interval was occasioned between them and the 76th., which had arrived within a hundred yards of the foe. In this situation the regiment was exposed to such a dreadful fire, and was losing so many men, that the Commander-in-Chief placing himself at its head, led it forward to the attack, supported by only one battalion and six companies of Sepoys, namely, the second battalion of the 12th., and six companies of the second battalion of the 16th. Bengal Native Infantry.

"As soon as this handful of heroes," wrote General Lake, "were arrived within reach of the enemy's canister shot, a most tremendous fire was opened upon them." Their loss was

---

* Colonel Thomas Pakenham Vandeleur rode a celebrated race-horse, of a jet-black colour. Long after the melancholy fate of his rider, this horse kept his place with the regiment, and afterwards became the property of Cornet Burrowes, who took great care of him until the regiment left India, when he was shot, that he might not fall into unworthy hands.

so severe, that the enemy's cavalry advanced to the charge, but were gallantly repulsed by this steady and invincible band. Rallying, however, at a short distance, they assumed so menacing a posture, that the General directed an attack by the British cavalry. This was executed with admirable intrepidity, while the infantry fell upon the Mahratta line, which, after a vigorous resistance, at length gave way. By four o'clock in the afternoon the work of destruction had ceased.

The British loss amounted to one hundred and seventy-two killed, and six hundred and fifty-two wounded, while that of the enemy was most severe; his numerous French-officered battalions of infantry—the boasted "Deccan Invincibles"—were annihilated; his cavalry dispersed; and the baggage and camp equipage, elephants, camels, and bullocks, with forty-four stand of colours, seventy-two guns, sixty-four tumbrils of ammunition, three laden with treasure, and two thousand prisoners, remained in the hands of the victors; five thousand stand of arms were collected on the field.

By this victory, which was mainly gained by the gallantry of the 76th., that regiment acquired great honour, and its "heroic bravery" was borne testimony to in the official despatches. During this campaign the regiment acquired a gurrah, or Indian gong of great value, which was afterwards carried about by the corps; being usually planted opposite the guard room, and a sergeant regularly striking the hours on it.

This decisive action terminated the campaign of 1803 and the war with Scindiah, a treaty of peace highly advantageous to the East India Company being concluded on the 30th. of December.

Hindoostan inscribed around the elephant on the colours of the 76th., keeps in remembrance the services of the regiment in the East at this period. LESWARREE was, however, authorized for the guidons and appointments of the 8th. Hussars, which is the only corps that bears the word. General Lake gained a peerage, being created Baron Lake of Delhi, Leswarree, and Aston Clinton. Several Indian titles were also conferred upon him, which being translated from the Persian, signified Saviour of the State, the hero of the land, the lord of the age, and the victorious in war.

BATTLE OF ARGAUM.
29TH NOVEMBER, 1803

A series of active movements in pursuit of the Rajah of Berar were re-commenced on the 25th. of October, 1803; and on the 29th. of November, Major-General Wellesley, having been joined by the subsidiary force under Colonel Stevenson, encountered the united armies of Scindiah and the Rajah of Berar, on the plains of Argaum. Although late in the day, the Major-General resolved to attack; he formed his army in two lines, the infantry in the first, the cavalry in the second, and supporting the right; and the Mogul and Mysore cavalry the left, nearly parallel to that of the enemy, with the right rather advanced, in order to press upon his left. When formed, the whole advanced in the greatest order; the 74th. and 78th. Highlanders were attacked by a large body, supposed to be Persians, who were all destroyed. "These two regiments," wrote the British general, "had a particular opportunity of distinguishing themselves, and have deserved and received my thanks." The enemy's line retired in disorder, leaving thirty-eight pieces of cannon and all their ammunition; whereupon the British cavalry pursued them for several miles, destroying great numbers, and capturing several elephants and camels, with a considerable quantity of baggage. One hour more of daylight, and not a man would have escaped.

In the orders thanking the army for its exertions on this day, the 74th. and 78th. were particularly mentioned; Colonel Harness being very ill, Lieutenant-Colonel Adams, of the 78th., commanded the right brigade in the action, and Major Scott being in charge of the pickets as field officer of the day, the command of the regiment fell to Captain Fraser. In this battle, as at Assye, a scarcity of officers occasioned the colours of the 78th. to be carried by sergeants, and it is somewhat extraordinary that not a shot penetrated either colour in the two actions; at the latter it was probably owing to the high wind, in consequence of which they were carried rolled close round the poles. The names of the non-commissioned officers who carried them on these memorable occasions were at Assye, Sergeant Leavock, paymaster's clerk, afterwards quarter-master, and Sergeant John Mc Kenzie, senior sergeant, and immediately afterwards quartermaster-sergeant. At Argaum Sergeants Leavock and Grant; the latter was regimental clerk, and was subsequently promoted to a commission in the 78th. Highlanders.

The regiments of the crown engaged were the 19th. Light Dragoons, and the 74th., 78th., and 94th. regiments. The European loss was fifteen killed, and one hundred and forty five wounded; the native troops had thirty-one killed and one hundred and forty-eight wounded.

SIEGE AND STORM OF GAWILGHUR.
15TH. DECEMBER, 1803.

After the victory of Argaum. Major-General the Honourable Arthur Wellesley, resolved to lose no time in commencing the siege of Gawilghur, a strong fort situated on a range of mountains between the. sources of the rivers Poorna and Taptee; he accordingly marched on, and arrived with both divisions at Ellichpoor on the 5th. of December, whence, after establishing an hospital for the men wounded at Argaum, both divisions advanced upon Gawilghur, on the 7th of that month. The heavy ordnance and stores were dragged by hand over mountains and through ravines, for nearly the whole distance, by roads which the troops had to make for themselves. The batteries were opened against the place on the morning of the 13th., and the breach of the outer fort being reported practicable on the following night, the storm took place on the 15th. of December. All the troops advanced about ten in the morning, and an entrance was effected without difficulty. The wall in the inner fort, in which no breach had been made, had then to be carried; when Captain Campbell with the light infantry of the old 94th. escaladed the wall; opened the gates for the stormers, and the fort was shortly in their possession. This service was effected with slight loss, but vast numbers of the enemy were killed, especially at the different gates. The garrison was numerous, comprising a great portion of the infantry which had escaped after the battle of Argaum, and were all armed with the Company's new muskets and bayonets.

The 74th. and 78th. had only two men wounded during the siege; the 94th. had three men killed, and two sergeants and fifty-one men wounded. The total loss of Europeans was limited to five killed and fifty-nine wounded; the Native troops had eight killed and fifty-one wounded.

This led to a treaty with the Rajah of Berar on the 17th. of December, and on the 30th. of the same month, peace was signed with Scindiah.

DEFENCE OF DELHI.
OCTOBER, 1804.

This defence of Delhi by Native troops, under British superintendence, presents a striking contrast to that made by them during the recent Indian Mutiny, against their former instructors in the art of war, and deservedly met with a different result.

As General Lord Lake advanced upon Muttra, Holkar secretly despatched his infantry and artillery for the purpose of surprising Delhi, leaving his cavalry to engage the attention of the British Commander. From its great extent and unprotected state, Holkar expected an easy conquest: his troops arrived before the city on the morning of the 8th of October. Colonel Ochterlony, the resident, at once made the most judicious preparations for its defence; his garrison amounted to nearly two thousand two hundred men, and consisted entirely of Native troops. Lieutenant-Colonel Burn, as senior officer, commanded, and the resident's time was fully taken up in preserving peace within the city, with the Mahomedan population of Delhi. Lieutenant Rose, with two hundred of the 14th. native infantry, one hundred and fifty irregulars, and a reserve of fifty men and a six-pounder, made a sortie during the evening of the 10th., and succeeded in storming the enemy's battery, of which he gained possession, and having spiked the guns, withdrew, with trifling loss. At daybreak on the 14th. of October, under cover of a heavy cannonade, the enemy assaulted the Lahore gate, but were repulsed, leaving the ladders behind, which were drawn up over the walls by the Sepoys. After this defeat Holkar's troops became dispirited, and before the following morning, his whole force had retired from the place. This successful defence by so small a force, was highly applauded, and it is a circumstance worthy of record, that as the men could not be frequently relieved, the resident caused provisions and sweetmeats, of which the natives are specially partial, to be distributed to them.

BATTLE OF DEIG.
13TH. NOVEMBER, 1804.

The British army which had marched from Muttra on the 12th. of October, arrived at Delhi on the 18th., and encamped under its walls. On the 5th. of November the main body of the infantry, of which the 76th. was the only King's regiment, with some corps of native cavalry, and the park of artillery, proceeded under the command of Major-General Frazer towards Deig, on the right bank of the Jumna, where the enemy's infantry and guns were assembled. Although numerically the foe was superior, it was determined to attack him, and about daybreak on the 13th. of November, the action commenced. Major-General Frazer received a dangerous wound from a cannon shot, which carried away his right foot and part of the leg, and resulted in his death eleven days after; whereupon the Honourable Colonel Monson assumed the command. According to the most reliable statements the opposing force consisted of twenty-four battalions, from five to seven hundred men each, a numerous body of cavalry, and one hundred and sixty guns. In this battle the 76th. acquired additional renown; its "undaunted bravery and steadiness" being specially adverted to in the despatches. About two thousand of the enemy were killed and drowned in attempting to escape. Eighty-seven pieces of cannon were captured, including some which Colonel Monson had previously lost.

Sixty-four Europeans were killed, and two hundred and four wounded. The native troops had eighty four killed, and three hundred and fourteen wounded.

CAPTURE OF DEIG.
23RD. DECEMBER, 1804.

When the troops of Holkar fled before the British in the action of the 13th. of November, the guns of the garrison of Deig, which belonged to the Rajah of Bhurtpore, were opened upon the pursuers, and the fugitives were sheltered within the fort. Accordingly an order was issued for the annexation of all his strongholds and territories, to the dominions of the Company; and the army encamped within ten miles of the strong fortress of Deig, on the 3rd. of December. The siege commenced on the 14th. of that month. A fortification had been erected by the foe on an eminence named Shah Bourj, or King's redoubt, which commanded the town and forts; and the besieged had also entrenched themselves in its front, throwing up batteries in the best situations. The possession of this eminence being deemed essential, at half-past eleven o'clock in the night of the 23rd. of December, the flank companies of His Majesty's 22nd. and 76th. Foot, and those of the 1st. European regiment, and the first battalion of the 8th. Native Infantry, were ordered to storm it. In one hour the gallantry of this heroic party had surmounted every obstacle, and completely succeeded in the enterprise. The two other columns were equally fortunate, notwithstanding that the enemy's gunners offered a strenuous resistance; fighting desperately with their tulwas or swords, and being mostly bayoneted at their posts. About half-past twelve the moon arose, and enabled the assailants to secure the guns they had so nobly captured. An attempt was now organized for the assault of the citadel, but during the night of the 24th. it was evacuated; and on Christmas morning the British flag was hoisted on the fortress. Considering the nature of the operations the loss was small; consisting of Europeans, twenty-eight killed, and seventy-eight wounded;

and of natives one hundred and one killed, and one hundred and six wounded. One hundred guns, sixteen of which were brass, became the trophies of the victors. The flank companies of the 22nd., and 76th. Foot, represented the King's troops on this service.

WAR IN NEPAUL, 1816.

In consequence of the Rajah of Nepaul having refused to ratify the treaty which had been signed by his ambassadors, an army was collected under the command of Major-General Sir David Ochterlony, K.C.B., with a view to coerce this refractory ruler. There were three King's regiments with this force: the 24th. belonged to the first brigade, the 66th. to the second brigade, and the 87th. Royal Irish Fusiliers to the third brigade. The first brigade, commanded by Colonel Kelly, of the 24th., was to penetrate by Hurryhurpore; the second brigade, under Lieutenant-Colonel Nicol, of the 66th., was to enter the hills at Ramnuggur, and by a circuitous route join Sir David Ochterlony before Muckwanpore. The third brigade, under Lieutenant-Colonel Miller, of the 87th., remained with the fourth brigade, (native troops,) under Sir David Ochterlony, who marched through the forest at the foot of the Nepaul Hills on the 9th. of February.

The troops, in marching towards their respective points for penetrating the forest opposite to the entrances of the passes they were ordered to force, had to proceed with extreme caution, and could move on but slowly, from the impediments, both natural and artificial. Objects of the strangest nature continually attracted attention. Magnificent trees, covered with fruit, of various unknown species; birds of rich plumage but most discordant notes; bands of monkeys, chattering as the troops marched under the huge trees, in which these denizens of the forest had remained undisturbed for ages, excited the surprise of the soldiers. Great difficulty was also experienced in carrying the guns through the forest, which was accomplished by the personal exertions of each individual.

On the 27th. of February, the advance guard arrived at Muckwanpore, and on the following day the brigade was ordered to take possession of the heights of Sierapore; an action ensued, which commenced about noon, and terminated at six o'clock, leaving the British in possession of the heights for a considerable distance from Sierapore, and of one field-piece.

For this affair, Lieutenant-Colonel Francis Miller, of the first battalion of the 87th., and Lieutenant Fenton, who had performed very arduous duties, having been placed in charge of the advanced guard, composed of the light company of his regiment and those of the native infantry, with two guns, received the public thanks of the authorities in India. The 87th. had ten men killed and above thirty wounded, several of whom died. The enemy's loss was very considerable.

Colonel Kelly, with the first brigade, encountered the Rajah's troops on the heights of Hurryhurpore, on the 1st. of March, in which action the 24th. had four privates killed, three officers, one sergeant, and twenty-two privates wounded.

Convinced of the inutility of further opposition, the Rajah sued for peace, and a treaty was eventually concluded on the 4th. of March, which terminated the war in Nepaul.

BATTLE OF KIRKEE, AND BATTLE AND CAPTURE OF POONA.
November, 1817.

On the 2nd. of November accounts were received of the Peishwah's renewed treachery, when the division under Brigadier-General Lionel Smith, C.B., was instantly put in motion, and on arrival at Ahmednuggur on the 8th., it was ascertained that the gallantry of the troops at Poona under Lieutenant-Colonel Burr, of the 7th. Bombay infantry, had successfully resisted the Peishwah's attempt to annihilate them, in their position at Kirkee, on the 5th. of November. After some slight skirmishing on the road, the force under Brigadier-General Smith, (of which the King's 65th. regiment formed a portion,) joined the Poona brigade at their position on the 13th. of November, when immediate preparations were made for attacking the enemy's camp, which was on the opposite side of the Moottah Moola. The force moved down before daybreak on the 14th. of November, but finding the river too deep to cross, it again encamped. The ford having been more particularly ascertained under some skirmishing and trifling loss, the left wing under the command of Lieutenant-Colonel Mimes, of the 65th., crossed on the evening of the 16th., in face of the enemy, whose artillery and matchlocks occasioned considerable loss during the passage and advance to a position on the right of the Peishwah's camp. The casualities amounted to fifteen killed and seventy-six wounded; the foe leaving about five hundred on the field.

During the night the Peishwah abandoned his capital, and moved to the southward. The inhabitants made their submission, and about noon on the 17th. of November, the British flag was hoisted on his palace, under a royal salute.

The 65th. regiment, for the above and subsequent services, has received authority to bear on its colours and appointments the figure of the Royal Tiger, with the word India above, and Arabia beneath.

BATTLE OF SEETABULDEE, AND BATTLE AND CAPTURE OF NAGPOOR.
NOVEMBER AND DECEMBER, 1817.

Without any previous declaration of hostilities, or the slightest act of aggression on the part of the Indian government, the Rajah of Berar attacked the troops at Nagpoor; consisting of two weak battalions of the Madras Native Infantry, and three troops of cavalry, in the evening of the 26th. November; and after an action which lasted eighteen hours was repulsed. Lieutenant-Colonel Scott at the requisition of the Resident had taken post on the hill of Seetabuldee, overlooking the city of Nagpoor, when the attack took place, in which the three troops of the 6th. regiment of native cavalry, and the 1st. battalions of the 20th. and 24th. Madras Native Infantry, were highly distinguished.

Reinforcements immediately marched on to the seat of war, of which eight companies of the 2nd. battalion of the 1st. Royals, formed part of the second division, under Brigadier-General Doveton. Upon his arrival the Rajah was desirous of treating for peace, and agreed to surrender his guns and disperse his troops; but the treachery he had already evinced made the Brigadier-General dispose his troops in order of battle, when he advanced to take possession of the guns. This precaution was not in vain. No opposition was encountered in obtaining the first battery, but on the soldiers entering the plantation, a sharp fire of musketry was treacherously opened upon them. The Rajah had formed an army of twenty-one thousand men, of which fourteen thousand were horse; the position being marked by irregularities of the ground, and clusters of houses and huts, and a thick plantation of trees, with ravines and a large reservoir. In the action of the 16th. of December, which ensued, the 2nd. battalion of the 1st. Foot added to the former honours of that corps. The batteries were carried with great gallantry, the enemy driven from all his positions and pursued a distance of five miles; his camp equipage, forty elephants and seventy five guns being captured. The battalion had nine men killed and twenty-six wounded.

After this success the siege of the city of Nagpoor was commenced. The troops which defended this place, consisting of about five thousand Arabs and Hindoostanees, insisted upon extraordinary terms, and these not being acceded to they determined on a desperate defence. On the 23rd. of December a breach was made in one of the gates, when an assault was resolved upon. At half-past eight o'clock in the morning of the 24th. of December the stormers advanced, but the breach being found untenable, the troops were withdrawn, although the parties had gained the desired points. On the following day the Arabs renewed their offer, and their terms being granted, they marched out of the city on the 1st. of January, 1818; being permitted to go where they pleased, with the exception of proceeding to Asseerghur.

The Royals had Lieutenant Bell and ten men killed, and two sergeants and forty-nine men wounded.

"Nagpore" on the regimental colours of the Royals commemorates the foregoing services.

BATTLE OF MAHEIDPORE.
21ST. DECEMBER, 1817.

While the eighth battalion companies of the Royals had been engaged at Nagpoor, the two flank companies, commanded by Captain Hulme, had shared in the movements of the first division of the army of the Deccan. On the 8th. of December the troops arrived near Maheidpore, where the army of Mulhar Rao Holkar, one of the coalesced Mahratta powers against the British interests in India, was assembled. After various fruitless negotiations the Anglo-Indian troops advanced against the enemy on the morning of the 21st. of December, and as they were crossing the ford of the Soopra river they were exposed to a powerful and concentrated cannonade. About half a mile beyond the river stood the troops of Holkar, and after passing the stream Brigadier-General Sir John Malcolm proceeded with two brigades of infantry to attack their left, and a ruined village situated on an eminence near the centre. They were completely routed, and in the general orders of Lieutenant-General Sir Thomas Hislop, Bart., Commander-in-Chief of the army of the Deccan, dated 22nd. of December, the charge of the squadron of the 22nd. Light Dragoons, under Captain Vernon, and the intrepid courage and animated zeal of the flank companies of the Royals under Captain Hulme, were specially commended. The Royals had Lieutenant Donald M'Leod, one sergeant and seven rank and file killed; Lieutenants John M'Gregor and Charles Campbell, four sergeants, one drummer, and twenty-seven men wounded.

In commemoration of the conduct of the flank companies the word "MAHEIDPORE" was authorized to be inscribed on the regimental colours of the Royals.

DEFENCE OF CORYGAUM.
1st. January, 1818.

This eminent service was confined to the Company's troops. The Peishwah having advanced towards Poonah, Colonel Burr, commanding in that city, requested a reinforcement from Seroor; accordingly Captain Staunton, of the second battalion 1st. regiment of Bombay Native Infantry, was despatched with that corps, barely six hundred strong, a few Madras artillery, with two six-pounders, and about three hundred auxiliary horse. The Peishwah's army, estimated at twenty thousand horse and about eight thousand infantry, was encamped on the right bank of the Beemah, above the village of Corygaum. Captain Staunton, upon coming in sight of this overwhelming force, on the 1st. of January, immediately moved upon Corygaum, and had scarcely succeeded in reaching the village, when he was attacked by three divisions of infantry, supported by immense bodies of horse, and two pieces of artillery. The enemy obtained immediate possession of the strongest posts of the village; and the remaining position was most obstinately contested from noon until nine at night, after a fatiguing march of twenty-eight miles. Ultimately the enemy was forced to abandon the village, after sustaining great loss. During the night of the 2nd., the detachment returned unmolested to Seroor, which was reached at nine o'clock on the following morning, without having partaken of any refreshment since the evening of the 31st. of December. Nearly all the wounded were brought in, and both the guns, and the colours of the regiment were preserved.*

WAR IN AVA.
1824 to 1826.

The repeated acts of aggression of the Burmese governors

---

* The following officers were engaged in this brilliant affair:—*Madras Artillery.*— Lieutenant Chisholm, killed ; Assistant-Surgeon Wylie. *2nd. Battalion 1st. Regiment Bombay Native Infantry.*—Captain Staunton; Lieutenant and Adjutant Pattinson, died of wounds; Lieutenant Connellau, wounded; Lieutenant Jones, 10th. regiment, doing duty with the 2nd. battalion 1st. regiment; Assistant-Surgeon Wingate, killed. *Auxiliary Horse.*—Lieutenant Swanston, Madras Establishment, wounded.

in the country adjacent to the British territory, at length rendered it necessary to demand an explanation from the Court of Ava. This terminated by a mutual declaration of war, and troops were assembled to penetrate the Burmese empire. His Majesty's 13th. and 38th. regiments, and two companies of artillery, and the 40th. Native Infantry, amounting to two thousand one hundred and seventy-five men, proceeded from Bengal, while His Majesty's 41st. and 89th. Foot, the Madras European regiment, and the 9th., 12th., 28th., and 30th. Madras Native Infantry, and artillery embarked from Madras,— making in all eleven thousand four hundred and seventy-five men. The troops from Bengal embarked in April and May, 1824.* To occupy Rangoon and the country at the mouth of the Irrawaddy was the first object. Brigadier-General Sir Archibald Campbell with his troops took possession of Rangoon on the 12th. of May, without the loss of a man; and Cheduba, on the Arracan coast, was also captured by storm on the 17th. of May, by a detachment under Brigadier-General Mc Creagh, of the 13th. Light Infantry, three companies of the regiment being employed on this service.

Meanwhile the Burmese army continued in great force in the vicinity of Rangoon, under the fortifications of wood called stockades, and of the dense jungle which covered the country. In carrying the stockades without ladders on the 28th. of May, portions of the 13th. and 38th. regiments were specially noticed. On the 10th. of June Kemmendine was assaulted; when about two miles from the town, the head of the column was stopped by a strong stockade, full of men, against which the artillery opened fire, and in half an hour a breach was made. The 41st., and part of the Madras European regiment, stormed the works in front; and the detachments of the 13th. and 38th. assaulted the rear face, which was ten feet high. The soldiers being encouraged and animated by the spirited conduct of Major (afterwards Sir Robert) Sale, who was the first on the top, climbed the works, one helping another

---

* Additional troops proceeded from Madras in the autumn, and before the close of the year His Majesty's 47th., with the governor-general's body-guard, had joined the expedition, which then amounted to about thirteen thousand men.

up, and entering simultaneously with the party by the breach, they bayoneted every man that opposed them.

This point being gained, the column advanced about a mile, and at four o'clock in the afternoon took up a position against the principal stockade. Batteries were erected during the night, and the artillery opened a heavy fire at daylight, when the Burmese forsook their works and fled.

An attack was made upon the British pickets on the 1st. of July, which was repulsed. The Burmese position in the rear of the great pagoda was assaulted on the 5th. of July, and a general attack was made on the 8th. of that month, one column advancing by land, under Brigadier-General M'Bean, while the other column proceeded by water. Major Wahab, with the Native Infantry, landed and immediately attacked the breach; Lieutenant-Colonel Henry Godwin, of the 41st., entered the work higher up by escalade; Major Sale encountered the Burmese commander-in-chief in the works, and slew him in single combat, taking from him a valuable gold-hilted sword and scabbard. Eight hundred of the enemy were killed on this occasion, and thirty-eight pieces of artillery, forty swivels, and three hundred muskets were captured.

The terror of these attacks caused the Burmese troops to remove to a greater distance; and the difficult character of the country, rainy weather, inundations, and the necessity for procuring a large supply of provisions before the army advanced, detained the British some time in the neighbourhood of Rangoon. An expedition was sent on the 11th. of October against Martaban, on the Saluen river, under the command of Lieutenant-Colonel Godwin, of His Majesty's 41st. regiment, and the place was captured on the 30th. of that month.

Meanwhile the Burmese recovered from the consternation into which they had been thrown, and a veteran chief, named Maha Bandoola, being appointed their commander, he approached the British position on the 1st. of December, with upwards of fifty thousand foot, a body of Cassay horse, and three hundred pieces of artillery, and commenced forming entrenchments. Major Sale advanced against the left of the Burmese line with two hundred of the 13th. Light Infantry, under Major Dennie, and two hundred and fifty of the 18th.

Native Infantry, under Captain Ross, and stormed the entrenchments in sight of the whole army. The soldiers of the 13th. led the charge with great intrepidity; they burst through the entrenchments, and overcame all opposition; this example was followed by the native infantry, when the Burmese fled, and the British troops returned to their posts laden with trophies.

This victory was followed by another over the left wing of the Burmese army, on the 5th. of December. The first advantage was followed up, the enemy was overthrown, and of the three hundred pieces of ordnance which they had in position, two hundred and forty were brought into the British camp.*

On the 7th. of December the trenches were assaulted in four columns of attack, under the superintendence of Lieutenant-Colonel Miles, the second in command, and led by Lieutenant-Colonels Mallet, (both of the 89th.,) Parlby, Brodie, and Captain Wilson, of the 38th. regiment. At a quarter before twelve every gun that would bear upon the breaches opened fire. Major Sale at the same time made a diversion on the enemy's left and rear. At noon the cannonade ceased, and the columns moved forward to their points of attack, when the total defeat of Bandoolah's army ensued, his loss being estimated at five thousand men.

In an attack on the enemy's corps of observation, on the Dalla side of the river, on the 9th. of December, the 89th. regiment highly distinguished itself.

Rallying his broken legions, the Burmese commander called reinforcements to his aid, and took up another position, which he fortified with great labour and art. These formidable works were attacked on the 15th. of December, when two hundred of the 13th., under Major Sale, with three hundred of the 18th.

---

* "All their artillery, stores, and reserve depots, which had cost them so much labour to get up, with a great quantity of small arms, gilt chattahs, standards, and other trophies fell into our hands. Never was victory more complete or decided, and never was the triumph of discipline and valour, over the disjointed efforts of irregular courage and infinitely superior numbers, more conspicuous. Majors Dennie and Thornhill, of the 13th. Light Infantry, and Major Gore, of the 89th., were distinguished by the steadiness with which they led their men."—*Brigadier-General Sir A. Campbell's despatch.*

and 34th. Madras Native Infantry, formed the right column of attack under Brigadier-General (afterwards Sir Willoughby) Cotton; this made a detour round the enemy's left to gain the rear of his position at Kokien, which was to be attacked in front by another column. Sir Archibald marched with the left column, which consisted of five hundred Europeans, from the 38th., 41st., 89th., and Madras European Regiment, with portions of native infantry, to attack the foe in front. Of this column two divisions were formed, the command of one being given to Lieutenant-Colonel Miles, of the 89th., and the other to Major Evans, of the 28th. Madras Native Infantry. On arriving in front of the position it presented a very formidable appearance; but when the signal was given, the soldiers rushed forward, and in less than fifteen minutes they were in full possession of these stupendous works. Major Sale received a severe wound in the head, and was succeeded by Major Dennie, who although wounded in the hand, continued at the head of the 18th. regiment until the action was over. The Burmese after a short resistance, fled in a panic, leaving their camp standing, and abandoning all their baggage, together with a great portion of their arms and ammunition.

The British casualties amounted to three lieutenants, one jemadar, two sergeants, and twelve rank and file killed; two majors, three captains, six lieutenants, two ensigns, one subadar, one jemadar, five sergeants, one drummer, and ninety-one rank and file wounded.

These successes, connected with those of the royal navy, had produced important results; the maritime provinces of Mergui, Tavoy, Yeb, and Martaban, had been captured, and seven hundred pieces of artillery had been taken from the Burmese. Lieutenant-Colonel Elrington, with a small detachment, consisting of a portion of the 47th., with some seamen and marines, carried by storm the factory and stockades of Syriam on the 11th. and 12th. of January, 1825. To wrest additional territory from the court of Ava, Major Sale proceeded against the city of Bassein, in the south-west part of the ancient kingdom of Pegu, which constituted part of the Burmese empire. The troops, after a tedious passage, arrived in the evening of the 24th. of February, off Pagoda Point, Great Negrais. On the 26th. the expedition entered the river, and the 13th., 38th., and 12th. Native Infantry landed and captured a stockade. The force afterwards re-embarked, and proceeded to the next stockade, which the Burmese abandoned as the soldiers went on shore to storm the works; so great was their consternation, that the city of Bassein was set on fire and abandoned, the enemy retiring on Donabew.

Brigadier-General Cotton, in the interim, with a detached force, of which the 47th. and 89th. regiments formed a part, had attacked the pagoda stockade in advance of Donabew, on the 7th. of March. The troops were formed in two columns, under Lieutenant-Colonel O' Donaghue, 47th., and Major Basden, 89th. regiment. All were exposed to a heavy fire, which was kept up to the last, with greater spirit and perseverance than was usual. The operations against the second defence, distant about five hundred yards from the pagoda stockade, were not successful, and the force was re-embarked on the 18th., after the enemy's cannon had been spiked and his arms destroyed.

Meanwhile, a force of eleven thousand men, under Brigadier-General Morrison, of the 44th., of which that regiment and the 54th. formed a portion, had been assembled at Chittagong towards the end of September of the preceding year, moved forward early in January, in order to penetrate through Arracan and across the mountains into Ava, where it was to effect a junction with the army at Rangoon. The first attack at Arracan, on the 29th. of March, failed, owing principally to a dense fog, which prevented the great strength of the position from being discovered. On the night of the 31st, Brigadier Richards proceeded by a circuitous route, and gained the summit of the range unperceived; and on the morning of the 1st. of April the Burmese were attacked in flank, while the front was assailed by the main body. In a short time the heights were abandoned, and Arracan was gained.

Donabew was taken possession of by Sir Archibald Campbell on the 2nd. of April; Maha Bandoolah having been killed by a rocket, the other chiefs could not prevail on the garrison to remain, and the place was evacuated during the night of the 1st. of April. Several desperate sorties were made by the Burmese during the siege, which commenced on the 25th. of March, but they were quickly repulsed.* The 1st. Royals, 38th., 41st., 47th., and 89th. here sustained several casualties.

After this success the march was resumed to Prome, where the army arrived on the 25th. of April, the Burmese having evacuated the town after setting it on fire, but the decisive measures adopted saved the place from a general conflagration.

In consequence of the season of military operations being over, the army remained inactive at Prome, and in the autumn overtures of peace were made by the Burmese, but hostilities were resumed in the middle of November; and the army of Ava, having repulsed the attack of three bodies of sepoys, became suddenly elevated with a high idea of its own power, and advanced to attack the British troops at Prome, which had been reinforced by the detachments left at Rangoon.

About sixty thousand Burmese environed six thousand Anglo-Indian troops; but undismayed by this formidable host, four native regiments were left for the defence of Prome, and the remainder advanced on the 1st. of December to attack the enemy's left wing at Simbike. This post was gallantly stormed by the troops under Brigadier-General Cotton, and the works were carried in ten minutes. The flank companies of the Royals, under Captain Thomas John Harvey, with the 41st. and 89th. regiments, commanded respectively by Major Peter Latouche Chambers and Brevet-Major Henry Ross Gore, supported by the 18th. Madras Native Infantry, and led by Lieutenant-Colonel Godwin, performed this service.

After a harassing march of about twenty miles, the troops bivouacked at Ze-ouke, and at daylight on the morning of the 2nd. of December they were again in motion, to attack

---

* "In one of these sorties a scene at once novel and interesting presented itself in front of both armies. Seventeen large elephants, each carrying a complement of armed men, and supported by a column of infantry, were observed moving down towards our right flank. I directed the body-guard, under Captain Sneyd, to charge them, and they acquitted themselves most handsomely; mixing boldly with the elephants, they shot their riders off their backs, and finally drove the whole back into the fort."—*Brigadier-General Sir Archibald Campbell's despatch.*

the formidable position occupied by the enemy's centre division on the Napadee Hills. Arriving in the vicinity, the British artillery commenced a sharp cannonade; Brigadier-General Elrington's troops drove the enemy from the jungle, and six companies of the 87th. Royal Irish Fusiliers carried the posts at the bottom of the ridge; the Burmese were driven from the valley to their principal works on the hills, which appeared very formidable; as the heights could only be ascended by a narrow road, commanded by artillery, and defended by stockades crowded with men armed with muskets. When the artillery had made an impression on the works, the 13th. and 38th. regiments, the latter leading, rushed into them, overthrew all opposition with the bayonet, and forced the Burmese from hill to hill, over precipices that could only be ascended by a narrow stair, until the whole of the position nearly three miles in length, was captured. Scarcely a shot was fired in return to the enemy's continued volleys, and the six companies of the 87th. advancing through the jungle to the right, drove everything before them on that side.

On the 5th. of December the enemy's right wing was driven from its post. The division employed under Brigadier-General Cotton consisted of two hundred and fifty of the Royal Regiment, two hundred and seventy of the 41st., two hundred and sixty of the 89th., the light company of the 28th. Madras Native Infantry, and one hundred pioneers; The immense army of Ava was thus forced from its positions, and the Burmese legions sought safety in flight. After this success the army continued to advance; the Burmese evacuated Meeaday, and took post at Melloon, at the same time they renewed their offers for terminating the war; but this appeared to be with the view of gaining time to re-organize their forces for a more determined resistance.

The conditions of peace not being ratified by the stipulated time, hostilities were resumed on the 19th. of January, 1826, on which day the 13th. and 38th. regiments embarked in boats under Lieutenant-Colonel Sale, to assault the main face of the enemy's fortifications at Melloon. At the same time Brigadier-General Cotton, with the flank companies of the 47th. and 87th. regiments, and the 89th., under Lieutenant-Colonel

Hunter Blair, the 41st. regiment and the 18th. Madras Native Infantry, under Lieutenant-Colonel Henry Godwin, commanding the first brigade of Madras troops, and the 28th. Madras Native Infantry, with the flank companies of the 43rd. Madras Native Infantry, under Lieutenant-Colonel Parlby, were to cross above Melloon, and, after carrying some outworks, were to attack the northern face of the principal work. The whole of the boats quitted the shore together; but the current and breeze carried the 13th. and 38th. to their point of attack before the other divisions could reach the opposite bank of the river, and Lieutenant-Colonel Sale was wounded in his boat; but the two regiments landed, formed under the command of Major Frith, of the 38th., (who was wounded in the assault,) and rushed forward with such intrepidity that they speedily became masters of these formidable works. When Brigadier-General Cotton saw that they were carried, he ordered the brigade under Lieutenant-Colonel Blair, of the 87th., to cut in upon the enemy's line of retreat, which was performed with much effect.

On the 28th. of January, the 87th., with the flank companies of the 28th. Native Infantry, and detachments of the Governor-General's body-guard and artillery, under Brigadier Hunter Blair, were sent from Tongwyn, to attack the position of Moulmein, eleven miles distant. The position, being a great annoyance to the surrounding country, was destroyed, and the troops returned to camp the same evening.

The army advanced upon the Burmese capital, and the legions of Ava resolved once more to try the fortune of war. They met the British in the open fields near Pagahm Mew, where an action took place on the 9th. of February. The 13th. Light Infantry led the right attack, supported by the 38th. and 89th. regiments. That on the left was supported by the 41st. Part of the Burmese troops, broke by the 38th., retired into a well-constructed field-work, but were so closely pursued that they had not time to form for its defence: here from three to four hundred of them perished either by the bayonet or plunging into the river to escape. The result was another defeat to the enemy.

After this victory the army continued its advance upon

Ummerapoora, the capital, situated upon the shores of a beautiful lake; and when within four days' march of that city the king of Ava sent the ratified treaty, paying the expenses of the war, and relinquishing a considerable portion of territory. In one of the conferences the negotiators had objected to the payment of money, and stated, that by using great economy, they might furnish a million baskets of rice within a year, but they did not grow rupees; and if the British had any objection to the rice, there was abundance of fine trees in the forests, which they might cut down and take away in lieu of the money.

On the conclusion of this campaign, the following statement appeared in general orders:—"While the Governor-General in Council enumerates, with sentiments of unfeigned admiration, the 13th., 38th., 41st., 89th., 47th., 1st., (or Royals,) 87th., and 45th. regiments, the Honorable Company's Madras European regiment, and the Bengal and Madras European artillery, as the European troops who have had the honour of establishing the renown of the British arms in a new and distant region, His Lordship in Council feels that higher and more justly-merited praise cannot be bestowed on those brave troops than that, amidst the barbarous hosts whom they have fought and conquered, they have eminently displayed the virtues, and sustained the character, of the British Soldier."*

---

* In the same general orders it was announced that "Medals also, bearing a suitable device, are to be distributed to the native troops which at any period during the war, were employed under the command of Major-General Sir Archibald Campbell, including the officers and men of the gunboats serving in the Irrawaddy." This medal, also designed by William Wyon, Esq., contained on the obverse a quaint device—the Asiatic elephant crouching to the British Lion. It was not conferred on the regiments of the Crown, and therefore does not come within the scope of this work. When the medal for services in India from 1808 to 1826 was authorized, a bar inscribed AVA was granted.

The 1st., 13th., 38th., 41st., 44th., 45th., 47th., 54th., 87th, and 89th. King's regiments were permitted to bear the word AVA on their colours, in commemoration of their gallantry during this service.

SIEGE AND STORM OF BHURTPORE.
January, 1826.

Baldeo Singh had become attached to the British government, with which he formed an alliance offensive and defensive, and procured a guarantee for the succession of his youthful son, Bhulwunt Singh, to the throne; but among many of the rajah's subjects a strong feeling of hostility to the British existed, particularly in the army, and his nephew, Doorjun Sal, headed a party opposed to the alliance. After the rajah's decease his nephew gained possession of the capital, and assumed the sovereign power. Sir David Ochterlony assembled a force (of which the 59th. formed part) and marched on Bhurtpore; but the government having disapproved of the measures taken, the troops returned to Cawnpore. Sir David in consequence resigned, and died at Meerut in July, 1825, his decease being, it is considered, hastened by this event.

It was, however, afterwards determined to carry into effect the engagements entered into with the late rajah, by placing his son on the throne. An army was assembled under General Lord Combermere, the Commander-in-Chief in India, and the siege of the capital, the fortified city of Bhurtpore, was determined upon. Great confidence was placed by the natives in the strength of this place, the fort being upwards of five miles in circumference, and having, in 1805, withstood four attacks of Lord Lake's army, wherein were five king's regiments, which had been repulsed with great loss.

On the 10th. and 11th. of December, 1825, the British appeared before this celebrated city and fortress. The army amounted to twenty-five thousand three hundred men, of which His Majesty's 11th. and 16th. Light Dragoons, and the 14th. and 59th. regiments formed part, the remainder being made up of Native corps. The garrison was nearly equal in numbers to the besieging force. The Bhurtporees had cut a sluice into the embankment of a lake near the town, to fill the ditch round the works with water, but they were speedily driven from the spot; the sluice was stopped, and the embankment was turned into a military post, which was entrusted to a company of the 14th. Foot and some sepoys. About eighteen inches of water only had flowed into the ditch, and this sudden seizure of the embankment facilitated the progress of the siege by keeping the ditch nearly empty, and thus prevented the enemy from filling it with water, as was done in Lord Lake's time. The several corps took up their ground, and the investment became complete, orange and date trees from the groves being converted into fascines and gabions.

At an early hour on the morning of the 24th. of December, the fires of two batteries were opened on the town; additional works were constructed, the batteries became more numerous, and the siege was prosecuted with vigour. It was, however, found extremely difficult to effect practicable breaches in the peculiarly-constructed walls of Bhurtpore, as they were in many places thickly studded with large trees of a very tough description of timber, which offered a remarkable resistance to shot. The process of mining was adopted; several explosions took place, and the result soon rendered it evident that the horrors of an assault were drawing near. Great bravery and perseverance were evinced by the garrison; they exposed themselves resolutely to the fire of besiegers, and built up in the night the works which were knocked down during the day, labouring under a ceaseless fire, and evincing a firm determination to persevere in the defence.

Considerable progress having been made towards effecting practicable breaches, it was determined to attempt the storming of the place on the morning of the 18th. of January, 1826, the explosion of the mine under the north-east angle being the signal for the assault. The 14th. and 59th. regiments headed the two attacks, and they were directed to wheel as soon as they had entered the breaches, one to the right and the other to the left, and, continuing their career round the ramparts, to drive the enemy before them till they met. Some delay occurred in the mine, and the soldiers stood seven hours anxiously waiting for the moment to commence the assault, during which time the thunder of the artillery was tremendous. The mine having exploded in an unexpected direction, several men of the 14th., at the head of the column of attack, were killed, and Brigadier-General John M'Combe, (of that regiment,) and other officers received severe contusions.

As soon as the tremendous crash was over the troops rushed through the cloud of smoke and dust, and commenced ascending the breach, and, the summit, after some opposition, was gained. Here a short pause ensued from the native corps appointed to support not being near, when the enemy opened a heavy fire from the buildings near the breach, and sprang a mine, which killed several of the soldiers. The Bhurtpore artillerymen fought with great desperation, and the defenders of the walls exhibited much bravery; but in two hours the whole rampart surrounding the town, together with the command of the gates, were in possession of the British. The citadel surrendered about four o'clock, and the 14th., (at the head of which the Commander-in-Chief entered it,) was placed there in garrison, as a compliment to the gallantry of the corps.

General Viscount Combermere, G.C.B., in his despatch stated, "I must particularly remark the behaviour of His Majesty's 14th. regiment, commanded by Major Everard, and the 59th., commanded by Major Fuller; these corps, having led the columns of assault, by their steadiness and determination decided the events of the day." His lordship also specially adverted to the services rendered by Brigadier, now General Sir James Wallace Sleigh, K.C.B., commanding the cavalry; the general good and active conduct of the cavalry, and the spirited manner in which they had volunteered their services when it was anticipated (before the arrival of the 1st. European regiment) to employ them in the storm were also mentioned.*

Considering the service on which the troops had been employed the casualties were comparatively few; of Europeans

---

* In consequence of the scarcity of European infantry with the infantry, it was deemed necessary to call for volunteers from the cavalry, each King's regiment to furnish three officers and eighty rank and file. This number was at once obtained. The officers' names were Captain Browne, Lieutenant Windus, and Cornet Pearson, of the 11th. Dragoons and Captain Luard, and Lieutenants Mc Conchy and Walker, of the 16th. Lancers. Viscount Combermere had formerly served in the latter regiment.

and natives killed there were one hundred and three, and wounded four hundred and sixty-six. The enemy's loss was estimated at seven thousand.

Thus was accomplished the capture of this city, regarded throughout the East as impregnable, the natives being accustomed to remark that India was not subdued because Bhurtpore had not fallen. The usurper Dooljun Sal was captured while attempting to escape, and the young Rajah was placed on the throne. The 14th. had Brigadier-General Edwards and Captain Armstrong killed, and the 59th. lost Captain Pitman, and had Major Fuller and other officers wounded.

The state of the Burmese war at this period rendered it of the highest importance that Bhurtpore should be captured, as a failure in that object would have paralyzed British domination in the East.*

BHURTPORE was authorised by the Sovereign to be borne on the standards and colours of the 11th. and 16th. Light Dragoons, and the 14th. and 59th. regiments.

Lord Combermere, whose earliest services had been connected with the siege of Seringapatam, in 1799, and who had commanded the British cavalry during the Peninsular war, under Wellington, was made a Viscount for this capture.

THE INDIAN WAR MEDAL, 1799–1826.

This medal, the design of which is extremely chaste and beautiful, has on the obverse the Queen's head, with the inscription VICTORIA REGINA, similar to the Crimean and other medals. The artist, the late William Wyon, Esq.,† R.A.,

----

* From the 24th. of December, 1825, to the 18th. of January, 1826, the expenditure of shot and shells during the twenty-six days was as follows:– Shot 42,215, shells 17,060, shrapnells 1,096, grape 693, case 404, carcasses 4; in all 61,472.

† I have to express my great obligations to his son, Leonard C. Wyon, Esq., who was appointed modeller and engraver to Her Majesty's Mint in 1852, the title of chief engraver having been discontinued. This gentleman has most kindly furnished me with descriptions of the several medals, and is the designer of those struck for the second Burmese war, the Baltic and Kaffir campaigns, and the Indian mutiny. When it is

THE INDIAN WAR MEDAL 1799–1826.
THE GHUZNEE MEDAL 1839.

was the chief engraver to the Royal Mint from the latter portion of George the Fourth's reign until his decease in 1851, and is considered the most accomplished medallist of modern times. He has represented the figure of Victory, on the reverse, as seated, considering that quiet posture the most fitting to commemorate services long past, the medal not being engraved until 1850. In her left hand is a laurel wreath, and in her right an olive branch. A lotus-flower,* emblematic of India, is at her side, a trophy of Oriental arms and a palm-tree forming the back-ground. It is superscribed To THE ARMY OF INDIA; in the *exergue* 1799-1826. The ribbon is pale blue. The various services specified at page 1, are commemorated by clasps. On those belonging to the medal from which the engraving has been made are the words ALLIGHUR, BATTLE OF DEIG, and CAPTURE OF DEIG; the medal granted to the Duke of Wellington contained bars for ASSYE, ARGAUM, and GAWILGHUR.

---

considered that there is a great restriction to the same class of designs, such as figures of Victory or Britannia, the merit of such medals as the above, and those for the Kaffir campaigns and Indian mutiny, can be better appreciated. The Crimean Medal is by Benjamin Wyon, Esq.; and that for Waterloo is by Thomas Wyon, Esq., Jun., who was chief engraver to the mint at the time of the great re-coinage in 1816. He was a young man of great promise, but died at the early age of twenty-five. Benjamin Wyon, his brother, was an eminent medallist, and succeeded his father, Mr. Thomas Wyon, as chief engraver of His Majesty's seals in 1830. He died in 1858. The Peninsular War Medal and others engraved in this work for Indian services, are by Mr. William Wyon, with the exception of that for the first capture of Ghuznee in 1839, and that for Jellalabad, of the mural crown pattern.

* Prior to the Indian mutiny the lotus-flower was circulated amongst the native regiments of Bengal as a symbol of conspiracy. According to the interpretation of the Hindoo priests, the lotus rising from the water is typical of the world issuing from the ocean of time. The goddess Asteria (or Justice) is depicted in Egyptian Mythology as rising from this flower; and in representations of the Judgment of the Dead, the lotus of knowledge, or tree of life, the great serpent, the vase of nectar, and the table of ambrosia, emblems of Paradise, are introduced before Osiris, who, clad in the white habiliments of the grave, with a red girdle, sits upon a throne of black and white spots, emblematic of good and evil. The figures of Buddha at the Indian Museum, now in Whitehall Yard, have a lotus-flower in the left hand. It is cultivated by the Buddhist priests and placed in vases in their temples, and the veneration of the Chinese extends also to this sacred flower. In the new Indian Order, recently instituted, the lotus is prominently introduced.

FIRST AFFGHAN CAMPAIGN.
1839.

Shah Soojah-ool-Moolk had been driven from the throne of Affghanistan, and his kingdom divided among several chiefs. A Persian army besieged Herat, on the Affghan frontier, and the court of Persia claimed an extensive portion of territory, which, lying between India and Persia, appeared to menace the safety of the British dominions in the East Indies. These circumstances, and the unprovoked attack made on a British ally, Runjeet Singh, by Dost Mahomed Khan, occasioned a tripartite treaty to be concluded between the British, Runjeet Singh, and Shah Soojah, for the purpose of effecting the restoration of the dethroned monarch, and a British force designated the "ARMY OF THE INDUS," was assembled to effect this object. In addition to the native corps, it comprised the 4th. and 16th. Dragoons, (the cavalry being commanded by the late Lieutenant-General Sir Joseph Thackwell, G.C.B., then Major-General,) and the 2nd., 13th., and 17th. regiments of the regular army. The Bengal column was placed under Major-General Sir Willoughby Cotton, K.C.B., and the Bombay one under Major-General Willshire. General Sir Henry Fane was to have commanded the whole, but on information being received in October, 1838, that the siege of Herat had been raised by the Persian monarch, who had marched therefrom towards his capital, the force was reduced, and the second Bengal division was left at Ferozepore. Lieutenant-General Sir John (afterwards Lord) Keane, was consequently appointed to the command.

The plan of operations was thus arranged:—Major-General Sir Willoughby Cotton was to march near Scinde, through the Bolan Pass to Candahar, and proceed thence to Ghuznee and Cabool. The Bombay division of the army commenced its march from the mouth of the Indus, through the country occupied by the Ameers of Scinde, who, refusing permission for the troops to pass through their territory, a passage had to be effected by force. Hyderabad, the capital, was captured;

Kurrachee was occupied; and the Ameers were brought to submission early in February, 1839. The army then continued its march, passed the Indus on a bridge of boats near the fortress of Bukkur, (which had been delivered up as a place of arms during the war in Affghanistan,) and entered upon regions never before traversed by British troops, but which are interesting from their association with the operations and reverses of Alexander the Great.

Advancing from Shikarpore the troops arrived in the middle of March, at Dadur, situated a few miles from the Bolan Pass, through which they marched between mountains covered with snow. In these wild regions bands of Beloochees lurked to avail themselves of every opportunity to follow their predatory habits, and they murdered several camp followers, and plundered some baggage. Issuing from this gloomy defile of more than fifty miles in length, the army entered the Dush-i-be-doulut, or the unhappy desert, and halted a short time at Quettah, situated in the centre of the valley of Shawl, of which it is the capital. Supplies of provisions could not be procured in these sterile regions; the issue of grain for the horses ceased, the soldiers were placed upon half rations, the native followers upon quarter, and several men, who were searching for forage at a distance from the camp, were sacrificed by the natives, who availed themselves of every opportunity of destroying small parties.

All these hardships were borne with fortitude, and in the early part of April the army commenced its march through the vale of Shawl; it descended the picturesque height of Kotul into the valley of Koochlak; forded rivers; traversed a difficult country spangled with flowers of every hue, some of which reminded the soldiers of their own distant home; and passed the height of Kozak, where the men had to drag the artillery over the precipice with ropes. Surmounting every obstacle with patient perseverance, the troops continued to press forward; the rulers of Affghanistan, struck with dismay, fled from the capital, leaving the country to the Sovereign whom the British were advancing to restore. As the army proceeded on its way, various classes of individuals tendered their submission, and on the 27th. of April it arrived at Candahar, the capital of western Affghanistan, where provisions and repose were obtained. The tents were pitched in the grassy meadows, among enclosures covered with crops of grain. The watery exhalations from the low grounds however proved injurious to the health of the men, and the great heat experienced in the tents, with a saline impregnation in the water, augmented the number of the sick.

CAPTURE OF GHUZNEE.
23RD. JULY, 1839.

Breaking up from Candahar on the 27th. of June, to reduce the remainder of the Shah's dominions to obedience, the army advanced along a valley of dismal sterility to the Turnuk river; then proceeding up the right bank, traversed the country of the Western Ghilzees, and arrived on the 21st. of July before Ghuznee, a strong fortress garrisoned by three thousand Affghans, under Prince Mahomed Hyder Khan, who were well provided with stores, and had determined on a desperate defence, having blocked up every gate with masonry excepting one.

Not having a battering train of sufficient power to proceed by the regular method of breaching the walls, Lieutenant-General Sir John Keane resolved to storm the place without delay, and a reconnoisance was made on the 21st. of July, when it was determined to blow open the gate, and accordingly during the night of the 22nd. of July a quantity of gunpowder was secretly brought to the one not blocked up with masonry, which was to be destroyed by an explosion before daylight on the following morning.

To the 13th. Foot was assigned the duty of covering the operations, in blowing open the gate, and they paraded at two o'clock, a.m. Three hundred pounds of gunpowder (in twelve sand-bags) were used for this purpose. The regiment proceeded in advance of the storming party to the causeway of the gate under cover of the darkness of the night, and the fire of the batteries of the assailants, six men of the leading company being told off to assist in carrying the powder-bags. On reaching the causeway, the 13th. extended in light order along the ditch, and by their fire distracted the enemy's attention from the gate. After the explosion a company of the regiment, under Lieutenant Jennings, moved up with the engineer officer to ascertain if the operation had been attended with success; on which the light company of the 2nd. (or Queen's Royal,) No. 9 company of the 13th., under Captain Vigors, the light companies of the 17th. and of the Bengal European Regiment, which had been named to form the advance of the storming column, immediately pressed forward under the command of Brigadier Donnie, and despite a heavy fire gained an entrance into the fort. These were quickly followed by the main storming column under Brigadier Sale, (who was severely wounded on this occasion,) which consisted of the 2nd. Queens, under Major Carruthers, and the Bengal European Regiment, under Lieutenant-Colonel Orchard; to these succeeded the 13th. Light Infantry, under Major Fraser, as they collected from the duty of skirmishing, with which they were directed to commence, and the 17th., under Lieutenant-Colonel Croker. The whole were soon established in possession of the fort.

After this the garrison rushed some to the citadel and others to the houses, from which they kept up an annoying fire, when the 13th. and 17th. regiments were directed against the former, but which unexpectedly was found evacuated. Large supplies of grain, ammunition of all kinds, and several guns and military weapons, with about two thousand horses, fell into the hands of the victors. A company of the 13th., under Lieutenant Arthur Wilkinson, succeeded in capturing the redoubt, (or outwork,) and took two standards and about sixty prisoners. A standard was captured by the 17th., but was afterwards lost by the wreck of a transport, in which a part of the regiment was embarked.

The loss sustained in the assault of Ghuznee by the Queen's regiments, (the 2nd., 13th., and 17th. Foot,) was limited to five men killed, and six officers and sixty-three men wounded.

When the Affghan horsemen, who had assembled in the neighbourhood, learnt the fate of the fortress, they abandoned their camp equipage and baggage, and fled towards Cabool, the capital of Eastern Affghanistan, in the direction of which city the British forces immediately advanced.

Dost Mahomed Khan, the ruler of the country, assembled a formidable host in position near Ughundee; but ascertaining that his soldiers had resolved to abandon him, he fled with a body of select cavalry, leaving his artillery in position; and the British army advancing to the capital, replaced Shah Soojah-ool-Moolk, on the 7th. of August, in the possession of the palace of his forefathers, from which he had been an exile many years. The conquest of a kingdom was thus achieved with trifling loss, and the troops pitched their tents in a rich valley near Cabool.

An order of merit was instituted by the Shah, called the Order of the Dooranee Empire, the decorations of which were conferred on the general and field officers. The following regiments of the Queen's army received authority to bear the words AFFGHNISTAN and GHUZNEE for the foregoing services—4th. and 16th. Light Dragoons, and the 2nd., 3rd., and 17th. Foot.

THE GHUZNEE MEDAL.

A medal was presented by the restored monarch to the officers and soldiers present at the storming of Ghuznee, which The Queen authorized them to receive and wear. This permission was thus announced to the army in India:—

"24th. June, 1841.

"The Commander-in-Chief has the gratification to publish the following letter, addressed to Lord Hill by the Marquis of Normanby, Secretary of State for the Home Department, whereby 'Her Majesty has been graciously pleased to permit the officers and soldiers engaged in the assault and capture of the fortress of Ghuznee, on the 21st. and 23rd. of July, 1839, to accept and wear the medal conferred upon them by Shah Soojah-ool-Moolk, in approbation of their services on that occasion."

"Whitehall, 22nd. March, 1841.

"My Lord,

"The Shah Soojah-ool-Moolk, King of Affghanistan, having conferred a medal upon the officers and soldiers engaged in the assault and capture of the fortress of Ghuznee, on the 21st. and 23rd. of July, 1839, in approbation oì their services on that occasion, I have the honour to acquaint your Lorship, that Her Majesty has been graciously pleased to permit these officers and soldiers to accept and wear the medal in question.

"I have, etc.,

"The Right Honourable NORMANBY."

Lord Hill, G.C.B."

The medal is of silver, and has on one side a representation of the fortress, with the word GHUZHEE in a scroll beneath, (vide page 47;) on the other side, within a wreath of laurel,

is a mural crown, with the date 23rd. July above, and the year 1839 below, as shewn in the accompanying engraving. The ribbon is crimson and green.

FIRST CHINESE WAR.
1840–1842.

In consequence of the Chinese government having commenced summary measures without sufficient previous notice, the British superintendents of trade applied to the Governor-General of India for a number of ships of war and armed vessels for the protection of life and property. Although the introduction of opium into China was prohibited, the local authorities did not enforce the law. Ultimately Captain Elliot and the merchants at Canton were confined to the factories as prisoners, and in June the Chinese High Commissioner and other officers proceeded to Chunhow, near the Bocca Tigris, and commenced destroying vast quantities of the prohibited drug, besides offering insult to Captain Elliot, R.N., the Queen's representative. Hostilities became unavoidable, and the 18th., 26th., and 49th. regiments, a native corps of Bengal volunteers, and detachments of artillery and sappers from the presidency of Madras, were embarked under Brigadier-General George Burrell, of the Royal Irish. It became important to gain possession of a portion of the Chinese territory as a *point d' appui* for subsequent operations; and the governor of Chusan, an island lying off the coast, was summoned to surrender in the beginning of July. He, however, made dispositions to defend the place, and on the morning of the 5th. of July the shore, landing-place, wharf, and adjoining hill were crowded with Chinese troops. The British shipping silenced the war-junks and batteries; and the right wing of the 18th. regiment, commanded by Major Henry William Adams, with the Royal Marines of the fleet, forming the advance, landed. They were followed by other corps, and the British troops, commanded by Brigadier-General George Burrell, Lieutenant-Colonel of the 18th., took up a position in front of the fortified city of Ting-hae-hien, whence a sharp fire was sustained for some time; but before the following day the Chinese soldiers fled in a panic, and the city was taken possession of, but the climate proved injurious to the health of the troops.

This success was followed by negotiations; the tardy councils of the Chinese being expedited by the activity of the British naval force, and in the early part of 1841 they agreed to give up the island of Hong-Kong, pay an indemnity of six million dollars, and open a direct intercourse for trading upon an equal footing. Accordingly the island was occupied; but the authorities appeared to have had no intention of fulfilling the other stipulations of the treaty. Hostilities were in consequence resumed, and the force embarked in February with the expedition up the Canton river. In less than an hour the fleet silenced the batteries of Wantong, and a body of troops, consisting of detachments of the 26th. and 49th. regiments,

Royal Marines, and the 37th. Madras Native Infantry, and Bengal volunteers, commanded by Major Pratt, of the 26th., landing, the island was captured without the loss of a man, thirteen hundred Chinese soldiers surrendering prisoners of war. Continuing the voyage, the fleet arrived at the bar, destroying the war-junks, the works being stormed and captured by the marines and seamen. As the expedition pursued its way up the river, the Chinese abandoned several batteries and armed rafts, and solicited terms of peace; but procrastination seemed to be their only object, and the British fleet advanced. The forts in front of Canton soon fell under the fire of the artillery, the Chinese flotilla was destroyed, and peace was again requested. While negotiations were pending, bodies of Tartar troops were arriving at Canton, which shewed the object of the enemy; and on the 24th. of May the troops landed, and on the following day they advanced against the fortified heights on the north of the city, when dispositions were made for the attack. About half-past nine o'clock the advance was sounded, and by a spirited effort the heights were carried,—the 18th. and 49th. being emulous which should first reach their appointed goals,—and the British colours waved triumphantly on the captured forts.

A fortified Chinese camp had been established on the high ground on the north-east of Canton, and from this bodies of the enemy advanced against the British troops. The 18th., 49th., and a company of marines, met and repulsed the principal attack, and, following the fugitives along a causeway, stormed and captured the entrenched camp in gallant style. It was afterwards burnt, and the magazines destroyed.

On the following morning (26th. of May) a flag of truce was seen on the walls, and hostilities were suspended; but delay still appearing to be the object of the Chinese, preparations were made to attack the city by storm, when six millions of dollars were agreed to be paid for the redemption of Canton, and opening the port for trade.

Disregarding the stipulations of treaties, the Emperor of China issued a mandate for the extermination of the British who dared thus to insult his coasts and capture his towns, offering, at the same time, immense rewards for the heads of the commanders, and even a large sum for that of a private soldier. His decrees were responded to by depriving him of a further extent of territory; and on the 22nd. of August an expedition proceeded against the island and city of Amoy, situated in a fine gulf in the province of Fokein, the great tea district of China. On the 25th. of August the fleet arrived before Amoy, which was defended by five hundred pieces of cannon and a numerous force; but nothing could withstand the combined efforts of the British naval and land forces. On the following day the works were bombarded for two hours, and a landing was effected about three o'clock, when the Chinese and Tartar soldiers fled in dismay, after firing a few shots. The small island of Koolangsoo was captured on the preceding day.

On the 5th. of September the expedition sailed for the recapture of Chusan, which island had been given up in consequence of the stipulations of the first treaty. The place was found more strongly fortified than before, and a resolute but unavailing stand was made by the Chinese. A landing in two columns was effected on the 1st. of October; the first, about fifteen hundred strong, was accompanied by Major-General Sir Hugh Gough, and was under the command of Lieutenant-Colonel Craigie, of the 55th. Foot. The second, about one thousand strong, was commanded by Lieutenant-Colonel Morris, of the 49th. regiment.

The expedition proceeded on the 6th. against the city of Chinhae, the military depot of the province, situated on the mainland opposite Chusan, and surrounded by a wall of extraordinary height and thickness. The troops landed on the 10th. of October, advanced through a difficult country towards the city, and stormed the works covering the approach to the place. In this city an extensive arsenal, and cannon foundry, with military stores, fell into the hands of the captors. The force employed consisted of detachments of the 18th., 49th., and 55th. regiments, and of the Royal and the Madras Artillery.

From Chinhae the expedition proceeded up the river on the 13th. of October, against the fortified city of Ningpo, where no resistance was encountered. The troops landed, and formed on the ramparts, and possession was taken of the second city in the province of Che-Keang, containing three hundred thousand inhabitants.

On the 10th. of March, 1842, a large army of Tartars and Chinese made a sudden attack upon Ningpo, escalading the walls, and forcing some of the gates, with great spirit, when the few British in garrison, triumphed over their numerous opponents. A guard of the 18th. Royal Irish Regiment, consisting of Lieutenant Anthony Armstrong, one sergeant, and twenty-three rank and file, stationed at the West-gate, being attacked by large numbers, behaved steadily, and gallantly drove them back, capturing two banners, the bearers of which had been shot at the gate: the spirited behaviour of this officer was commended in the public despatches.

Five days afterwards the troops embarked from Ningpo, and sailed up the river to attack the enemy's posts. On the 15th. of March they were engaged at Tsekee, and the heights of Segaon, which were captured; the Chankee-pass was also forced, and the expedition, of which the 18th., 26th., and 49th. formed a portion, returned to Ningpo on the 17th. of March. This place was evacuated by the British in May, and an expedition proceeded against the fortified city of Chapoo, where a landing was effected on the 18th. of May. The 18th. and 49th. regiments composed the right column, under Lieutenant-Colonel Morris; and the 26th. and 55th. regiments were in the left, under Colonel Schoedde; the centre column under Lieutenant-Colonel Montgomerie, comprised detachments of the Royal and Madras Artillery, and the 36th. Madras Native Infantry. Lieutenant-Colonel Tomlinson met a soldier's death at the head of his regiment, the 18th. Royal Irish.

In June an expedition sailed up the Yangtse-Keang river, and the fortified posts of Woosung and Poonshau were captured. The city of Shanghae was afterwards taken possession of without opposition. Reinforcements arrived, including the 98th. regiment from England, and the expedition proceeded against Chin-Keang-foo, one of the strongest and most important cities of China. The fleet left Woosung on the 6th. of July, the Chinese troops were driven from Suyshan, and on the 20th. of July the armament approached Chin-Keang-foo. On the following day, after the reconnoissance had been completed, and the ships were in position, the landing commenced. The first brigade, consisting of the 26th., the Bengal Volunteers, flank companies of the 41st. Madras Native Infantry, and the 98th., was under the command of Major-General Lord Saltoun; the second (centre) brigade consisting of a detachment of the Royal Artillery, 55th., 6th. Madras Native Infantry, 36th. Madras Rifles, 2nd. Madras Native Infantry, and a detachment of Sappers, was commanded by Colonel, now Lieutenant-General Sir James Holmes Schoedde, K.C.B., (55th. Foot;) the third brigade comprised the 18th. and 49th., and the 14th. Madras Native Infantry, and was commanded by Colonel, afterwards Sir Robert Bartley, K.C.B., (49th. regiment,) both these officers having the local rank of Major-General.

Major-Generals Lord Saltoun and Schoedde commenced landing the troops before daylight, but considerable delay occurred from the rapidity of the current and the scattered state of the ships. The guns were next landed, followed by Major-General Bartley's brigade. Lord Saltoun moved forward with the troops of his brigade first landed, the 98th. under Lieutenant-Colonel Campbell, (now Lord Clyde), and some companies of the native regiments, to destroy the encampments, and cut off the enemy's communication with the city, between twelve and fifteen hundred of whom had shewn themselves. The soldiers drove them over the hills and destroyed the encampments. Major-General Schoedde escaladed the city walls at the north angle and carried the inner gateway, which was obstinately defended.

The 55th. highly distinguished itself on this occasion.* Lieutenant Cuddy, of that regiment, was the first to mount the walls, and was shortly afterwards severely wounded. Major (now Major-General Charles Warren, C.B.,) Warren, commanding the 55th., after he was himself wounded, cut down two of the enemy, and was personally engaged with a third.

---

* "The grenadier company of H.M. 55th. Foot, and two companies of the 6th. regiment of M.N.I. with the Sappers carrying the ladders, under the command of Brevet-Major Maclean, 55th. Foot, advanced against the north-east angle. The Sappers, commanded by Lieutenant Johnstone, with the greatest steadiness and gallantry reared their ladders against the wall, and in a few minutes the grenadiers of the 55th. had mounted, and dividing into two parties, proceeded to clear the ramparts, one party turning to the right, under Brevet-Major Maclean, and another to the left, under Lieutenant Cuddy, 55th."–*Major-General Schoadde's despatch.*

Every angle and embrasure had to be carried at the point of the bayonet. Brevet-Major Maclean commanded the storming party, and Captain Greenwood the Royal Artillery.

Meanwhile the west-gate had been blown in by Captain Pears, the commanding engineer. A body of Tartars having been driven into one division of the western outwork, refused to surrender, when most of them were either shot or destroyed in the burning houses, several of which had been set on fire by the enemy, or by the British guns. Major-General Bartley subsequently proceeded with a body of troops, consisting of the 18th. and part of the 49th. regiment, when a hot engagement ensued with about one thousand Tartars, who, under cover of some enclosures, opened a destructive fire on the soldiers as they were filing round the walls. The leading division of the 49th. dashing down the ramparts on their left, while the 18th. pushed on to turn their right, they were soon dispersed, although some fought with great desperation.

From the sun becoming so overpowering, it was found impossible to move with men already fatigued by their exertions, many of whom died from the intense heat.* The troops therefore remained in occupation of the gates until six o'clock, when several parties were pushed into the Tartar city and to the public offices. On passing through the city and suburbs the painful spectacle presented itself of hundreds of the dead bodies of men, women, and children, lying in the houses, numerous families having destroyed themselves sooner than outlive the disgrace of their city being captured by foreigners.

In the attack on the entrenched camp, and storm and capture of the city of Chin-Keang-foo, the total casualties were three officers, two sergeants, and twenty-nine men killed; fifteen officers, four sergeants, one drummer, and eighty-six men wounded. Of these numbers one gunner of the Royal Artillery, two men of the 49th., and thirteen men of the 98th., were killed by a stroke of the sun.

The Royal Artillery, 18th., 26th., 49th., 55th., and 98th. regiments shared in this service.

---

* Lieutenant-Colonel Stephens, commanding the 49th., Colonel Bartley being on the staff, with the local rank of Major-General, died in consequence of the great fatigue, and exposure to the sun.

Sir Hugh Gough proceeded to carry his victorious troops into the heart of the empire, and attack Nankin, the ancient capital of China, wherein the fugitives from Chin-Keang-foo had sought refuge. By the 9th. of August the British naval and land forces environed Nankin, and a great portion of the troops landed. This decisive step produced the desired results, and conditions of peace were acceded to; the Chinese paying an indemnity, and ceding a portion of territory to the British crown.

In consideration of the gallantry displayed by the troops employed on the coasts and rivers of China, Her Majesty was graciously pleased to permit the 18th., 26th., 49th., 55th., and 98th. regiments, to bear on their colours and appointments the word CHINA, and the device of the "Dragon."

THE FIRST CHINA MEDAL.

This Medal, authorized by the Queen, is by the late William Wyon, Esq., R.A., and has on the obverse the Queen's head, with the superscription VICTORIA REGINA; on the reverse is a palm tree, against which are placed the arms of England on a shield, with cannons, anchor, flags, etc.; and the motto ARMIS EXPOSCERE PACEM. In the *exergue* the word CHINA, 1842, underneath. The ribbon is crimson with yellow edges. Mr. Wyon made a very elaborate design for this medal, consisting of the Chinese Plenipotentiaries signing the treaty, and on the cloth of the table was a very minute pattern embroidered, representing the British Lion trampling on the dragon. So happy was the idea considered, that this portion instead of the whole of it was adopted for the reverse, over which was the above motto, and Nanking, 1842, beneath; but the present medal was ultimately struck, as the former was deemed offensive to the feelings of the conquered people.

SEQUEL TO THE FIRST AFFGHAN CAMPAIGN.

Shah Soojah's government became so unpopular that the Affghans determined to effect the expulsion of the British, by whose aid he had been reinstated, and whose presence in

Cabool was rendered necessary to support him on the throne. The crisis arrived in 1841. In October the Affghans broke out into open insurrection; the British envoy, Sir William Macnaghten, and Sir Alexander Burnes, were treacherously murdered, and the troops, including the 44th. regiment,* which occupied Cabool, being compelled to evacuate that place, and retreat towards Jellalabad, were cut to pieces on the march, Dr. Brydon of the Shah's forces, being the only officer who succeeded in reaching that place. It is remarkable that this officer was one of the heroes of Lucknow.

The 13th. regiment was more fortunate; under its gallant Lieutenant-Colonel, Sir Robert Sale, (serving with the local rank of Major-General), it reached Jellalabad, having at the breaking out of the insurrection been detached from Cabool with a force in order to reduce the insurgents, and after much hard fighting in the passes had taken possession of Jellalabad, the successful defence of which by his small garrison, forms so bright a feature in this terrible and gloomy history. Before describing this heroic defence, only equalled by that of Lucknow, it is necessary to show the manner in which the gallant band reached the place of safety. The 13th. and other troops left Cabool on the 11th. of October, in consequence of a body of insurgents having possessed themselves of the Khoord Cabool pass,† about ten miles from the capital, with a view to expel the rebels, and re-open the communication with India. On the 12th. of October the pass was

---

* The 44th. regiment arrived at Jellalabad in January 1841, and was moved to Cabool in May following. On the 1st of October of that year, the strength of the regiment in Affghanistan was 25 officers, 85 sergeants, 14 drummers, and 685 rank and file. The number killed at Cabool, and during the retreat, amounted to 22 officers and 548 men; three officers, Lieutenant-Colonel Shelton, and Lieutenants Evans and Souter, and 51 men were taken prisoners. The officers killed between the 10th. of November, 1841, and the 18th. of January, 1842, were Lieutenant-Colonel Mackrell, Major Scott, Captains Swayne, Mc Crea, Leighton, and Robinson; Lieutenants Dodgin, Collins, White, Wade, Hogg, Cumberland, Raban, Cadett, Swinton, Fortye, and Gray; Paymaster Bourke; Quartermaster Halahan; Surgeon Harcourt, and Assistant-Surgeons Balfour and Primrose. Lieutenant Souter, severely wounded, preserved the colours of the 44th. by tying them round his waist. 102 officers were killed at Cabool, and during the retreat.

† This was the place where the massacre of the British troops occurred, and not as too frequently stated, in the *Khyber* pass, which had they been able to reach, being on the Indian side of Jellalabad, they would have been safe.

forced, the troops under Sir Robert penetrating to Khoord (Little) Cabool.

Major-General Sir Robert Sale, Captain Hamlet C. Wade, (Major of Brigade,) Lieutenant George Mein, and Ensign Oakes were wounded. Lieutenant Mein being dangerously wounded, was obliged to be sent back in a litter to Cabool. Upon Sir Robert Sale being compelled to quit the field from the severity of his wound, the command of the troops devolved upon Lieutenant-Colonel Dennis, C.B., also of the 13th. The regiment then faced about, to return through the pass according to the plan for executing the operation, leaving the other corps at Khoord Cabool. Possession was then taken of Bootkhak, where the regiment was stationed until the 18th. of October. During this delay, incessant night-attacks were made by the enemy, called by them Shub Khoon, (night slaughter;) Sir Robert Sale's precaution in ordering the men to lie down on their alarm posts, as soon as the fire was opened on the camp, prevented much loss: his orders prohibiting any return-fire likewise saved many, and all the enemy's attempts to force an entrance therein were successfully resisted by the bayonet alone. Meanwhile the rebellion continued of a formidable character, and the 13th. were ordered to march to Tezeen, where they arrived on the 22nd. of October, and were engaged with a body of insurgents, whom they drove from some heights and strong positions. The regiment here lost Lieutenant Edward King, who fell at the head of his company, while gallantly charging the enemy, and Lieutenant R.E. Frere was wounded.

In consequence of orders from Cabool, the force under Major-General Sir Robert Sale marched for Gundamuck, and were continually pressed day and night, by insurgent bands hovering on their flanks and rear, which occasioned the fatigues and duties of the troops to be particularly harassing; the way led along defiles and over mountains, and when the soldiers halted, breast-works had to be thrown up to defend the bivouac ground from sudden attacks of the Affghan cavalry.

On the 29th. of October the rebels were found in force at the Jugdulluck Pass, and for some time they checked the advance of the column; but the skirmishers of the 13th. sprang forward, and driving the Affgbans from almost inaccessible heights protected by breast-works, enabled the British force to surmount every obstacle in the defile, and to arrive at Gundamuck on the following day. Lieutenants Jennings, Holcombe, and Rattray were severely wounded; Lieutenant-Colonel Dennie, Captains Wilkinson, Havelock, Wade, and Fenwick, were specially mentioned in the despatches. The 13th. regiment up to this period had ten men killed and seventy-five wounded.

Sir Robert Sale remained at Gundamuck with his troops until the 5th. of November, when they proceeded and captured the fort of Mamoo Khail in the neighbourhood, and returned on the 6th. to Gundamuck. There intelligence was received of the breaking out of a violent insurrection at Cabool, on the 2nd. of November, and of the probability that the rebellion would become general. Under these circumstances, two forced marches on Jellalabad were made, with a numerous enemy pressing on the flanks and rear; a body of insurgents were beaten at Futtehabad by the rear-guard under Lieutenant-Colonel Dennie; and Jellalabad, the chief town in the valley of Ningrahar, was seized by the British troops on the 12th. of November, to establish a post upon which the corps at Cabool might retire, if necessary, and thus restore a link in the chain of communication with India.

DEFENCE OF JELLALABAD.
12TH NOVEMBER, 1841, TO 7TH APRIL, 1842.

The fortress of Jellalabad was found to be in a very dilapidated state, and the inhabitants disaffected to the government of the Shah. The Affghans collected to about ten thousand, and the walls of the fort being without parapets, and the garrison having only one day and a half supplies, on half rations, a sally was made on the 14th. of November, which routed the enemy, and enabled the troops to collect provisions, and erect works for the defence of the fortress, which called forth the efforts of all. While thus employed, the Affgbans in great force again invested the place on the 27th. of November, but they were completely routed and dispersed by a sally of the garrison on the 1st. of December.

On the 9th. of January, 1842, the garrison was summoned to give up the fortress by the leader of the Affghan rebellion, in fulfilment of a convention entered into at Cabool with Major-General Elphinstone, who was taken prisoner at a conference, and died shortly afterwards; but Sir Robert Sale being fully assured of the bad faith of the insurgents, refused; the annihilation of the troops from the capital, in the Ghilzie defiles, by the severity of the climate, and the basest treachery on the part of those in whose promises they had confided, proved the correctness of the major-general's estimate of their character.

Captain Broadfoot, garrison engineer, and Captain Abbott, commissary of ordnance, aided by the indefatigable exertions of the troops, brought the works into a state of defence against any Asiatic enemy not provided with siege-artillery; but the place was kept in a continual state of alarm by the occurrence of one hundred shocks of an earthquake in the course of a month, one of which, on the 19th. of February, occasioned the parapets to fall, injured the bastions, made a breach in the rampart, destroyed the guard-houses, reduced other portions of the works to ruins, and demolished one third of the town. With that unconquerable spirit of perseverance for which the troops had already been distinguished, they instantly turned to the repair of the works. Sirdar Mahomed Akbar Khan, Barukzye, the assassin of the late Envoy, and the treacherous destroyer of the Cabool force, flushed with success, approached with a numerous army to overwhelm the little garrison; he attacked the foraging parties on the 21st. and 22nd. of February; but was astonished at finding the works in a state of defence, whereupon he established a rigorous blockade. From that time to the 7th. of April, the reduced garrison was engaged in a succession of skirmishes, in which the 13th. had opportunities of distinguishing themselves; particularly detachments under Captains Pattisson and Fenwick, Lieutenants George Wade and W. Cox.

Information was received on the 5th. of April, that the force under Major-General, now General Sir George Pollock, G.C.B., had experienced reverses in the Khyber, and had retraced its steps towards Peshawur; and on the 6th. a *feu-de-joie* and salute of artillery were fired by Mahomed Akbar, in honour of the event. It was also reported that the Ghazees had been defeated, and that the Sirdar had retreated into Lughman.

Sir Robert Sale resolved to anticipate the last-mentioned event, by a general attack on the Affghan camp, with the hope of relieving Jellalabad from blockade, and facilitating Major-General Pollock's advance. Directions were accordingly given to form three columns of infantry, the central one consisting of the 13th., (mustering five hundred bayonets,) under Colonel Dennie, C.B.; the left comprising a similar number of the 35th. Native Infantry, under Lieutenant-Colonel Monteath, C.B.; and the right composed of one company of the 13th., one of the 35th. Native Infantry, and the detachment of Sappers, under the command of Lieutenant Orr, (the severity of Captain Broadfoot's wound still rendering him non-effective,) amounting to three hundred and sixty men, was commanded by Captain (afterwards the celebrated Sir Henry) Havelock, of the 13th.; these were to be supported by the fire of the guns of No. 6 field battery under Captain Abbott, the whole of the small cavalry force being under Captain Oldfield and Lieutenant Mayne.

At daylight on the morning of the 7th. of April, the troops issued from the Cabool and Peshawur gates. The Sirdar, Mahomed Akbar Khan, had formed his force of about six thousand men in order of battle for the defence of his camp; its right resting on a fort, and its left on the Cabool river; even the ruined works within eight hundred yards of the place, but recently repaired, were filled with Ghilzie marksmen, who had evidently determined upon a stout resistance. The attack was led by the skirmishers and column under Captain Havelock; this drove the enemy from the extreme left of his advanced line of works, which it pierced at once, and proceeded to advance into the plain; the central column at the same time directed its efforts against a square fort, upon the same base, the defence of which was obstinately maintained. Colonel Dennie, while nobly leading his regiment to the assault, received a shot through his body, which, to the deep regret of officers and men, shortly after proved fatal.*

The rear of the work having been finally gained by passing to its left, orders were given for a combined attack upon the enemy's camp; this was brilliant and successful. The artillery advanced at the gallop, and directed a heavy fire upon the Affghan centre, while two columns of infantry penetrated his line near the same point, and the third forced back his left from its support on the river, into which some of his horse and foot were driven. The Affghans repeatedly attempted to check the advance by a smart fire of musketry—by throwing forward heavy bodies of horse, which twice threatened in force the detachments of infantry under Captain Havelock, and by opening three guns, screened by a garden wall; but in a short time they were dislodged from every point of their positions, their cannon taken, and their camp involved in a general conflagration.

By about seven o'clock in the morning the battle was over, and the enemy in full retreat in the direction of Lughman. Two Affghan cavalry standards were taken, besides four guns which had been lost by the Cabool army and Gundamuck forces. Great quantities of *matériel* and stores were, together with the enemy's tents, destroyed, and the defeat of Mahomed Akbar, in open field, by the troops he had boasted of blockading, was complete.

In addition to Colonel Dennie, killed, the 13th. had Lieutenant Jennings and Assistant-Surgeon Barnes wounded; eight privates were killed, and thirty-one rank and file wounded.

Armourer Sergeant Henry Ulyett, of the 13th., captured Mahomed Akbar's standard, which be took from a cavalry soldier, whom be killed. The standard is of scarlet cloth, with a green border, and crimson and yellow fringe. It is triangular in shape and swallow-tailed.

---

* Captain Wilkinson, of the 13th., on whom the charge of one of the infantry columns devolved on the lamented fall of Colonel Dennie, and Captain Hamlet Wade, (Brigade-Major,) were highly commended in Major-General Sir Robert Sales despatch; Lieutenant and Adjutant Wood made a dash at one of the enemy, and in cutting him down, his charger was so severely injured as to have been afterwards destroyed. Lieutenant Cox was the first of the party which captured two of the enemy's cannon. The conduct of these two officers, both of the 13th., was specially noticed. Major Wade presented to the United Service Museum an Affghan steel helmet, with chain-mail defence for the neck and eyes, and a nasal or bar to be raised or lowered for the defence of the nose. This was worn by one of the Afghan cavalry, and taken in the above action.

About the centre a patch of light blue cloth is introduced, on which are neatly sewn some characters in yellow cloth, being an extract from the Koran, signifying "The Omnipotent God! In the name of God, the clement and the merciful! With God as a helper, victory is nigh." This and two other flags, captured by the 13th. on the same day, were deposited in Chelsea Hospital.

In this successful enterprise the force employed amounted to about eighteen hundred men of all arms. The safety of the fortress was entrusted, during the action, to the ordinary guards of its gates, and one provisional battalion of followers of every description armed with pikes and other weapons, who manned the curtains, and made a respectable show of defence. Captain Pattisson, of the 13th., was left in command of this diminished garrison; towards the conclusion of the engagement a sally was made from the Cabool gate by Lieutenant George Wade, of the same regiment, into the fort before which Colonel Dennis had fallen, when it was observed that the enemy were abandoning the place; all it contained was set on fire, and some of the defenders were bayoneted.

The enemy's loss was very severe; the field of battle was strewed with the bodies of men and horses, and the richness of the trappings of some of the latter denoted that chiefs of rank (several being present and taking part in the action) had fallen.

In February following, the thanks of Parliament were accorded to the Governor-General of India, and to the officers and troops employed in Affghanistan, the resolutions being moved in the House of Lords by the Duke of Wellington, and in the House of Commons by Sir Robert Peel, who, after eulogizing the gallant conduct of Sir Robert Sale and the garrison of Jellalabad, (appropriately designated "ILLUSTRIOUS") specially deplored the death of Colonel Donnie,* justly described as "one of the most noble and gallant spirits, whose actions have ever added brilliance to their country's military renown."

---

* The following interesting circumstance was related by Lord Fitzgerald and Vesey in the House of Lords, in his speech on the 20th. of February, 1843, regarding the vote of thanks for the operations in Atfghanistan. The Adjutant-General of the Army in India, acting by the command of Lord Ellenborough,

On the 26th. of August, 1842, it was officially announced in the "London Gazette," that "In consideration of the distinguished gallantry displayed by the 13th. Light Infantry, during the campaigns in the Burmese empire and in Affghanistan, Her Majesty has been graciously pleased to approve of that regiment. assuming the title of the 13th., or Prince Albert's Regiment of Light Infantry;' and of its facings being changed from yellow to blue.

"Her Majesty has also been pleased to authorize the 13th. Regiment of Light Infantry to bear on its colours and appointments a 'Mural Crown,' superscribed 'Jellalabad,' as a memorial of the fortitude, perseverance, and enterprise, evinced by that regiment, and the several corps which served during the blockade of Jellalabad."

THE JELLALABAD MEDALS.

A silver medal was distributed by the Governor-General of India to every officer, non-commissioned officer, and private, European and Native, who belonged to the garrison of Jellalabad on the 7th. of April, 1842; on one side was a Mural Crown superscribed JELLALABAD, and on the other VII APRIL, 1842. Her Majesty's permission for the 13th. Light Infantry to wear this medal was dated 26th. of August, 1842. The ribbon, intended to represent the rays of the rising sun, was made expressly for the above medal, and is generally known as the rainbow pattern.*

Subsequently a silver medal, designed by William Wyon,

---

transmitted to the aged mother of Colonel Dennie that medal which her son would have worn, had he happily survived. In replying to the letter which accompanied this token, Mrs. Dennie beautifully said, that "she accepted it with pleasure and with pride, for she had a right to feel a pride in her son's life, and in his death." Lord Fitzgerald added, "that it was impossible to read that passage without honouring the lady, and even more deeply lamenting the fate of the son of whom she had so justly and truly written." Since 1842 it has been the invariable practice with regard to medals granted for service in India, to present them to the legal representatives of the deceased officers and soldiers.

* This medal, which was struck in India by order of Lord Ellenborough, is now very scarce. The accompanying engraving has been made from a specimen kindly lent to me by Captain A.C. Tupper, one of the Council of the Royal United Service Institution, from whom I have received several valuable hints during the progress of this work.

Esq., was struck. On the obverse was the Queen's Head superscribed
VICTORIA VINDEX. On the reverse a figure of Victory, with the Union
Jack in her left hand, and laurel wreaths in her right, flying over the
fortress of Jellalabad. Above the figure are the words JELLALABAD, VII
APRIL., in a semicircle; and in the exergue MDCCCXLII. (See page 91.)
This was exchanged for the first medal, the ribbon being the same in
both cases.

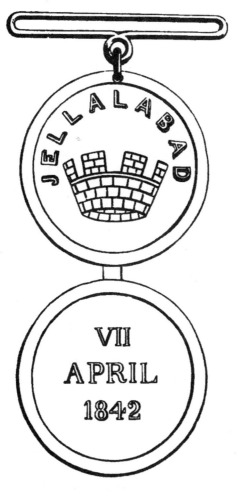

FIRST JELLALABAD MEDAL

SECOND AFFGHAN CAMPAIGN. 1842.

When the news of the Affghan tragedy reached India, it was resolved to rescue the gallant garrison, and to restore British supremacy beyond the Indus. Accordingly a force was collected at Peshawur, in the north of the Punjaub, under Major-General Pollock, early in 1842. Of this army the Queen's regiments consisted of the 3rd. Light Dragoons, and the 9th. and 31st. Foot. On the 5th. of April the Khyber Pass was forced, although strongly occupied, and its mouth having a breastwork of stones and bushes.

Precipitous and rocky hills, on the right and left, presented great natural obstacles to the ascent of troops, and it was an undertaking of no ordinary difficulty to gain the summit of such heights, defended, as they were, by a numerous body of the enemy; the columns destined to accomplish this most important object, moved off simultaneously with the main one intended to assault the entrance, but were compelled to make a considerable detour to the right and left, to enable them to commence the ascent. The right column, consisting of four companies of the 9th. Foot, and the same number of companies of the 26th. and 64th. Native Infantry, were under the command of Lieutenant-Colonel Taylor, of the 9th. regiment, and Major Anderson, of the 64th. Native Infantry. The left column, consisting of four companies of the 9th. Foot, a similar number of companies of the 26th. and 64th. Native Infantry, together with four hundred Jezailchees, commanded by Lieutenant-Colonel Moseley and Major Huish, commenced the ascent, led by Captain Ferris, of the regiment of Jezailcbees.

Both columns, after considerable opposition, succeeded in routing the enemy, and gaining possession of the crest of the hills on either side. While the flanking columns were in progress on the heights, Captain Alexander, in command of the artillery, placed the guns in position, and threw shrapnels among the enemy when opportunity offered, which assisted much in their discomfiture. Upon the heights being gained, the main column was advanced to the mouth of the Pass, and commenced destroying the barrier, which the enemy had evacuated on perceiving their position was turned; portions of the right and left columns were left to keep the heights, under the command of Lieutenant-Colonel Moseley and Major Anderson, and Major Huish and Lieutenant-Colonel Taylor continued their advance to crown the hills in front, and on each side, which were covered with the foe, who appeared determined to contest every inch of ground; but the gallantry of the troops carried everything before them.

Thus was accomplished without the payment of any tribute, the passage of the Khyber Pass,* and the road to Jellalabad was gained. The siege of that place (as already shewn) had been abandoned, when Major-General Pollock arrived on the 16th. of April, and found the garrison, after a siege which had lasted upwards of five months, in excellent health, with a plentiful supply of ammunition, and all most anxious to march on Cabool.

ADVANCE ON CABOOL. 1842.

Major-General Pollock urged upon Lord Ellenborough, the new Governor-General of India, the advance upon Cabool; the 31st. regiment, which had followed by forced marches, joined at Jellalabad on the 5th. of May, having undergone much privation on the way, and the loss of several men from famine and fatigue; while at Jellalabad the army was halted in wretched tents, the climate being so unhealthy during the summer, that the natives use it only as a winter residence. Soon the effect of this displayed itself; the days became so oppressive, that both officers and men were obliged to dig deep holes underground in which to shield themselves,

---

* It is remarkable that the Sikhs, afterwards such formidable opponents during the Sutlej and Punjab campaigns, were able supporters at this period, and during the recent Indian Mutiny they sustained their former character, the Sikh regiments being most valuable allies.

In a notification from the Governor-General, in Council, dated from Benares, on the 19th. of April, 1842, the following passage occurs:—"The Governor-General deems it to be due to the troops of the Maha Rajah Shere Shing, to express his entire satisfaction with their conduct, as reported to him, and to inform the army, that the loss sustained by the Sikhs in the assault of the Khyber Pass, which was forced by them, is understood to have been equal to that sustained by the troops of Her Majesty and of the Government of India."

in some slight measure, from the burning heat of the sun, the thermometer rising in the tents as high as 126°.

In consequence of the extreme heat the troops suffered a loss which the most sanguinary encounter with the enemy could not have exceeded. Neither was it in men alone that the army was daily losing its efficiency. From the valley of Jellalabad having been so long the seat of war, the fertile land had become a desert,–the wretched half-starved camels could find no forage on the bare face of the sand, and they died by hundreds; their dead bodies lying about in all directions, swollen with the sun, and emitting the most pestilential exhalations, together with the filth and dirt of a standing camp of fifty thousand men, added to the disease which raged among the troops.

Eventually it was found necessary to divide the force, and the fourth brigade, in which was the 31st. regiment, was ordered to march under Brigadier Monteath to Peshbolak, in the Shinwaree country, to punish some refractory tribes, who had attacked several convoys, and been guilty of many acts of murder and plunder. The warlike and turbulent Shinwaree tribes sheltered themselves in their strongholds, which were formed in a narrow valley, strengthened by many forts and stockaded enclosures, while the heights on either side were defended by numerous sunghas, or breastworks of large stones, which were so constructed as to enable them to dispute every inch of ground with an advancing force. The brigade having arrived, and encamped about two miles from this formidable position, a reconnoitring party was sent out, under the command of Captain Willis, of the 31st.; this party, having proceeded some four or five miles from the camp, was furiously attacked, and suffered severely from the enemy's fire; nevertheless the object sought was fully obtained, after which it returned, to the camp, sustaining a smart action the whole way back.

On the 26th. of July, Brigadier Monteath prepared to attack the enemy near Mazeena with his whole force; and accordingly, leaving the camp standing under an efficient guard, he moved towards the position occupied by the Affghans, who were prepared, and nothing loath to meet him. The engagement was commenced by the 31st. regiment, seconded by the 33rd. and 53rd. Native Infantry, ascending the heights, and driving the Shinwarees from their breastworks, and along the ridges of the hills, while the 10th. Light Cavalry, in the valley below, charged them whenever they showed front on level ground. The camp followers and pioneers had been furnished with combustibles to burn the forts, as the Shinwarees were driven out of them, which service was very efficiently performed. Meanwhile, on the heights, the enemy disputed every foot of ground until taken at the point of the bayonet, and Lieutenant M'Ilween, of the 31st., was killed in leading one of the attacks.

The Affghans being driven from their defences, the artillery, under the command of Captain Abbott, played upon them with great effect; and after contesting the day until every fort and place of defence had been taken and destroyed, they fled, dispersing themselves among the neighbouring hills, where it was impossible to pursue them. Their loss was very great, including most of their leaders.

After this action the brigade returned to Jellalabad, and on the 20th. of August the army marched in two divisions *en route* to Cabool. Three days afterwards the troops arrived at Gundamuck, when information was received that the enemy, under the Chiefs Hadji Ali and Khyroolah Khan, occupied the village and fort of Mammoo Khail, about two miles distant, and it was determined to attack them there on the following morning. Accordingly on the 24th. of August, at four o'clock, a.m., the troops advanced, and the attack on Mammoo Khail was attended with complete success.

Major-General Pollock left Gundamuck on the 7th. of September, and on the day after the troops were engaged with the forces of Mahomed Khan and the Ghilzie chiefs at the Pass of Jugdulluck; in the valley were seen the blackened remains of the unfortunate Cabool force. No further opposition was shown to the advance of the army until nearing the valley of Tezeen;—the road from this place to Khoord Cabool was through a succession of lofty hills, called the Haft Kotul, or Eight Hills.

On the 10th. of September, it having been ascertained that Akbar Khan, with twenty thousand men, had established himself in the Khoord Cabool Pass, in order to cover the capital and fight a pitched battle with the British, the second division was ordered to join the first by a forced march to Tezeen, where Major-General Pollock was encamped. This junction was effected on the 11th. of September, with little loss, although a running fight was kept up the greater part of the way. In fact, the advance to Cabool was a succession of skirmishes oftentimes by night as well as by day. The camp was attacked on the night of the 12th. of September, but the enemy made no impression, and little loss occurred.

Shortly after daybreak on the 13th. of September, the army moved off its ground towards the Tezeen Pass, the advanced guard being commanded by Sir Robert Sale. After moving carefully along the Pass for about two miles, the Affghans were discovered, in great force, occupying strong positions on the heights on either side, while their artillery and cavalry were formed some distance farther on in the Pass itself. The action commenced by a heavy fire on the advanced guard of the British; and the distance being too great for musketry, from the effect of which also the Affghans were covered by extensive sunghas, for the whole length of their position, it was judged necessary for the troops to ascend the heights and drive them from their posts at the point of the bayonet. This service was most effectively performed on the left heights by the 9th. and 31st. regiments, and on the right by the 13th. Light Infantry.

The companies ascended the face of the mountain under a most galling fire, from the effects of which many casualties occurred, and not returning a shot until the ledge was gained: a combined volley within ten yards of the enemy, followed by an immediate charge of bayonets, drove him from his defences with great slaughter, and the heights were gained.

Being reinforced by fresh troops, the British pushed on, and storming one entrenchment after another, threw the Affghans into great confusion. The artillery was now brought up, and played upon them with terrific effect, while the British cavalry, having charged and overthrown their horse, posted in the Pass, and taken their guns, together with the state tent of their commander, Mahomed Akbar Khan, victory, even at this early period was in favour of the British arms; but the war-like mountaineers continued the struggle with desperate valour. Attack after attack was made upon the troops occupying the posts from which the enemy had first been driven. Reckless of life, the stern fanatics came on to be shot down from the defences which they had themselves thrown up. In a series of desultory attacks the day declined, and the British having obtained possession of every height commanding the Pass, the remains of the Affghan army made a detour among the hills, and attacked the British rear-guard, commanded by Colonel Richmond, but they were warmly received, and entirely discomfited.*

So complete was the defeat of the Affghan army on the 13th. of September, that Akbar Khan escaped from the field accompanied only by a solitary horsemen. The enemy acknowledged to have lost fifty-three chiefs and persons of consequence and seven hundred men. The casualties on the part of the British amounted to one hundred and eighty-five.

No impediments now existed to the advance of the British on Cabool, at which city the army arrived on the 15th. of September, and encamped on the race-course. On the following morning the British colours were hoisted on the highest pinnacles of the battlements of the Balar Hissar, (upper fort,) on the spot most conspicuous from the city; the National Anthem was played, and a royal salute fired from the guns of the horse artillery, the whole of the troops present giving three cheers. The colours were left in the Balar Hissar to be hoisted daily as long as the troops should continue at Cabool.

All the objects of the campaign were thus gained, and the rescue of the prisoners effected, amongst whom were several officers† and ladies, (Lady Sale being of the number,) together

---

* Major Skinner, of the 31st., highly distinguished himself with the force which was detached under his command, and which proceeded, in the afternoon of the 12th. of September, across the hills towards the valley of Khoord Cabool by a route different from that of the main army. On the march, this officer came suddenly in presence of a greatly superior number of Affghans. Notwithstanding that the country was difficult and imperfectly known, by a series of skilful manoeuvres he extricated his troops from the perilous situation in which they were placed, and defeated the Affghans, who exceeded five times his force, with great slaughter, on the 13th. of September.

† One of these officers, Lieutenant Mein, was thus alluded to in reference to his conduct,

with thirty-six non-commissioned officers and men of the 44th. regiment—one hundred and five in all.

CANDAHAR. 1842.

As the 13th. Light Infantry are so intimately connected with the defence of Jellalabad, in like manner the 40th. regiment is associated with Candabar. Major-General Sir William Nott, like Sir Robert Sale, refused to obey the order from Major-General Elphinstone to surrender. After the insurrection at Cabool, a general rising took place throughout Affghanistan, and the insurgents in the neighbourhood of Candahar being headed by Prince Sufter Jung, the son of Shah Soojah, and brother of Prince Timour, (Governor of Candahar,) who had left on the 29th. of November, 1841, to place himself at the head of those whom Mahomed Atta Khan was

----

while serving with the army on its retreat from Cabool, by Sir Robert Peel, on moving the vote of thanks to the army employed in Affghanistan:—"I have said that, in the course of this campaign, instances of the most generous devotion, of friendly sympathy, and of desperate fidelity, were displayed, which deserve at least a passing notice. Lieutenant Eyre says: 'Lieutenant Sturt (son-in-law to Sir Robert and Lady Sale) had nearly cleared the defile, when he received his wound, and would have been left on the ground to be hacked to pieces by the Ghazees, who followed in the rear to complete the work of slaughter, but for the generous intrepidity of Lieutenant Mein, of Her Majesty's 13th. Light Infantry, who, on learning what had befallen him, went back to his succour, and stood by him for several minutes, at the imminent risk of his own life, vainly entreating aid from the passers by. He was, at length, joined by Sergeant Deane, of the Sappers, with whose assistance he dragged his friend, on a quilt, through the remainder of the Pass, when he succeeded in mounting him on a miserable pony, and conducted him in safety to the camp, where the unfortunate officer lingered till the following morning, and was the only man of the whole force who received Christian burial. Lieutenant Mein was himself at this very time suffering from a dangerous wound in the head, received in the previous October; and his heroic disregard of self, and fidelity to his friend in the hour of danger, are well deserving of a record in the annals of British valour and virtue; I think, Sir, it is but just that the name of Lieutenant Mein should be mentioned with honour in the House of Commons, and I do not regret having noticed this circumstance, as it has called forth so generous and general an expression of sympathy and approval.'"

The name and sufferings of Lady Sale will be ever connected with the disasters in Affghanistan; her extraordinary presence of mind, her generous consideration for the wants of her companions in captivity, and her noble example, displaying a total forgetfulness of self, endeared her to the country, and shed an imperishable renown on her sex, exhibiting to the world a remarkable instance of self-reliance and strength of mind, combined with the faithful performance of the duties of a soldier's wife. Her Journal is one of exciting and absorbing interest.

assembling on the eastern frontier. The insurgents under these two chiefs having approached within eight miles, Major-General Sir William Nott, G.C.B., moved out to attack them on the morning of the 12th. of January, 1842, the 40th. forming the advance. This regiment, during the previous year, had suffered severely from sickness, the number of deaths amounting to one hundred and fifty-nine. A strong position, with a morass in their front, had been taken up by the enemy, which rendered the approach of the troops difficult. The Affghans were, however, quickly routed. At this period, and until the 7th. of May, the soldiers remained accoutred every night.

During the month of February considerable numbers of Affghans, under the command of Prince Sufter Jung and other chiefs assembled in the vicinity of Candahar, plundering the villages, and by every possible means urging the inhabitants to join in an attack upon the British troops, especially those occupying the cantonments; but owing to the severity of the weather the Major-General was unable to move, and such a measure became impracticable till the 7th. of March, when, the enemy having approached closer, Sir William Nott marched with the remainder of his army against them; they were followed, and dispersed in every direction. While the force was thus absent, a strong detachment of the enemy made an attack on the city, and succeeded in burning the Herat gate, but were repulsed with great loss by the troops in garrison. On the 25th. of March, Sir William moved out with a force (of which the 40th. formed a part,) to the support of a brigade detached under the command of Colonel Wymer, C.B., of the Bengal army, to forage and to afford protection to the numerous villages, when the Afghans were driven across the Urghundaub in the greatest confusion.

Major-General (now Lieutenant-General Sir Richard) England, who had at first been unsuccessful in conveying stores to Candahar from Scinde, having been reinforced at Quetta, again advanced, and accomplished his object. On the 28th. of April he attacked the enemy's strong position in front of the village of Hykulzie. The 41st., which formed part of his force, was the only Queen's regiment that shared in this action; two out of the three columns of attack were led by

Majors Simmons and Cochran, the reserve being under Major Browne, all of the 41st. Foot.

On the 19th. of May, a force, composed of the 40th. and other corps, under Colonel Wymer, marched for the purpose of drawing off the garrison of Kelat-i-Ghilzie, a hill fort eighty-four miles from Candahar, on the road to Ghuznee. It arrived there on the 26th., but on the 21st. the fort had been attacked by four thousand Ghilzees, whom the defenders had gallantly defeated. The troops consequently were only occupied in destroying the defences, etc., till the 1st. of June, when they returned to Candahar.*

Major-General Nott moved with his army on the 10th. of August, upon Cabool. The 40th. and 41st. regiments formed a portion of his force, the wounded, sick, and weakly men being sent to India *via* the Kojuck Pass, with the troops under Major-General England.† Captain White, of the light company of the 40th., was appointed to command the advance, composed of the light companies of the 40th. and 41st.,

---

* A medal was granted to the gallant garrison of Kelat-i-Ghllzie for its heroic and successful defence, under Captain Craigie, bearing on one side a shield inscribed KELAT-I-GHILZIE within a wreath of laurel, and surmounted by a mural crown; on the other side a cuirass, helmet, flags, muskets, and cannon, arranged as a trophy, with the word INVICTA, and date MDCCCXLII underneath. The ribbon is of the rainbow pattern. This medal was also by William Wyon, Esq., R.A. No Queen's regiment formed part of the garrison, and therefore did not receive the above medal The Kelat-i-Ghilzie regiment is the only corps which bears the name of this fort on its colours, which place is sometimes mistaken for KHELAT, borne on the colours of the 2nd. and 17th. Foot, to commemorate the capture of the capital of Beloochistan by the troops under Major-General Sir Thomas Willshire, on the 13th. of November, 1839.

† Major-General England evacuated Quetta on the 1st. of October, and succeeded in withdrawing through the Kojuck and Bolan Passes into the valley of the Indus, a portion of the force which had been stationed at Candahar, and all the scattered garrisons of the intermediate places between the eastern face of the Kojuck mountains and the plains of Cutchee. Lord Ellenborough, in General Orders, remarked that, "This operation, less brilliant in its circumstances than that entrusted to Major-General Pollock and Major-General Nott, was yet one which demanded the greatest prudence in the making of every previous arrangement for securing the safe descent of the several columns, and which called into exercise many of the higher qualities which most contribute to form the character of an accomplished general."

"The Governor-General could not but regard with some anxiety the progress of this movement, requiring so much of delicate management in its execution; and it is a subject of extreme satisfaction to him, that the same complete success should have attended this, which has, during the present campaign, attended every other part of the combined operations of the armies beyond the Indus."—*General Orders by the Governor-General of India, Simla, October 20th.,* 1842.

and the 2nd., 16th., 38th., 42nd., and 43rd. regiments of Bengal Native
Infantry, and the regiment of Kelat-i-Ghilzie.

BATTLE OF GONINE.
30TH. AUGUST, 1842.

Shumshoodeen, the Affghan governor of Ghuznee, about three
o'clock in the afternoon, on the 30th. of August, brought nearly the
whole of his army, amounting to about twelve thousand men, into
the vicinity of the camp at Gonine, distant thirty-eight miles south-
west of Ghuznee, when Major-General Nott moved out with one-
half of his force, and after a short but spirited contest, defeated the
Affghans, capturing their guns, tents, ammunition, etc., and dispersing
them in every direction. One hour more of daylight, and the whole of
their infantry would have been destroyed. Shumshoodeen fled towards
Ghuznee, accompanied by about thirty horsemen. Major Hibbert, of
the 40th., was specially noticed in the despatches. Two officers were
killed and four wounded; thirty-six non-commissioned officers and men
were killed and sixty-two wounded.

RE-CAPTURE OF GHUZNEE.
6TH. SEPTEMBER, 1842.

Major-General Sir William Nott, on the morning of the
5th. of September, moved upon Ghuznee. Lieutenant-Colonel
Palmer, Political Agent, commanding at Ghuznee, upon promise
of honourable treatment and safety on the march to Cabool, and by
the orders of Major Pottinger and Major-General Elphinstone, had,
in March, 1842, capitulated. The garrison was exhausted by fatigue
and constant duty, and the men had suffered greatly from cold,
the thermometer having been fourteen degrees below Zero. Upon
Shumshoodeen, nephew of Dost Mahomed Khan, swearing on the
Koran that he would give the Sepoys a safe escort to Hindoostan, they
consented to deliver up their arms. The city was found to be full of
men, and a range of mountains running north-east of the fortress was

covered by heavy bodies of cavalry and infantry; the gardens and ravines in the vicinity being likewise occupied. A considerable reinforcement from Cabool, under Sultan Jan, had also been received by the enemy. Major Sanders, of the Bengal Engineers, was directed to reconnoitre the works; this brought on some smart skirmishing, and Captain White, of the 40th., commanding the light companies, was pushed forward, when the Major-General determined to carry the enemy's mountain positions before encamping his force. This was effectively performed by the troops, and the Affghans were driven before them until every point was gained. Two regiments and some guns were sent from the camp, (which had been pitched,) to occupy the village of Bullool, about six hundred yards from the walls of Ghuznee, upon the spur of the mountain to the north-east, as this appeared to be a desirable spot for preparing a heavy battery.

During the night of the 5th. of September, the engineers, sappers and miners, and infantry working parties were employed in erecting breaching batteries; before the guns, however, had reached the position on the morning of the 6th., it was ascertained that the fortress had been evacuated, and at daybreak the British colours were flying from the citadel. The 40th. had one private killed and three privates wounded; the 41st. had the same number wounded. In these operations the loss was much less than might have been expected, from the numbers and positions of the enemy, and from the fact of the troops being obliged to move under the range of the guns of the fortress. Three hundred and twenty-seven Sepoys, of the 27th. Native Infantry were here released from the state of slavery to which they had been reduced by the Affghans. A party was detained, under Lieutenant G. White, to take down the celebrated gates of Somnauth, concerning which so much discussion afterwards arose.

On the 10th. of September the troops continued their march on Cabool, when Shumshoodeen, Sultan Jan, and other chiefs having assembled about twelve thousand men, occupied, on the 14th. and 15th. of September, a succession of strong mountains, intercepting the advance at Beenee Badam and Mydan, but they were dislodged, and driven from their position.

No further opposition was encountered, and on the 17th. the troops, under Major-General Nott, reached Cabool, and joined the force under Major-General Pollock.

After the strong town of Istalif had been captured by the troops under Major-General Mc Caskill, on the 29th. of September, in which the 9th. Foot and the light companies of the 41st. bore a gallant part, the army broke ground on its return to India on the 12th. of October, the grand bazaar of Cabool, named the Chahar Chuttah, where the remains of the British envoy had been exposed to public insult, having been first destroyed. On arriving at Jellalabad, the fortress was destroyed.* During the march through the passes several attacks of the Affghans were repulsed. According to the wish of Lord Ellenborough, the Governor-General, the garrison of Jellalabad proceeded in advance of the rest of the troops, in order to make a triumphant entry. The medals (mural crown pattern) granted to the garrison for the defence and battle near Jellalabad had been forwarded a few days previously, in order that they might be worn on its entrance into Ferozepore, which took place on the 17th. of December.

The foregoing services are commemorated on the colours and appointments of the following Queen's regiments:—*Cabool*, 1842.– 3rd. Light Dragoons, 9th., 13th., 31st., 40th., and 41st. regiments. *Candahar and Ghuznee.*—40th. and 41st. regiments. *Jellalabad.*—13th. Light Infantry.

MEDALS FOR THE SECOND AFFGHAN CAMPAIGN.

The medals for the second Affghan campaign generally resembled that for meritorious service, of which an illustration has been given, except that the words CANDAHAR, GHUZNEE, CABUL, 1842, under each other, were engraved within the wreath of laurel, and beneath the imperial crown, instead of

---

* On the south face of the fort was a large bastion, close to which was an open space which had been converted into a burial ground; here the remains of Colonel Dennie, with many other gallant soldiers were laid, and the engineer officer in mining the bastion caused the whole mass to be thrown by the explosion over the graves, thus leaving a lasting and appropriate monument over them, and effectually preventing the bodies being disturbed by the Affghans.

For Meritorious Service. Where the recipient was entitled to the foregoing services but one medal was given. Some of these medals were only inscribed Candahar, 1842; and others Cabul, 1842. Such

as claimed for Ghuznee and Cabul had one inscribed with those words within a double wreath of laurel, as shewn in the accompanying engraving. On the obverse in each instance was the Queen's head, with the superscription Victoria Vindex. The ribbon was the same in all, being that known as the rainbow pattern. The artist was the late William Wyon, Esq., R.A. The authority for these medals to be worn by the Queen's troops was notified to the army in India on the 28th. of January, 1843.*

CAMPAIGN IN SCINDE. 1843.

The withdrawal of the troops from Affghanistan was considered by the Scindian princes as a sign of weakness, and

---

* "His Excellency the Commander-in-Chief in India has received the authority of His Grace the Commander-in-Chief to promulgate to the Army in India, that Her Majesty has been graciously pleased to permit such of the officers, non-commissioned officers, and privates of Her Majesty's regiments, as were engaged in the operations beyond the Indus, to receive respectively medals similar to those which will be issued by the Right Honourable the Governor-General to the Indian Army, in commemoration of the same services, and to wear such medals, suspended by the Indian ribbon, in all parts of Her Majesty's dominions."

they consulted how they might destroy the British power. Being feudatories of the Dooranee empire, they had been persuaded to take a bold part in what they considered the common cause. A force was consequently assembled under Major-General Sir Charles Napier, and its first employment was the destruction of the Fort of Emaun Ghur, in the desert, on the 14th. and 15th. of January, 1843.

This service was described by the Duke of Wellington in the House of Lords, "as one of the most curious military feats he had ever known to be performed, or had ever perused an account of in his life. Sir Charles Napier (added his Grace) moved his troops through the desert against hostile forces; he had his guns transported under circumstances of extreme difficulty, and in a manner the most extraordinary; and he cut off a retreat of the enemy which rendered it impossible for them ever to regain their positions."

As Emaun Ghur could only serve as a stronghold in which the Beloochees might be able to resist British supremacy, Major-General Sir Charles Napier determined upon destroying the fortress. It was a place of great strength, and was constructed of unburnt bricks, into which the shot easily penetrates, but brings nothing down, so that recourse was had to mining. The place was full of gunpowder and grain, and the former was employed in blowing up the fortress, which was effected on the 15th. of January. The 22nd. was the only Queen's regiment employed in this service, three hundred and fifty of that corps having been carried on camels.

After this difficult and harassing service, the troops returned on the 23rd. of January to Peer-Abu-Bekr, without the loss of a man, or without even a sick soldier, and the Ameers' plan of campaign was frustrated.

On the 14th. of February a treaty of peace was signed by these chiefs, and directions were sent by them to the British. political resident, Major Outram, to quit Hyderabad, the capital; but before this was complied with, eight thousand Beloochees, commanded by several Ameers in person, attempted to force an entrance into the enclosure of the British residency.

BATTLE OF MEEANEE.
17TH. FEBRUARY, 1843.

Having thus commenced hostilities, the Ameers assembled a numerous force to destroy the few British troops in the country. Sir Charles Napier, trusting to the valour of the force under his orders, advanced to meet the enemy. On the 17th. of February, twenty-two thousand Scindian troops were discovered in position behind the bank of a river at Meeanee. The British, mustering two thousand eight hundred men, advanced in echelon of regiments to attack their numerous opponents, and the 22nd., commanded by Lieutenant-Colonel (now Lieutenant-General Sir John) Pennefather, led the attack. A numerous body of Beloochees discharged their matchlocks and pistols at the 22nd., and then rushed forward sword in hand to close upon the British line; but these bold and skilful swordsmen went down under the superior power of the musket and bayonet.*

After a severe contest the Scindian army was defeated, and, on the day following the victory, six of the Ameers delivered their swords to the British General upon the field of battle. The Beloochees lost five thousand men, and all their guns, ammunition, and treasure were taken, together with their camp and standards.

In the Notification of the Right Honourable Lord Ellenborough, the Governor-General of India, it was directed, "That the

---

* The only Queen's regiment at Meeanee was the 22nd., and the following extracts from the despatch of Major-General Sir Charles Napier testify the part borne by it in this victory:—"Lieutenant-Colonel Pennefather was severely wounded, as, with the high courage of a soldier, he led his regiment up the desperate bank of the Fulaillee. Major Wyllie, Captains Tucker and Conway, Lieutenants Harding and Phayre, were all wounded while gloriously animating their men to sustain the shock of numbers. Captains Meade, Tew, and Cookson, with Lieutenant Wood, all fell honourably, urging on the assault with unmitigated valour. Major Poole, of the 22nd., and Captain Jackson, of the 25th. Native Infantry, who succeeded to the command of those regiments, proved themselves worthy of their dangerous posts. The Acting Assistant Quartermaster-General, Lieutenant Mc Murdo, of the 22nd. regiment, had his horse killed, and, while on foot leading some soldiers in a desperate dash down the enemy's side of the bank, he cut down a chieftain. He has greatly assisted me by his activity and zeal during the whole of our operations. Innumerable are the individual acts of intrepidity which took place between our soldiers and their opponents, too numerous for detail in this despatch, yet well meriting a record."

unserviceable guns, taken at Hyderabad, shall be sent to Bombay, and there cast into a triumphal column, whereon shall be inscribed in the English, and two native languages, the names of Major-General Sir Charles Napier, K.C.B., and of the several officers mentioned by His Excellency in his despatch, and likewise the names of the several officers, non-commissioned officers, and privates mentioned in the reports, that thus the names may be for ever recorded of those who, at Meeanee, obtained for themselves that glory in the field, which is the reward dearest to a true soldier." Sir Charles Napier set the example, which has since been more or less followed, in naming the non-commissioned officers and men who had specially distinguished themselves.

The loss of the 22nd. regiment was Captain J. Mc Leod Tew, one sergeant, and twenty-two rank and file killed; Lieutenant-Colonel Pennefather, Captain T.S. Conway, Lieutenants W.M.G. Mc Murdo and F.P. Harding, Ensigns R. Pennefather and H. Bowden, one sergeant, one corporal, and fifty privates wounded.*

BATTLE OF HYDERABAD.
24TH. MARCH, 1843.

The whole of the Ameers did not submit, and the chiefs who continued to resist assembled an army, which was commanded by Meer Shere Mahomed. The British advanced from Hyderabad at daybreak on the morning of the 24th. of March, and about half-past eight o'clock twenty thousand Scindian troops were discovered in order of battle behind a nullah. Arrangements were immediately made for commencing the

---

* Major Poole, commanding the 22nd. regiment, in consequence of Lieutenant-Colonel Pennefather having been severely wounded, stated in his report, respecting the soldiers of the regiment under his command, who had distinguished themselves in the battle of Meeanee, that the officers generally assert that they feel difficulty in making selections, where the conduct of every man of their companies was so satisfactory. In so general a field of action and persevering exertion, I equally feel at a loss where to draw a distinction ; but it may be proper to mention the names of Private James O'Neill, of the light company, who took a standard whilst we were actively engaged with the enemy, and Drummer Martin Delaney; the latter shot, bayoneted, and captured the arms of Meer Whullee Mahomed Khan, who was mounted, and directing the enemy in the hottest part of the engagement."

action, and the 22nd. regiment led the attack. Major Poole commanded the brigade, and Captain F.D. George the regiment, which advanced steadily against the enemy's left, exposed to a heavy fire of matchlocks, without returning a shot until arriving within forty paces of the entrenchment, when it stormed the position occupied by the Beloochees. Lieutenant Coote first mounted the rampart, seized one of the enemy's standards, and was severely wounded while in the act of waving it and cheering on his men; Lieutenant Powell seized another, and the gallant example of the officers stimulated the men to similar deeds. Privates J. Doherty, C. Lynar, E. Jobin, J. Mc Cartin, J. Wahmsley, G. Roberts, E. Watson, and J. Oakley shot the defenders, and then captured fourteen standards, making five of their opponents prisoners. Privates S. Cowen, S. Alder, and G. Banbury also captured colours; and Corporal Tim Kelly shot one of the Scindians, taking from him a silver-knobbed standard. The Belooohee infantry and artillery fought well, but were unable, although greatly superior in numbers, to resist the determined attack of disciplined soldiers.

Major-General Sir Charles Napier stated in his public despatch, "The battle was decided by the troop of Horse Artillery, and Her Majesty's 22nd. regiment."*

The loss of the enemy was very great, and eleven pieces of cannon were taken in position on the nullah, together with seventeen standards. The Beloochee force was completely defeated, and their commander, Meer Shere Mahomed, fled to the desert.† Among the killed was the great promoter of the war, Hoche Mahomed Seedee. Twenty-three rank and file of the 22nd. regiment were killed on this occasion; Lieutenants Chute, Coote, Evans, and Brennan, Ensign Richard Pennefather, six sergeants, one drummer, four corporals, and one hundred and twenty-three privates were wounded. At the battle of Hyderabad the regiment mustered only five hundred and sixty-two

---

* The words MEEANEE, HYDBRABAD, and SCINDE were authorized to be borne on the colours of the 22nd. regiment.

† In the pursuit of Meer Shere Mahomed, the following men of the 22nd., concealing their wounds received in the battle of Hyderabad, marched with their regiment the next day, thinking another action was at hand:— Sergeant Haney, John Durr, John Muldowney, Robert Young, Henry Lines, Patrick Gill, James Andrews, Thomas Middleton, James Mulvey, and Silvester Day.

rank and file; the remainder, being sick and convalescent, having been left at Sukkur, in Upper Scinde.

These successes gained for the troops the high honour of the thanks of Parliament, and the Order of the Bath for several of the officers.

MEDAL FOR MEEANEE AND HYDERABAD.

Her Majesty was graciously pleased to command that a medal should be conferred upon the officers, non-commissioned officers, and soldiers engaged in these battles. On the obverse is the Queen's bust, with the inscription "VICTORIA REGINA." On the reverse the words "MEEANEE," "HYDERABAD," "1843," enclosed within a wreath of laurel, and surmounted by the crown. The ribbon is the rainbow pattern, which is associated with the medals granted whilst Lord Ellenborough was Governor-General. The medal is similar to that accorded for Meritorious Service, of which an illustration is given in the second section of this work, the names of the two battles being inserted within the wreath, instead of the words "FOR MERITORIOUS SERVICE."

BATTLES OF MAHARAJPORE AND PUNNIAR.
29TH. DECEMBER, 1843.

A force named the "Army of Exercise" was assembled at Agra, in November, 1843, in consequence of affairs in the state of Gwalior, which had for some time required the attention of the Indian Government, although it was not anticipated that actual hostilities would take place. The events which led to the collision between the Anglo-Indian troops and those of the once powerful 'Mahratta kingdom, are as follow:— Upon the decease of Maharajah Thunkojee Rao Scindiah, the British Government promptly acknowledged as his successor the Maharajah Tyajee Rao Scindiah, who was nearest in blood to the late sovereign of Gwalior, and whose adoption by the Maharanee, his Highness's widow, was approved by the chiefs.

During the minority of the Maharajah, the office of regent was to be held by Mama Sahib. In a short time the regent was compelled by force to quit the Gwalior state, and the Dada Khasgee Walla succeeded to the confidence of the Maharanee without possessing generally that of the chiefs, and by his influence various acts were committed insulting and injurious to the British Government. The delivery of the Dada being peremptorily insisted upon as a necessary preliminary to the re-establishment of the customary relations with the Gwalior state, the Maharanee at length complied with the request, and the Governor-General, in order to give friendly support to the youthful Maharajah, directed the immediate advance of forces sufficient for the purpose. The Anglo-Indian troops entered the dominions of Scindiah, and a strong government having been established at Gwalior, they received orders to withdraw; but were not destined to return to their own territory without a severe conflict. Negotiations appeared proceeding to an amicable issue, but the design of the enemy to gain time to concentrate his forces became at length so evident, that active measures of hostility were determined upon.

The main division crossed the Koharee river early in the morning of the 29th. of December, and found the Mahratta forces drawn up in front of the village of Maharajpore, in a very strong position, which they had occupied during the night, and which they had carefully entrenched. The British were about fourteen thousand strong, with forty pieces of artillery, while the enemy mustered eighteen thousand men, including three thousand cavalry, with a hundred guns. Notwithstanding the extreme difficulty of the country, intersected by deep and almost impassable ravines, the whole of the Anglo-Indian troops were in their appointed positions by eight o'clock in the morning of the 29th. of December. The action commenced by the advance of Major-General Littler's column, which was exactly in front of Maharajpore; whilst Major-General Valiant's brigade took it in reverse, both being supported by Major-General Dennis's column, and the two light field batteries.

Her Majesty's 16th. Lancers, and the 39th. and 40th. regiments highly distinguished themselves. The 39th., forming part of Brigadier Wright's brigade, (Lieutenant-Colonel of the regiment, now Major-General,) in one of the charges, had their commanding officer, Major Bray, desperately wounded, by the blowing up of one of the enemy's tumbrils in the midst of the corps; but the regiment was ably brought out of action by Major (now Major-General Sir Charles Thomas) Van Straubenzee. A small work of four guns on the left of the entrenched main position of Chonda was long and obstinately defended, but subsequently carried; and the guns captured by the grenadiers of the 39th., under Captain Campbell, admirably supported by a wing of the 56th. Native Infantry, under Major Philips.

Not less distinguished was the conduct of the 40th.; this regiment in the attack on the enemy's entrenched positions, had two successive commanding officers, Major Stopford* and Captain Coddington, wounded at the very muzzles of the guns. Two regimental standards were captured by the 39th., and four by the 40th. regiment. Major-General Valiant was also wounded.

Major-General Churchill, C.B., Quarter-Master General of Her Majesty's forces in India, and Captain Somerset of the Grenadier Guards, Military Secretary to Lord Ellenborough, both received several wounds in personal rencontres. The former died after amputation of the leg. Major Henry Havelock, C.B., of the 13th. Light Infantry, Persian interpreter, served on Sir Hugh Gough's personal staff.

Brigadier Cureton's brigade of cavalry, of which the 16th. Lancers (under Lieutenant-Colonel Macdowell) formed part, took advantage of every opportunity, manoeuvring most judiciously on the right, and had it not been for an impassable

---

* Brigadier Stopford, C.B., of the 64th., who was killed on the 9th. of December, 1856, at the attack on Reshire, in Persia, commanded the 40th. at Maharajpore, and fell whilst leading on his regiment, dangerously wounded, at the very muzzles of the enemy's guns. For this service he was made Lieutenant-Colonel and a C.B. He lay for a considerable time wounded on the field, among the dying and the dead, men and horses, and might have fallen a victim to his own generosity. When his dooly or stretcher was sent for him from the rear, and he perceived Major-General Churchill lying near him mortally wounded, with both legs carried away by a cannon ball, like another Sidney, he said, "Oh! General you are worse than I am, you'll bleed to death, you must go on this dooly." Colonel Stopford was at last carried to the rear, and was only in time to bid farewell to the general who died immediately afterwards.

ravine, would have cut off the retreat of the whole. The cavalry division was under the orders of Major-General Sir Joseph Thackwell, K.C.B.

In this action fifty-six guns, and the whole of the enemy's ammunition waggons were captured.

Major-General Grey, who had been directed to push on with the left wing as rapidly as practicable to Punniar, twelve miles south-west of Gwalior, gained also a complete victory on the same day as the battle of Maharajpore was fought, namely, the 29th. of December.

About four o'clock in the afternoon the enemy was observed to have taken up a strong position on a chain of lofty hills, four miles eastward of the camp. The Major-General determined immediately to attack him, and the 3rd. Buffs, with a company of sappers and miners, were detached to occupy a position on an opposite ridge, followed afterwards to the right by five companies of the 39th. Native Infantry, until the troops, amounting to two thousand and seven men, could be brought up, and an attack made upon the enemy's left flank and centre. Owing to the lateness of the day, it was some time before this force could be supported. The Buffs, under Lieutenant-Colonel Clunie, and the sappers attacked the centre, exposed to a galling fire from the guns, and gallantly carried every position, driving the enemy from height to height, and capturing eleven of his guns with a standard. The second infantry brigade under Acting-Brigadier Anderson, of the 50th., arrived in time to put a finish to the action; forming on the crest of the hill, he, by a gallant and judicious movement, attacked the enemy's left, and completely defeated him, taking the remainder of his guns. Major Petit commanded the 50th., and distinguished himself by the charge he made down the hill at the head of that regiment. The 50th. Native Infantry shared in the above movement. Major White commanded the latter, and took the second infantry brigade out of action upon Brigadier Anderson being wounded.

A portion of the first cavalry brigade, under Brigadier Campbell of the 9th. Lancers, accompanied the force as far as the ground would admit, but no opportunity was afforded for actively employing them.

THE SECOND JELLALABAD MEDAL.
THE MAHARAJPOOR STAR.

These victories were not gained without severe loss,* owing to the enemy's force greatly exceeding the British, particularly in artillery, and to the commanding position of his guns, which were well served and resolutely defended both by gunners and infantry; the peculiar difficulties of the country gave also additional advantages to the gallantry of the Mahratta troops, whose casualties were exceedingly heavy.

Punniar is borne by the 9th. Lancers, and the 3rd. and 50th. regiments of the Line; and Maharajpore by the 16th. Lancers, 39th. and 40th. Foot.

STAR FOR MAHARAJPOOR AND PUNNIAR

The Government of India, as a mark of its grateful sense of their distinguished merit, presented to every general and other officer, and to every soldier engaged in these battles, an Indian star of bronze, appropriately made from the captured guns.

Both stars are similar, the only difference being that one has MAHARAJPOOR the silver face, the other PUNNIAR, the date of course being the same. These were permitted to be worn by the Queen's regiments, and the ribbon used is that before described for the Affghan and Scinde campaigns, namely the rainbow pattern.

THE SUTLEJ CAMPAIGN.
1845–1846.

The Sikh army which had been formed by Runjeet Singh, and trained by French and Italian refugees in his service,

---

* Loss sustained by Her Majesty's regiments; the total casualties, including the Native corps, exceeded a thousand killed and wounded:—

MAHARAJPORE.	Officers.		Men.		PUNNIAR.	Officers.		Men.	
	K.	W.	K.	W.		K.	W.	K.	W.
16th Lancers.......	...	...	2	7	9th. Lancers........	...	...	...	...
89. Regiment......	1	10	29	174	3rd. Foot...........	1	3	10	58
40th. "	...	8	23	151	50th. "	1	1	8	32
Total......	1	8	54	332	Total.....	2	4	18	90

according to European tactics, had, since the decease of that politic ruler in 1839, become the dominant power, and finally coerced, or induced the Lahore authorities to commence hostilities. Accordingly the Sikh army, having crossed the Sutlej on the 11th. of December, 1845, invested Ferozepore on one side, and took up an entrenched position at the village of Ferozeshah, about ten miles in advance of Ferozepore, and nearly the same distance from Moodkee, the enemy placing in this camp one hundred and eight pieces of cannon, with a force exceeding fifty thousand men.

So unexpected and unprovoked an aggression, in a time of profound peace, rendered a series of difficult combinations for the protection of the frontier indispensable; and accordingly several regiments were hastily assembled under the personal command of the Commander-in-Chief in India, General Sir Hugh Gough, in order to repel the invasion. The Sikhs remained inactive in the vicinity of Ferozepore for some days, which may be regarded as a providential circumstance, as instead of annihilating Major-General Sir John Littler's weak divisions, they contented themselves with stopping the daks, and plundering the country, until the 17th. of December, when they marched to intercept the approach of the "Army of the Sutlej," then advancing to the relief of Ferozepore from Umballa.

BATTLE OF MOODKEE.
18TH. DECEMBER, 1845.

After a harassing march of one hundred and fifty miles, along roads of heavy sand, the troops arrived at Moodkee, on the 18th. of December, having endured every kind of privation, the incessant labour required of them admitting scarcely an hour's uninterruped repose before being called upon for renewed exertions. About three o'clock in the afternoon, the army, suffering severely from the want of water, and in a state of great exhaustion, received intelligence of the advance of the Sikhs on Moodkee, and the troops had 'scarcely time to get under arms, and to move to their positions, before the information was confirmed. The horse artillery and cavalry were immediately pushed forward, the infantry and field batteries moving in support. Two miles were scarcely passed, when the enemy, consisting of about twenty thousand infantry, and an equal number of cavalry, with forty guns, were discovered in position, which they had either just taken up, or were advancing in order of battle. The country at this spot was a dead flat, dotted with sandy hillocks, and covered at short intervals with a low thick jungle, forming an excellent screen for the infantry and guns of the enemy, from which they opened a severe cannonade upon the advancing troops, which was vigorously replied to by the horse artillery under Brigadier Brooke. After the manoeuvres of the cavalry on the left and right flanks of their opponents, the infantry commenced their participation in the fight, and advancing under Major-Generals Sir Harry Smith, Walter Gilbert, and Sir John Mc Caskill, attacked in echelon of lines the Sikh infantry, the wood and approaching darkness of night rendering them almost invisible. The great superiority of numbers of the enemy necessarily caused their extended line to outflank the British, but the movements of the cavalry counteracted this advantage. Desperate was the opposition experienced, but the roll of fire from the infantry soon convinced the Sikhs of the inutility of resistance; their whole force was driven from position to position with great slaughter at the point of the bayonet; night only saved them from further disaster, this stout conflict being maintained for an hour and a half of dim starlight, objects being rendered still more obscure from the clouds of dust which arose from the sandy plain. Darkness alone prevented the pursuit of the foe; and the force bivouacked on the field for some hours; returning to their encampment, when it was ascertained that they had no foe before them.

In this manner was achieved the first of a series of victories over the Sikh troops; troops that had fought with the British army only three years previously, in the advance on Cabool, and had been thanked in general orders for their services, sustaining as they did, at the forcing of the Khyber Pass, a loss equal to that of the Anglo-Indian force, as stated at page 71; it appears therefore but reasonable to infer, that much of the skill evinced by them in the disposition and arrangement of their army may be in some degree attributed to the experience they gained by their co-operation in the Affghan campaign; proving themselves unquestionably at Moodkee, and in the succeeding conflicts, one of the best disciplined and most powerful antagonists the British had ever encountered in India.

This victory was not gained without considerable loss; several gallant officers fell, and amongst them the hero of Affghanistan, Major-General Sir Robert Sale, who, towards the conclusion of the action, had his thigh shattered with a grape-shot, from the effects of which he died. Major-General Sir John Mc Caskill, K.C.B., who had served with the 9th. Foot in that country, was also amongst the slain.

MOODKEE was authorized for the colours and appointments of the 3rd. Light Dragoons, 9th., 31st., 50th., and 80th. regiments.

BATTLE OF FEROZESHAH OR FEROZESHUHUR.
21ST. AND 22ND. DECEMBER, 1845.

On the 19th. of December the army was concentrated at Moodkee, no further operations taking place until the 21st., when it moved by its left on Ferozepore; and having on the march been reinforced by Major-General Sir John Littler's division of five thousand men from that place, General Sir Hugh Gough formed his forces in order of battle. It was then resolved to attack the enemy's entrenched camp at Ferozeshah, or Ferozeshuhur, where they were posted in great force, and had a most formidable artillery; their camp was a parallelogram, about a mile in length, and half that distance in breadth, the shorter sides looking towards the Sutlej and Moodkee, and the longer towards Ferozepore, and the open country. The plains, as at Moodkee, were covered with low jhow jungle; this added to the difficulty of the advance, which was made in four divisions; the left wing under the direction of the Governor-General, (Lieutenant-General Sir Henry Hardinge,) who had volunteered his services as second in command. One hundred guns of the enemy, nearly one half of battering calibre, opened a heavy cannonade, which was checked, but not silenced, by the far less numerous artillery of the assailants. In spite of this storm of shot and shell, the infantry gallantly advanced, and boldly carried the formidable entrenchments, throwing themselves upon the guns, and wresting them from the enemy. These exertions, however, only partially gained the batteries, and the soldiery had to face so dense a fire from the Sikhs from behind their guns, that the most heroic efforts could only succeed in carrying a portion of the entrenchment. Darkness did not bring a total cessation of hostilities, for about the middle of the night the Sikhs caused one of their heavy guns to bear upon that part of the field gained, and on which the troops had bivouacked. The gun was soon captured by the 80th. regiment;* but the enemy, whenever moonlight revealed the position, still continued to harass the troops by the fire of their artillery.

At length the long night wore away, and with daylight of the 22nd. of December came retribution. The infantry formed into line, supported on both flanks by horse artillery, whilst a fire was opened from the centre, aided by a flight of rockets. Here a masked battery played with great effect, dismounting the pieces and blowing up the tumbrils of the British, but at this juncture Sir Henry Hardinge placed himself at the head of the left wing, the right being led by Sir Hugh Gough. Unchecked by the opposing fire, the line advanced, and drove the foe rapidly out of the village of Ferozeshah, and the encampment; then changing front to the left, continued to sweep the camp, bearing down all opposition. Eventually the Sikhs were dislodged from their whole position. The line now halted, and the two brave leaders rode along its front, amid the cheering of the soldiers and the waving of the captured standards of the Khalsa army.

The British, masters of the entire field, now assumed a position on the ground they had so nobly won; but their

---

* "Near the middle of it, one of their heavy guns was advanced, and played with deadly effect upon our troops. Lieutenant-General Sir Henry Hardinge immediately formed Her Majesty's 80th. Foot and the 1st. European Light infantry. They were led to the attack by their commanding officers, and animated in their exertions by Lieutenant-Colonel Robert Blucher Wood, (Aide-de-Camp to the Lieutenant-General,) who was wounded in the outset; the 80th. captured the gun, and the enemy dismayed by this counter-check, did not venture to press on further."— *General Sir Hugh Gough's Despatch.*

labours were not ended, for in less than two hours Sirdar Tej Singh brought up from the vicinity of Ferozepore fresh battalions, and a large field of artillery, supported by thirty thousand Ghorechurras, previously encamped near the river. Driving in the cavalry parties, he made strenuous efforts to regain the position at Ferozeshah; this attempt was defeated; but the Sirdar renewing the contest with fresh troops, and a large artillery, commenced the attack by a combination against the left flank; and after being frustrated in this attempt, essayed such a demonstration against the captured village, as compelled the British to change the whole front to the right. Meanwhile an incessant fire was maintained by the foe without being answered by a single shot, the artillery ammunition being completely expended in these protracted encounters. The almost exhausted cavalry were now directed to threaten both flanks at once, the infantry preparing to advance in support; this soon caused the Sikhs to discontinue firing, and to abandon the field, precipitately retreating towards the Sutlej, large stores of grain and the *materiel* of war being abandoned by the enemy.*

---

* A vivid picture of this sanguinary struggle was given by the late Viscount Hardinge, in a letter to a member of his family, which was quoted by Sir Robert Peel, when the vote of thanks to the army was proposed in Parliament. "It was the most extraordinary of my life. I bivouacked with the men, without food or covering, and our nights are bitter cold. A burning camp in our front, our brave fellows lying down under a heavy cannonade which continued during the whole night, mixed with the wild cries of the Sikhs, our English hurrah, the tramp of men, and the groans of the dying. In this state, with a handful of men, who had carried the batteries the night before, I remained till morning, taking short intervals of rest by lying down with various regiments in succession, to ascertain their temper, and revive their spirits. I found myself again with my old friends of the 29th., 31st., 50th., and 9th., and all in good heart. My answer to all and every man was, that we must fight it out, attack the enemy vigorously at daybreak, beat him, or die honourably in the field. The gallant old General, kind-hearted and heroically brave, entirely coincided with me. During the night I occasionally called upon our brave English soldiers to punish the Sikhs when they came too close, and were imprudent; and when morning broke we went at it in true English style. Gough was on the right. I placed myself, and dear little Arthur by my side, in the centre, about thirty yards in front of the men, to prevent their firing, and we drove the enemy without a halt from one extremity of their camp to the other, capturing thirty or forty guns as we went along, which fired at twenty paces from us, and were served obstinately. The brave men drew up in an excellent line, and cheered Gough and myself as we rode up the line, the regimental colours lowering to me as on parade. The mournful part is the heavy loss I have sustained in my officers. I have had ten aides-de-camp *hors-de-combat*, five killed and five wounded. The fire of grape was very heavy from 100 pieces of cannon. The Sikh army was drilled by French officers, and the men the most warlike in India."

It is not surprising that the British casualties were numerous. Within thirty hours an entrenched camp had been stormed, a general action fought, and two considerable conflicts sustained with the enemy. Thus in less than four days, sixty thousand Sikh soldiers, supported by upwards of one hundred and fifty pieces of cannon, were dislodged from their position, and received a just retribution for their treacherous proceedings, without provocation or declaration of hostilities.

The 3rd. Light Dragoons, 9th., 29th., 31st., 50th., 62nd., and 80th. regiments bear the word FEROZESHAH on their colours and appointments. In the official despatch there were no regiments particularized, for all were equally exposed during this protracted conflict.*

BATTLE OF ALIWAL.
28TH. JANUARY, 1846.

On the 16th. of January, 1846, the first brigade, with a few guns and some native cavalry, received sudden orders to march on the following morning in the direction of Loodiana, under the command of Major-General Sir Harry Smith. By a forced march on the 17th., the fort of Dhurrumkote was surprised, and the garrison, consisting of about three hundred men, laid down their arms, and were sent prisoners to head-quarters. On the 20th. of the same month this division was reinforced near the fort of Jugraon by the 16th. Lancers, the 53rd. Foot, a detachment of recruits of the Queen's regiments, and a troop of horse artillery. The Major-General decided on attempting the relief of Loodiana, which was but slightly garrisoned, and was threatened by a large body of the enemy. The troops commenced their march about one

---

* "The Governor-General's thanks are due to all the infantry regiments of Her Majesty, and to the 1st. European Light Infantry of the East India Company's service, all of which regiments distinguished themselves by the most devoted courage in braving the destructive fire of the enemy's batteries, and valiantly capturing their guns. The Governor-General offers his thanks more especially to Her Majesty's 3rd. Dragoons, who, on all these occasions, sought opportunities of useful conflict with the enemy, and fought with that superiority over their opponents which skill and discipline impart to brave and determined men" *—General Orders by the Right Honourable the Governor-General.*

o'clock in the morning of the 21st.; about eleven, the enemy was observed to be drawn up, parallel with the British line of march, in a strong position at Buddiwal, his front covered by a ridge of low sand-hills, bristling with forty pieces of artillery, which were so placed that it was necessary, in order to gain Loodiana, either to risk a battle to dislodge him from a strong position,—which, with troops fatigued by a long march, under a burning sun, and greatly inferior in numbers, would have been a hazardous proceeding,—or to proceed along the entire front of his position under a galling fire.

Having a just confidence in the steadiness of his troops, Sir Harry Smith chose the latter course. The infantry, formed in open column of companies right in front (the grenadier company of the 31st. leading,) and ready at any moment to form line, preceded by the artillery, and covered by the cavalry, marched at a distance of five hundred yards, along the front of this formidable line, receiving the fire of each battery as it bore upon them. The Sikh position being passed, and the enemy declining to follow, by three o'clock in the afternoon the troops arrived at Loodiana, thus effecting the desired object.

On the 22nd. and 23rd. the soldiers were permitted to rest themselves after their late fatigue, and on the 24th. the enemy retired to Aliwal, a village on the Sutlej. The British moved to the ground lately occupied by them at Buddiwal, where they were reinforced by the second brigade of Sir Harry Smith's division, consisting of the 50th. Foot and 48th. Native Infantry, with some cavalry and infantry from Loodiana.

At daylight on the 28th. Sir Harry Smith marched with his whole force to attack the Sirdar Runjoor Singh and the Rajah of Ladwa in their camps at Aliwal, the enemy being drawn up in line of battle with his left resting on the village. From information afterwards received, it appeared that the Sikhs were about to march upon Jugraon that very morning, for the purpose of getting between Sir Harry Smith's force and the heavy guns coming up from Delhi under a very slender escort. The march having been previously conducted in column of brigades at deploying distance, each brigade deployed on its leading company, and thus formed one long line. About ten o'clock in the morning the action commenced by a heavy cannonade from the Sikh artillery, which was principally directed on the British centre. The village of Aliwal was filled with infantry, supported by cavalry in the rear, and further defended by two guns on its left. The village was carried, and the two guns were captured,* but the line being in consequence somewhat disarranged, it was quickly re-formed, and advanced in excellent order, overcoming all opposition. The attack of the enemy by the left wing was equally successful; the line advanced, making a steady and successful charge, and the Sikhs, being beaten in every quarter, fled towards the river in the utmost confusion, leaving their camp and fifty-two pieces of artillery, as trophies in the hands of the victors.

The Queen's regiments which bear the word ALIWAL are the 16th. Lancers, 31st., 50th., and 53rd. Foot.

BATTLE OF SOBRAON.
10TH. FEBRUARY, 1846.

Although the intelligence of the victory of Aliwal, and the sight of the numerous bodies which floated from the vicinity of that battle-field to the bridge of boats at Sobraon, apparently disheartened the enemy, and caused many of them to return to their homes, yet in a few days they appeared as confident as ever of being able in their entrenched position, to defy the Anglo-Indian army, and to prevent the passage of the Sutlej.

The heavy ordnance having arrived on the 8th. of February, the day on which the forces under Major-General Sir Harry Smith

---

* Shortly after the storming of the village of Aliwal, an European officer in the Sikh service was given in charge to the 31st. regiment, having surrendered himself as a prisoner to an officer of one of the cavalry regiments in the Company's service. He said his servant had galloped off with his charger, and, being rather stout, preferred giving himself up to the chance of running away; his name was John Potter, a native of Maidstone, in Kent; he had deserted from the Company's Artillery twenty years before, and was now a Colonel of Artillery in the Sikh service, having a native wife and family at Lahore. The Governor-General afterwards permitted him to hold an appointment in the Sikh service.

rejoined the main body of the army, it was determined at once to storm their entrenchments, and finally drive them out of Hindoostan. This was no ordinary undertaking, as, from observations made during the time the head-quarters of the army were stationed at the village of Nihalkee, it was ascertained that the position at Sobraon was covered with formidable entrenchments, and defended by thirty thousand of the *elite* of the Khalsa troops; besides being united by a good bridge to a reserve on the opposite bank of the river, on which was stationed a considerable camp, with artillery, which commanded and flanked the Sikh field-works on the British side of the Sutlej.

About daybreak on the 10th. of February, the mortars, battering guns, and field artillery were disposed on the alluvial land, embracing within their fire the enemy's works. As soon as the sun's rays cleared the heavy mist which hung over the plain, the cannonade commenced; but notwithstanding the admirable manner in which the guns were served, it would have been visionary to expect that they could, within any limited time, silence the fire of seventy pieces of artillery behind well-constructed batteries, or dislodge troops so strongly entrenched. It soon therefore became evident that musketry and the bayonet must ultimately decide the contest.

The British infantry, formed on the extreme left of the line, then advanced to the assault, and in spite of every impediment, cleared the entrenchments, and entered the enemy's camp. Her Majesty's 10th., 53rd., and 80th. regiments, with the 33rd., 43rd., 59th., and 63rd. Native Infantry, moving at a firm and steady pace, never fired a shot till they had passed the barriers opposed to them, to which was attributed the success of their first effort, and the small loss sustained by them. When checked by the formidable obstacles and superior numbers to which the attacking division was exposed, the second division, under Major-General Gilbert, afforded the most opportune assistance by advancing to the attack of the Sikh batteries, entering the fortified position after a severe struggle, and sweeping through the interior of the camp. A very severe loss was inflicted by this division upon the retreating enemy. The same gallant efforts, attended by similar results, distinguished the attack of the enemy's left by the first division, under Major-General Sir Harry Smith, in which the troops nobly sustained their former reputation.*

Fighting with the energy of desperation, the Sikhs, even when some of their entrenchments were mastered with the bayonet, endeavoured to recover with the sword the positions they had lost. It was not until the weight of all three divisions of infantry, in addition to several regiments of cavalry, with the fire of every piece of field artillery that could be sent to their aid, had been felt, that the enemy gave way. The Sikh regiments retreated at first in tolerable order, but the incessant volleys soon caused them to seek safety in a rapid flight. Masses of them precipitated themselves on their bridge, which, being broken by the heavy fire, was incapable to sustain the multitudes pressing forward; the sudden rise too of the Sutlej rendered the ford almost impassable, adding another obstacle to their escape. A dreadful carnage ensued. The stream was red with the bodies of men and horses, the bridge in many places had given way, and it is considered that at least a third of the Sikh army perished in this battle; sixty-seven of their guns were captured, together with two hundred camel-swivels (zumboorucks,) numerous standards, and vast munitions of war.

In this manner ended the battle of Sobraon; at six in the morning it commenced; at nine it became a hand to hand conflict; and by eleven it was gained. Major-General

---

* A most gallant act was performed by Sergeant Bernard Mc Cabe, of the 31st. Foot. Lieutenant Tritton, bearing the Queen's colour, was shot through the head, and Ensign Jones, who carried the regimental one, was nearly at the same time mortally wounded. The regimental colour, falling to the ground, was seized by Sergeant Mc Cabe, who, rushing forward, crossed the ditch, and planted it on the highest point of the enemy's fortifications, maintaining his position under a most tremendous fire, the colour being completely riddled with shot. The men, cheering, scrambled into the works as best they could, and drove the enemy into the river, Lieutenant Noel bearing the Queen's colour, the staff of which was shivered in his hand. Sergeant Mc Cabe was appointed to an ensigncy in the 18th. Royal Irish Regiment, on the recommendation of the late General Sir Harry Smith, who pronounced this deed to be one of the most daring he ever witnessed, and which he considered tended much to shorten the struggle. Captain Mc Cabe, of the 32nd., to which regiment he was afterwards promoted, died of wounds, received while leading his fourth sortie, at Lucknow, on the 1st. of October, 1857.

Sir Robert Dick, K.C.B., the former leader of the 42nd. Royal Highlanders in Spain, fell at the moment of victory; Brigadier Taylor, C.B., the beloved commanding officer of the 29th. regiment, who commanded the third brigade of the second division, was also killed. In these several battles the British loss amounted to six thousand two hundred and seventy-two officers and men killed and wounded.*

Of the Queen's regiments, besides those already mentioned, the 31st. and 50th. were described in orders as having greatly distinguished themselves. The gallant conduct of the 9th., 29th., and 62nd. regiments, was also specially noticed, and the cavalry were not forgotten.†

SOBRAON, on the colours and appointments of the following regiments, commemorates this decisive victory, namely,—3rd., 9th., and 16th. Light Dragoons; 9th., 10th., 29th., 31st., 50th., 53rd., 62nd., and 80th. Foot; their conduct, and that of the officers, received the thanks of Parliament.

Ten days after the battle of Sobraon the British arrived before Lahore. So complete was the discomfiture of the Sikhs, that no further opposition had been experienced; and on the 22nd. of February a brigade of troops took formal possession of the palace and citadel of Lahore. A treaty was afterwards signed, which, while it evinced the moderation and justice of the paramount power of India, appeared calculated to secure the frontier against similar acts of aggression.

---

*

	KILLED.		WOUNDED.	
	Officers.	Men.	Officers.	Men.
Moodkee	15	200	48	609
Ferozeshuhur	54	640	96	1625
Aliwal	7	151	31	413
Sobraon.	16	304	140	1923
Total	**92**	**1295**	**315**	**4570**

† "Major-General Sir Joseph Thackwell has established a claim on this day to the rare commendation of having achieved much with a cavalry force, where the duty to be done consisted entirely of an attack on field-works, usually supposed to be the particular province of infantry and artillery. His vigilance and activity throughout our operations, and the superior manner in which our outpost duties have been carried on under his superintendence demand my warmest acknowledgments."—*General Sir Hugh Gough's despatch.*

THE PUNJAB CAMPAIGN.

SIEGE OF MOOLTAN.
7TH. SEPTEMBER, 1848, TO 2ND. JANUARY. 1849.

Major-General Sir John Littler had been selected to command the garrison of about ten thousand men which had been left at Lahore, to protect the chief sirdars from their own turbulent countrymen, while re-constructing the government, and everything appeared to be progressing in a satisfactory manner, when, in April, 1848, Moolraj, the Dewan of Mooltan, having apparently agreed to the arrangement for appointing Sirdar Khan Singh his successor as governor of that town, Mr. Vans Agnew, of the Civil Service, and Lieutenant Anderson, of the Bombay Army, who had been sent to Mooltan, were murdered. This was followed by a general outbreak at Lahore, and endeavours were made to expel the British from the Punjab. In this capital Maharaj Singh, a Gooroo or priest, raising the standard of rebellion, soon collected a numerous body of the disbanded Sikhs, and thus prevented the British troops at Lahore from marching against Mooltan, which was occupied by the enemy at the commencement of hostilities.

It was at this juncture that Lieutenant Edwardes* accomplished that for which he gained such just renown. By his gallantry and judicious skill he not only raised forces, but exerted so wise an influence that he succeeded in holding Moolraj in check until succours could be afforded; and having

---

* A superb gold medal, designed by William Wyon, Esq., was presented to this officer by the Honourable East India Company. The obverse bears the head of the Queen, superscribed Victoria Regina, and on the reverse are Victory and Valour crowning the arms of Major Edwardes; these figures are resting on the lotus flower, and beneath is the infant Hercules strangling the serpents, in allusion to the youth of the hero; within the border thus formed is the following inscription;—From the East India Company to Lieutt. and Brevt.-Major H.B. Edwardes, C.B., for his services in the Punjab, AD. MDCCCXLVIII.

united his troops with those of Colonel Cortlandt, several encounters took place with the insurgents, until they were in July compelled to shelter themselves within the walls of Mooltan. Major-General Whish arrived from Lahore in the vicinity of Mooltan, on the 18th. of August, 1848, with a force of which Her Majesty's 10th. Foot formed part, and on the next day was joined by a column from Ferozepore, with which was the Queen's 32nd. regiment. The village of Ramteerut was taken possession of on the 7th. of September, and the working parties having made good progress, it was resolved to attack the outworks on the 12th. of that month, when Shere Singh deserted with five thousand Sikhs to the enemy. This defection made it necessary to raise the siege on the 15th. of that month, and a position was taken up some miles distant. Lieutenant-Colonel Pattoun, of the 32nd., who commanded the attack, was killed, and also Quartermaster Taylor, of that regiment, together with Major Montizambert, of the 10th. Foot.

Meanwhile Lord Gough was marching into the Punjab, and the advance force, under Brigadier-General Campbell, C.B., (now Lord Clyde,) was engaged at Ramnuggur on the 22nd. of November, 1848. Here the gallant Brigadier-General Cureton, C.B., commanding the cavalry division, (the flaxen-haired boy of the Peninsula,) and Lieutenant-Colonel William Havelock, K.H., were killed. The brilliant charges of the 3rd. and 14th. Light Dragoons, and of the 5th. and 8th. regiments of Light Cavalry, against the enemy's horsemen, numbering between three and four thousand men, was specially noticed in general orders.

This engagement was followed by the action of Sadoolapoor, on Sunday, the 3rd. of December, 1848, by the troops under Major-General Sir Joseph Thackwell, K.C.B., in which the 3rd. Light Dragoons, and the 24th. and 61st. regiments shared. The enemy's loss was severe, but the British casualties were comparatively small, amounting to only seventy-three killed and wounded.

A gallant and successful attack was made with little loss, on a strong position of the enemy on the eastern side of the Grand Canal, by the troops under Brigadier-General F. Markham, on the morning of the 7th. of November.* This is known as the action of Sooroojkhund, in which the 10th. and 32nd. regiments shared, (the latter being commanded by Major Inglis, afterwards the heroic defender of Lucknow,) when the enemy's strongly entrenched position was carried, and four of his guns captured without firing a shot.

While these events were occurring Major-General Whish renewed the siege of Mooltan; and having been joined on the 26th. of December by Brigadier the Honourable H. Dundas, C.B., of the 60th. Rifles, with the Bombay column, which, in addition to native corps, comprised the 60th. Royal Rifles, an attack was made on the entrenchments on the 27th. of December; and the enemy being driven from the suburbs, a position was taken up by the British within four hundred yards of the walls. The gallantry and discipline of the 60th. Rifles were specially noticed; they had Major Gordon killed, and Major Dennis wounded. Three companies of the 32nd. shared in the re-occupation of the suburbs on this occasion.

By a shell from one of the mortars on the 30th. the principal magazine in the citadel was blown up, destroying the grand musjid and several houses, and costing the lives of about eight hundred of the garrison. Nowise dismayed by this misfortune, Moolraj continued the defence; but breaches were effected during the nights of the 30th. and 31st., one near the Delhi gate, and the other near the Bohur gate. A sortie was made by the garrison on the last day of the year, but this was repulsed by Major Edwardes and Lieutenant

---

* Brevet-Major Edwardes, C.B., in his despatch to Major-General Whisb giving such details of the action of the 7th. of November as concerned the Irregular Auxiliary Force under his command, and Lieutenant Lake, stated:– "I regret to say that the head of the British line reached the east side of the nullah as our Irregulars arrived at the passage in the canal, which connected the entrenchments on the east and west, and a party of Sheikh Emamoodeen's Rohillas, disregarding in the heat of the action the orders they had received to keep on their own side of the nullah, crossed over and had captured a gun on the eastern bank, when they were mistaken by the Sepoys for Moolraj's troops, and two were shot down before the error could be explained.

"I deem it my duty to bring to your notice the noble conduct of a private of Her Majesty's 82nd. Foot, who at this juncture, perceiving what was going on, leaped down the canal, and putting himself in front of my Pathans, faced the British troops, and waved his chako on the end of his bayonet as the signal to cease firing. Thus many friendly lives were saved. The name of this brave man is Howell."

Lake, the enemy being driven back with severe loss. The place was eventually stormed in the afternoon of the 2nd. of January, 1849.

Colour-Sergeant John Bennett, of the 1st. Bombay Fusiliers, performed a most gallant act. He planted the Union Jack in the crest of the breach, standing beside it until the troops had passed. Both colour and staff were riddled with balls. The suburbs between the Delhi gate and the left breach were occupied by pickets from the first brigade, under Major Dennis, of the 60th. Rifles, a company of that regiment, under Captain Douglas, being stationed in the houses opposite the breach in the Khoonee Boorj, to cover the advance of the storming party, and two companies, under Captains Young and Sibthorp, to perform the same office for the Bengal column.

Two practicable breaches having been made, orders were issued to storm the citadel (into which Moolraj had retired) on the 22nd.; and when the British troops were about to commence, the Sikh chief, with the whole of the garrison, surrendered. Moolraj was subsequently tried for the murder of Mr. Agnew and Lieutenant Anderson, but the capital sentence was changed into imprisonment for life. This siege cost the British a loss of nearly one thousand two hundred killed and wounded. After this brilliant success Major-General Whish proceeded with a considerable portion of his troops, to join the army immediately under the command of Lord Gough.

MOOLTAN is borne by the 10th., 32nd., and 60th., in commemoration of their distinguished services during these operations. These three regiments, after the fall of the place, proceeded to join the army under Lord Gough, and by forced marches succeeded in being in time to share in the final struggle at Goojerat.

BATTLE OF CHILIANWALA.
13TH. JANUARY, 1849.

Lord Gough having received information on the 10th. of January of the fall of the fortress of Attock, which had been defended for a lengthened period by Major Herbert, and of the advance of Chuttur Singh in order to unite his forces with those under his son, Shere Singh, resolved to attempt the overthrow of the Sikh army in his front; and, accordingly, at daylight on the morning of the 12th., moved on the Dingee from Loah Tibba, and thence on the following morning towards the village of Chilianwala, the army making a considerable detour to the right, partly to distract the enemy's attention, but chiefly with the view of keeping as clear of the jungle as possible. The village was reached about noon, when a strong picket of the enemy's cavalry and infantry was discovered on a mound close to it. This was at once dispersed, and from the elevation was obtained a very extended view of the country and of the enemy drawn out in order of battle. The ground in front, although not a dense was still a difficult jungle; and, as the day was so far advanced, Lord Gough decided to take up a position in rear of the village.

While ground was being selected for the encampment the enemy advanced some horse artillery, and opened a fire on the skirmishers in front of the village. Orders were given for this fire to be silenced by a few rounds from the heavy guns, which was instantly returned by that of nearly the whole of the enemy's field artillery, thus exposing the position of his guns, which had hitherto been concealed by the jungle. As it was evident that the Sikhs intended to fight, and would probably advance their guns so as to reach the encampment during the night, the British were at once drawn up in order of battle. After about an hour's fire that of the enemy appeared to be, if not actually silenced, at least sufficiently disabled to justify an advance upon his position and guns.

The left division was then ordered to advance. This had to move over a greater extent of ground, in front of which the foe appeared not to have many guns. Shortly afterwards Sir Walter Gilbert was directed to advance, Brigadier Pope being instructed to protect the flank and support the movement. Brigadier Penny's brigade was held in reserve, while the Irregular Cavalry, under Brigadier Hearsey, with the 20th. Native Infantry, was ordered to protect the provisions and baggage.

Brigadier Pennycuick's brigade having failed in maintaining the position it had carried, Brigadier Penny's reserve was ordered to support; but Brigadier-General Colin Campbell, (to use Lord Gough's own words,) "with that steady coolness and military decision for which he is so remarkable, having pushed on his left brigade and formed line to his right, carried everything before him, and soon overthrew that portion of the enemy which had obtained a temporary advantage over his right brigade."

This last brigade mistook for the signal to move in double time the action of their brave leaders, Brigadier Pennycuick and Lieutenant-Colonel Brookes, who waved their swords over their heads as they cheered on their gallant troops. This unfortunate mistake caused the Europeans to outstrip the native corps, which were unable to keep pace, and arriving, completely blown, at a belt of very thick jungle, got into some confusion, and Lieutenant-Colonel Brookes, heading the 24th., was killed between the Sikh guns. At this moment a numerous body of infantry, which supported their guns, opened so destructive a fire that the brigade was compelled to retire, but not before having lost their gallant leader, Brigadier Pennycuick,* and the three other field officers of the 24th., together with nearly half the regiment;† the native corps also suffered severely.

Major-General Sir Joseph Thackwell, on the extreme left and rear, charged the enemy's cavalry wherever they shewed

---

* When Brigadier Pennycuick fell mortally wounded, a Sikh was mangling the body; on seeing which his son rushed forward, dealt an avenging blow, and across his father's corpse endeavoured to protect the remains; but it was in vain, and the heroic youth fell overpowered by, numbers. Like Lord Talbot and his son, in Shakspere's "Henry VI.," where, however, the younger is the first slain, the words used by the elder are fully applicable in the above instance; in a gallant termination, such souls, "coupled in bonds of perpetuity," despite of "antick death," "shall 'scape mortality."

Another father and son met a like fate in this campaign. Colonel Cureton was killed at Ramnuggur, and his son, Lieutenant A.J. Cureton, of the 14th. Light Dragoons, fell at Chilianwala.

† The loss of the 24th. was fearful; it was the central regiment of the fifth brigade, under Brigadier Pennycuick, which formed the right brigade of the third division, under Brigadier-General Colin Campbell. Lieutenant-Colonels Brookes and Pennycuick, C.B., Major Harris, Captains Lee, Travers, Harris, and Shore, Lieutenants George Phillips, Payne, Woodgate, and Ensigns William Phillips, Collis, and Pennycuick were killed; Major Paynter, Captains Brown and Bazalgette, Lieutenants Williams, Croker,

themselves, and the right attack of infantry, under Major-General Sir Walter Gilbert, was most successful, whilst the left brigade, under Brigadier Mountain, was highly distinguished. Brigadier Godby ably supported the advance with the right brigade.*

Lord Gough remained with Brigadier-General Campbell's division, which had been reinforced by Brigadier Mountain's brigade, until nearly eight o'clock, in order to effect the bringing in of the captured ordnance, and of the wounded.

The loss of the Sikhs, principally among their old and tried soldiers, was computed at three thousand killed, and four thousand wounded. With the exception of Sobraon, it was remarked by Lord Gough that he never remembered seeing so many of an enemy's slain upon the same space. The British casualties were likewise heavy.†

In this battle the "undaunted bravery" of Her Majesty's 29th. regiment, under Lieutenant-Colonel Congreve, was specially noticed, and the conduct of the 61st. was equally distinguished.

BATTLE OF GOOJERAT.
21ST FEBRUARY, 1849.

After the battle of Chilianwala, the enemy, owing to want of supplies, quitted their entrenchments, and took up a position between Goojerat and the Chenab. It appears to have been their intention to cross this river, and, after plundering the Rechna Doab, to have marched to Lahore; but this was

---

Berry, Thelwall, and Hartshorn (Adjutant,) Macpherson, and Archer (96th. Foot,) were wounded. Of the men the casualties were returned as four hundred and ninety-seven killed or wounded; two hundred and twenty-seven of these were killed in action, and nine subsequently died of their wounds.

* "This division nobly maintained the character of the Indian Army, taking and spiking the whole of the enemy's guns in their front, and dispersing the Sikhs wherever they were seen."—*Lord Gough's despatch.*

† Ramnuggur:— Two officers and fourteen men killed, nine officers and fifty-three men wounded, and twelve missing. Chilianwala:— Thirty-eight officers and five hundred and sixty-four men killed, ninety-four officers and one thousand five hundred and fifty-seven men wounded, and one hundred and four missing. Goojerat:–Six officers and ninety men killed, thirty-nine officers and six hundred and sixty-seven men wounded, and five missing.

prevented by Major-General Whish, who had detached a brigade to guard the fords above and below Wuzeerabad, in which direction Lord Gough had moved.

At half-past seven o'clock in the morning of the 21st. of February, the army advanced with the precision of a parade movement. The Sikhs opened their fire at a very long distance, which exposed to the artillery both the position and range of their guns. The infantry was halted just out of fire, and the whole of the artillery were advanced, covered by skirmishers.

The Sikh guns were served with their accustomed rapidity, and the enemy well and resolutely maintained his position, but the terrific force of the British fire obliged him, after an obstinate resistance, to fall back. The infantry were then deployed, and a general advance was directed, the movement being covered, as before, by artillery.

Burra Kalra, the left village of those of that name, wherein the enemy had concealed a large body of infantry, and which was apparently the key of their position, lay immediately in the line of Major-General Sir Walter Gilbert's advance, and was carried in the most brilliant style by a spirited attack of the third brigade, under Brigadier Penny, consisting of the 2nd. Europeans, and 31st. and 70th. regiments of Native Infantry, which drove the enemy from their cover with great slaughter. A very spirited and successful movement was also made about the same time against a heavy body of troops in and about the second or Chotah Kalra, by part of Brigadier Hervey's brigade, most gallantly led by Lieutenant-Colonel Franks, of the 10th. Foot.

The heavy artillery continued to advance, taking up successive forward positions, driving the enemy from those he had retired to, whilst the rapid advance and beautiful fire of the horse artillery and light field batteries, which were strengthened by bringing to the front the two reserved troops of horse artillery, under Lieutenant-Colonel Brind, Brigadier Brook having the general superintendence of the whole of the horse artillery, broke the enemy's ranks at all points. The whole infantry line then rapidly advanced, and drove their opponents before it. The nullah was cleared, several villages stormed, the guns that were in position carried, the camp captured, and the foe routed in every direction; the right wing and Brigadier-General Campbell's division passing in pursuit to the eastward, and the Bombay column to the westward of the town.

Thus hotly pursued, the retreat of the Sikh army soon became a perfect flight, all arms dispersing over the country, rapidly followed by the troops for a distance of twelve miles, their track strewed with their wounded, their weapons and military equipments, which they threw away to conceal that they were soldiers.

Throughout these operations the cavalry brigades on the flanks were threatened and occasionally attacked by vast masses of the enemy's cavalry, which were in every instance put to flight by their steady movements and spirited manoeuvres, most ably supported by the troops of horse artillery attached to them, from whom the foe received the severest punishment.

On the left a most successful and gallant charge was made upon the Affghan cavalry, and a large body of Goorchurras, by the Scinde Horse and a party of the 9th. Lancers, when some standards were captured. The determined front shewn by the 14th. Light Dragoons and the other cavalry regiments on the right, both regular and irregular, completely overawed their opponents, and contributed much to the success of the day; while the conduct of all, in following up the fugitives received high commendation.

Thus were defeated the forces brought by the Sikhs into the field, amongst whom were the *elite* of the old Khalsa army. Their numbers were estimated at sixty thousand men of all arms, and fifty-nine pieces of artillery, under the command of Sirdar Chuttur Singh and Rajah Shere Singh, with a body of one thousand five hundred Affghan Horse, led by Akram Khan, son of the Ameer Dost Mahomed Khan.

For the first time the Sikhs and Affghans had combined together, but this last victory being so complete, shewed the futility of the compact. Amongst the fifty-three guns captured were recovered those lost at Ramnuggur and Chilianwala. It was also a gratifying circumstance that the casualties of the British were less than could be expected.

Major-General Sir Walter Gilbert, in command of a competent force, resumed the pursuit towards the Jhelum on the following morning, with a view of cutting off the enemy from the only practicable gun-road to that river. Another division of infantry, under Brigadier-General Colin Campbell, advanced on the road to Bimber, scouring the country in that direction to prevent their carrying off the guns by that route, and a body of cavalry, under Lieutenant-Colonel Bradford, successfully pushed on several miles into the hills, and twenty-four from Goojerat, accompanied by Captain Nicholson, a most energetic political officer, with the same object, whilst Lord Gough remained in possession of the field for the purpose of supporting these operations, covering the fords of the Chenab, and destroying the vast magazines of ammunition left scattered in all directions. These combinations were entirely successful, the detached parties coming at every step on the wreck of the dispersed and flying foe.

GOOJERAT was authorized to be borne by the 3rd., 9th., and 14th. Light Dragoons; 10th., 24th., 29th., 32nd., 53rd., 60th., and 61st. regiments. The thanks of parliament were unanimously voted for the operations in the Punjab.

Major-General Sir Walter Gilbert, K.C.B., crossing the Jhelum on the 3rd. of March, came up with a portion of the retreating army, under Shere Singh and Chuttur Singh, at Hoormuck, where they surrendered on the 11th. of March; the sirdars and the remainder of his troops, amounting to sixteen thousand men, laid down their arms at Rawul Pindee three days afterwards. Forty-one pieces of artillery were given up. Dost Mahomed was energetically pursued through Attock and Peshawur, as far as the Khyber Pass.

Sir Charles Napier, who had been selected at a moment's notice, and had proceeded to India, thus found on his arrival that the British arms had gained the ascendancy in that country, and the consequence of Lord Gough's crowning victory was the annexation of the Punjab. A pension was granted to Maharajah Dhuleep Singh; and the celebrated diamond, the Koh-i-Noor, or Mountain of Light, taken from Shah Sooja by Runjeet Singh, was presented to Her Majesty.

THE SUTLEJ MEDAL.   THE PUNJAB MEDAL.

THE SUTLEJ AND PUNJAB MEDALS.

The Sutlej and Punjab medals were designed by William Wyon, Esq., and both have on the obverse the head of the Queen, with the superscription VICTORIA REGINA. On the reverse of the Sutlej medal is a figure of Victory standing, offering a laurel wreath with her right hand, and holding a palm branch in her left, a trophy of Sikh arms being at her feet. The words ARMY OF THE SUTLEJ are arranged round the rim. In the *exergue* of the specimen from which the engraving is taken, occurs the word MOODKEE, 1845, so that a recipient in the four actions would have but three clasps. The same plan was followed for one, two, or three actions; some would consequently have FEROZESHUHUR, ALIWAL, or SOBRAON, 1846, beneath the figure of Victory. The ribbon is dark blue with crimson edges.

The reverse of the Punjab medal is unique. The Sikhs are represented as laying down their arms before Lord Gough, a field of battle at the termination of a victory, being depicted; in the background are the troops, together with a group of palm trees and other accessaries, indicative of an Indian landscape. The figure of Lord Gough, on his charger, is exceedingly spirited, the latter, a beautiful Arab, having been modelled from the life. Clasps were granted for MOOLTAN, CHILIANWALA, and GOOJERAT. The ribbon is blue with yellow edges. The superscription is TO THE ARMY OF THE PUNJAB, and in the *exergue* is the year MDCCCXLIX.

SECOND BURMESE WAR.
1852–53.

The King of Ava having refused redress for injuries inflicted on British subjects at Rangoon, in violation of the treaty of Yandaboo, concluded at the termination of the first Burmese war, after an ineffectual attempt at negotiation, hostilities commenced. Troops were collected from Bengal and Madras, and placed under the command of Major-General Godwin, who had borne a prominent part in the first war with Ava. The Queen's regiments which formed part of the force were the 18th., 51st., and 80th.* Major-General Godwin embarked with the force under his command on the 28th. of March, 1852, and three days afterwards the destruction of the stockades on the banks of the river Irrawaddy was effected. The next service was the attack and capture of Martaban, on the 5th. of April, in which portions of the 18th. and 80th. shared. Captain Campbell commanded the wing of the 18th., and Major Lockhart that of the 80th. Captain Gillespie in command of the grenadiers of the former regiment was first on the walls, and the soldier following him received three wounds. About seven o'clock in the morning the troops landed, and the storming party was soon under the walls and over them, when Lieutenant-Colonel Reignolds at once took possession, after some skirmishing, of the pagodas on the height, and by eight o'clock a.m. Martaban was won. The storming party from the 80th. was commanded by Captain Christie of that regiment.

At this period the Madras division (comprising the 51st. regiment) had not arrived at Rangoon, but by the 7th. of April it reached the rendezvous at the mouth of the Rangoon river; on the 11th., (Sunday,) Rangoon was bombarded, and at day-break on the following morning the troops commenced landing. They had not proceeded far when some guns were opened on the British, and shortly afterwards skirmishers showed themselves in the jungle. This was a new mode of fighting with the Burmese, as no instance occurred in the former war of their attacking the flanks or quitting their stockades. Now they were not only good shots, but bold in their operations, and clever in selecting their ground and covering themselves. A strong outwork named the White House Redoubt was assaulted; the storming party, of which four companies of the 51st. Light Infantry, under Lieutenant-Colonel St. Maur, formed

---

* 18th., eight hundred and fifty men; 51st., nine hundred; 80th., four hundred and sixty; Artillery, five companies, five hundred and seventeen; Native Infantry, three regiments, two thousand eight hundred; Gun Lascars, seventy; Sappers and Miners, one hundred and seventy; in all five thousand seven hundred and sixty-seven men.

part, carried the stockade, but in consequence of the intense heat of the sun, which occasioned the death of two officers, it was not until the 14th. of April that the fortified town and pagoda of Rangoon were stormed and captured.

The 80th. and 18th. formed the advance, and the 51st., under Major Errington, Colonel St. Maur having been compelled to quit the field from a stroke of the sun, were in reserve. After an advance for about a mile the ground became very difficult, barely admitting of the 80th. and 18th. occupying it in close order. The troops also suffered from a heavy fire, when an immediate assault was determined upon. The storming party was formed of a wing of the 80th., under Major Lockhart, two companies of the 18th., under Lieutenant Hewitt, and two companies of the 40th. Bengal Native Infantry, under Lieutenant White, the whole commanded by Lieutenant-Colonel Coote, of the Royal Irish; Captain Lutter accompanying the party to show the road. Captain J. Wood, who was specially mentioned, commanded the 18th. regiment. The Pagoda was soon carried, and all the country round fell with it, the once strong post of Kemmendine having been abandoned and destroyed.

During the attack and storming of Rangoon, on the 11th., 12th., and 14th. of April, the British had two officers and fifteen men killed, and fourteen officers and one hundred and eighteen men wounded.

Major Errington with his force, of which four hundred of the 51st. formed a portion, advanced on the chief Pagoda on the 19th. of May, and carried it in gallant style—the citadel, a strong mud fort, was next assaulted by a company of the 51st. and two of the Madras Native Infantry, under Captains Rice and Borthwick. Captain Rice, whilst gallantly leading his company, was shot through the lower part of the neck, when his place was taken by Lieutenant Carter, who, followed by his men, was the first on the parapet; here he was struck down by a musket-ball, and rolled over the exterior slope, but still insisted upon being carried into the work. Although the defence was obstinate, yet in forty minutes after the landing, the whole of the works were in the possession of the British. This dashing operation occasioned the officers and men of Captain Rice's company to be specially thanked in orders. Major Errington, who commanded the troops, was wounded. After leaving a garrison in Bassein the remainder of the troops returned to Rangoon.

Martaban was attacked by a Burmese force of upwards of one thousand men on the 26th. of May, but they were gallantly repulsed by the garrison, consisting of the 49th. Madras Native Infantry, under Major Hall. The 51st. regiment, which had been sent to reinforce the garrison, assisted in driving back the enemy from the stockade, and pursued him some distance.

During the middle of September, the 18th. and 80th. regiments embarked at Rangoon for Prome, and arrived there on the morning of the 9th. of October. The troops were landed in the evening in a suburb to the north of and beyond the town. As they advanced towards the position selected for the night, a very smart fire of musketry and jingalls was simultaneously opened from some jungle and houses on the British left, and a small pagoda in the front. The grenadiers of the 80th. under Captain Christie, and two companies of the same regiment under Captain Welsh, accompanied by Brigadier Reignolds, Lieutenant-Colonel of the 18th. regiment, in a short time most gallantly drove the enemy from their position. The remainder of the troops were landed on the following morning, when the place was found evacuated by the Burmese. Thus the important city of Prome was gained, with the small loss of one killed and eight wounded.

On Sunday, the 21st. of November, Pegu was attacked by a force under Brigadier Mc.Neill, of the Madras Army, composed of the 1st. Bengal Fusiliers, under Lieutenant-Colonel Tudor, three hundred; 1st. Madras Fusiliers, Major Hill, three hundred; 5th. Madras Native Infantry, Major Shubrick, four hundred; seventy Sappers; and thirty-two Artillery.

When the news of the capture of this city was received at Calcutta, a proclamation was issued annexing the whole province of Pegu to the British territories.

On the 8th. of December the enemy attacked Prome in force, but were repulsed with loss; the engagement lasted from midnight until four o'clock in the morning of the 9th.

The 51st. shared in this action.

The small garrison left in Pegu was constantly harrassed by the attacks of the Burmese army, encamped at a short distance, which were gallantly repulsed by Major Hill, of the Madras Fusiliers. A reinforcement of twelve hundred men, left Rangoon on the 11th. of December, and arrived at Pegu on the 14th; when, after a toilsome march through a close country without a road, and an attack from a large body of skirmishers, the relief was effected. A further advance into the country, with a view to bring on a general action, was made on the 17th., and an attack subsequently ensued, when the Burmese rapidly abandoned their entrenched position and took to flight; after a further march of two days, the enemy avoiding a general engagement, the state of the commissariat forced the British general to return to Pegu, and subsequently to Prome.

An expedition proceeded under Brigadier-General Sir John Cheape, K.C.B., to the Donabew district of Pegu, in order to reduce the stronghold of Myat-toon, a robber-chief. The force was actively engaged on the 17th., 18th., and 19th. of March, 1853; after a severe struggle of four hours' duration the place was stormed and destroyed. The left wing was commanded by Lieutenant-Colonel Sturt, of the 67th. Bengal Native Infantry, and the right wing by Major Wigstone, of the 18th. Royal Irish, who was severely wounded. The total loss amounted to twenty-two killed, and one hundred and eight wounded, fourteen being officers. The casualties sustained by the 18th., 51st., and 80th. regiments, amounted to thirteen killed and sixty-five wounded.

On the 30th. of June, 1853, the termination of the war was officially announced, and although the king of Ava refused to sign a formal treaty of peace, yet as all the concessions demanded were agreed to, the Governor-General proclaimed that hostilities would not be resumed so long as the British possession of Pegu remained undisputed. All the captives in Ava were released, and the navigation of the Irrawaddy was declared to be free for the purposes of trade between the two countries.

The word PEGU has been authorized for the colours of the 18th., 51st., and 80th. regiments.

THE PERSIAN CAMPAIGN.
1856-1857.

A rupture occurred with Persia, in consequence of that Power having taken possession of Herat on the 25th. of October, and war was declared on the 1st. of November following. An expedition accordingly proceeded to the Persian Gulf, under Major-General Stalker, C.B., and the Island of Karrack was taken formal possession of on the 3rd. of December without opposition. The troops landed on the 7th. at Ras Halala, about fifteen miles below Bushire, and two days afterwards stormed the position at the old Dutch fort of Reshire, which was taken, the place being carried at the point of the bayonet.* The casualties were principally confined to the officers, amongst whom was Brigadier James Stopford C.B., of the 64th., killed.

On the morning of the 10th. the British marched on Bushire, a walled town, which surrendered unconditionally, after a bombardment of upwards of four hours. No loss was sustained; sixty-five guns, with large quantities of ammunition and warlike stores, were here captured. The garrison, consisting of about two thousand, (a large number having previously effected their escape, and several drowned in the attempt,) grounded their arms in front of the British line, and were on the following morning escorted by the cavalry some distance into the country, and then set at liberty. Her Majesty's 64th., under Major Stirling, shared in this success.

---

* Captain John Augustus Wood, of the 20th. Bombay Native Infantry, gained the Victoria Cross for his gallantry on the 9th. of December. On that day he led the grenadier company, which formed the head of the assaulting column. He was the first man on the parapet of the fort, where he was instantly attacked by a large number of the garrison, who suddenly sprang on him from a trench cut in the parapet itself. These men fired a volley at Captain Wood and the head of the storming party, when only a yard or two distant; although struck by no less than seven musket-balls, he at once threw himself upon the enemy, passed his sword through the body of their leader, and, being closely followed by the men of his company, speedily overcame all opposition, and established himself in the place. This officer's decision, energy, and determined valour contributed in a high degree to the success of the attack. His wounds compelled him to leave the force for a time; but, with the true spirit of a good soldier, he rejoined his regiment, and returned to his duty at Bushire before the wounds were properly healed.

A stronger expedition subsequently proceeded from Bombay, commanded by Lieutenant-General Sir James Outram; this was composed of two divisions, one of which was under Brigadier-General Havelock, and the other under Major-General Stalker; the 78th. Highlanders were added to this force. On the evening of the 3rd. of February, 1857, Sir James Outram marched against Sooja-ool-Moolk, strongly posted in an entrenched camp at Borazgoon. Each man carried his great coat, blanket, and two days' provisions, but without any tents or other equipage; the rain fell heavily, and the nights were bitterly cold. The position was reached in the afternoon of the 5th. of February, when the place was found to be abandoned, but on the return march during the night of the 7th., the rear-guard was attacked by the Persians, who were kept in check until daybreak, when the enemy, amounting to between six and seven thousand men, were perceived drawn up near Koosh-ab. An action ensued, the brunt of which fell upon the cavalry and artillery, and by ten o'clock the defeat of the Persian troops was complete.*

After this victory the British bivouacked for the day close to the battle-field, and at night, by another route, accomplished a march of twenty miles, over a country rendered almost impassable by the incessant heavy rains. After a rest of six hours, the greater portion of the infantry continued their march to Bushire, which was reached before midnight, thus performing another most arduous march of forty-four miles under incessant rain, besides fighting and defeating the enemy during its progress, within the short period of fifty hours. On the morning of the 10th. the cavalry and artillery arrived in camp.

---

* Lieutenants Arthur Thomas Moore (Adjutant,) and John Grant Malcolmson, of the 3rd. Bombay Light Cavalry, here gained the Victoria Cross. On the occasion of an attack on the enemy on the 8th. of February, 1857, led by Lieutenant-Colonel Forbes, C.B., Lieutenant Moore, the Adjutant of the Regiment, was, perhaps, the first of all by a horse's length. His horse leaped into the square, and instantly fell dead, crushing down his rider, and breaking his sword as he fell among the broken ranks of the enemy. Lieutenant Moore speedily extricated himself, and attempted with his broken sword to force his way through the press; but he would assuredly have lost his life had not Lieutenant Malcolmson, observing his peril, fought his way to his dismounted comrade through a crowd of enemies, and, giving him his stirrup, safely carried him through everything out of the throng. The thoughtfulness for others, cool determination, devoted courage, and ready activity shewn in extreme danger by this young officer, Lieutenant Malcolmson, were most admirable.

The loss in the action at Koosh-ab on the 8th. of February was limited to sixteen killed and sixty-two wounded. Lieutenant Frankland, of the 2nd. European regiment, was the only officer killed.* This officer together with Captain Forbes, commanding the 3rd. regiment of Light Cavalry, and Lieutenant Doveton Downes Greentree, of the 64th. regiment, both severely wounded, (the latter losing his leg,) received special mention in the Governor-General's Notification.

For some months the Persians had been engaged in fortifying their position at Mohammerah, and Lieutenant-General Outram resolved to attack them. Their army, estimated at thirteen thousand men, with thirty guns, was commanded by the Shah Zadu, Prince Khauler Mirza, in person; whilst the Anglo-Indian troops consisted of about five thousand. This place was bombarded on the 26th. of March. Brigadier-General Havelock landed the troops, but no portion of the military force was actively engaged, except some European riflemen sent on board the war-vessels, as the Persians fled from their entrenched camp without waiting an attack. Meanwhile a treaty of peace had been in progress, the ratifications of which were exchanged at Bagdad on the 2nd. of May, whereby Herat was agreed to be evacuated, and all interference with the internal affairs of Affghanistan was to be avoided.†

In honour of this campaign, in a country believed to contain the site of the Garden of Eden, and memorable for the

---

* "To Lieutenant-General Sir James Outram, and to his brave companions in arms, the Governor-General in council desires to offer an early assurance of the warm approbation and thanks which they have so well merited. These are especially due to Major-General Stalker, C.B., and to Colonel Lugard, C.B., chief of the staff, who are described by Sir James Outram as having guided the troops to victory in the time-most happily not of long continuance—during which he was disabled by a severe fall of his horse. But they are due to all of every rank who have taken share in this signally successful exploit, which has called for extraordinary exertions from all, and in which all have borne themselves with gallantry."—*Notification, Fort William, Foreign Department, March 12th., 1857.*

Major-General Stalker and Commodore Ethersey both destroyed themselves at Bushire, while labouring under mental aberration; the former on the 14th. of March, 1857, and the latter three days afterwards.

† The Persian titles are remarkable; "His Majesty the Shah of Persia, His Excellency the Abode of Greatness, the favorite of the King, Ferokh Khan, Ameen Oolmoolk, the Great Ambassador of the Mighty State of Persia, the Possessor of the Royal Portrait, and of the Blue Cordon, the Bearer of the Diamond-studded Girdle," &c., &c.

MEDALS FOR SECOND BURMESE AND CHINESE WAR

exploits of Alexander the Great, the following Queen's regiments were authorized to bear on their colours the words—BUSHIRE, 64th. Foot; KOOSH-AB, 64th. and 78th. regiments; RESHIRE, 64th. regiment.

THE SECOND BURMESE AND PERSIAN MEDAL.

The medal and ribbon for these two services are the same. On the obverse is the Queen's head, similar to that for the Indian Mutiny, and on the reverse is represented Victory crowning an antique warrior. In the *exergue* is the lotus. This medal was designed by Leonard C. Wyon, Esq. The ribbon is bright scarlet, with two dark blue stripes. A clasp with the word PEGU was issued with the medal for services in Burmah, and that for the Persian campaign had one inscribed PERSIA.

THE INDIAN MUTINY MEDAL.
1857–1858.

This medal, which is by L.C. Wyon, Esq., is a work of great merit. The obverse has the Queen's head with the superscription VICTORIA REGINA, and on the reverse Britannia is represented in an erect position, instead of being seated, and above is the word INDIA; the drapery is most judiciously arranged. In her right hand, out-stretched, is a laurel wreath. The usual shield with the Union is on the left arm, and in the hand are other wreaths. The British Lion forms an appropriate background. The ribbon is French-white, with two red stripes. It was granted to all engaged in operations against the rebels or mutineers, and was also conferred on non-military persons who had borne arms as volunteers against them. There are five bars attached, respectively inscribed DELHI, DEFENCE OF LUCKNOW, RELIEF OF LUCKNOW, LUCKNOW, and CENTRAL INDIA. The first clasp was granted to the troops employed in the operations against, and at the assault of, Delhi; that for the DEFENCE OF LUCKNOW was conferred on all of the original garrison, under Major-General Inglis, and to those who succoured them, and continued the defence under Major-Generals Sir Henay Havelock and Sir James Outram, until relieved by Lord Clyde; Relief of Lucknow was authorized to the troops engaged in the operations against that place, under the immediate command of Lord Clyde, in November, 1857; and the clasp Lucknow was awarded to the force engaged under his lordship's immediate command in March, 1858, in the final capture of the town, and in all operations connected therewith; Central India was granted to the column under Major-General Sir Hugh Rose, G.C.B., engaged in the operations against Jhansi, Calpee, and Gwalior, and also to the troops, which, under the command of Major-Generals Roberts and Whitlock respectively, performed such important service in Central India.

SIEGE OF DELHI.
30th. May to 14th. September, 1857.

Sunday, the 10th. of May, 1857, will never cease to be remembered in India. An outbreak, for some time contemplated, broke out at Meerut in the afternoon of that day. A century had elapsed since Clive's celebrated battle of Plassey, the forerunner of so many victories gained in India, by the valuable co-operation of Native troops, when the latter, forgetful of their former glories and of their loyalty, burst out into mutiny, with the view of overthrowing British supremacy in the East; the outbreak of Vellore, in the Madras Presidency, in 1806, having been the only exception to the long-continued fidelity of the Sepoy soldier. During the operations against Persia the Court of Delhi had entered into correspondence with the Shah, and Dost Mahomed, the Sovereign of Cabool, had been urged to invade the Punjab, when, by the secession of the Bengal native army, the time should be opportune. The grievance of the greased cartridges was indeed urged, but the combination had been for some time forming, and the name of the King of Delhi, over eighty years of age, was imagined to be a "tower of strength" in the endeavour to be made to restore the supremacy of the Mogul dynasty.

There is no doubt the rebellion was prematurely commenced;

scenes of the most heart-rending descriptions occurred, and several officers, ladies, and even children fell victims to the brutality of the Sepoys. Outbreaks occurred at Allahabad, Jhansi, Azimghur, Bareilly, Lucknow, Cawnpore, Benares, and other places; the European women and children being, in many of them, murdered, and the several mutinous regiments all made for Delhi, hastening thither, as a central point, from all quarters, and committing the greatest outrages.

When the mutineers had seized Delhi, and proclaimed a descendant of the Mogul as king, their next object was to gain the chief magazine in that city. After a gallant defence it was exploded by order of Lieutenant Willoughby, who died of his wounds. Scully and Buckley were the two gunners, and the former, who fired the train, escaped, together with the other heroes Lieutenants Forrest and Raynor.

At this momentous period the Commander-in-Chief in India was General the Honourable George Anson, who had proceeded to Simla to escape the heat of the plains. Immediately upon receiving intelligence of the mutiny, he hurried to Umballa, and collecting all the available troops,* marched on Delhi,

---

* Queen's Regiments in India on the 1st. of May, 1857:—6th. Dragoon Guards, 9th. and 12th. Lancers, and 14th. Light Dragoons. 8th. Foot, 10th., (first battalions,) 24th., 27th., 29th., 82nd., 85th., 43rd., 52nd., 53rd., 60th., (first battalion,) 61st., 64th., 70th., 74th., 75th., 78th., 81st., 83rd., 84th., 86th., and 87th. Regiments. Strength:—seven hundred and fifty-seven officers and twenty-two thousand four hundred and seventy-one men. The East-India Company's Troops raised this force to two hundred and seventy-seven thousand seven hundred and forty-six; the Native Troops included therein amounting to two hundred and thirty two thousand two hundred and twenty-four, and the Europeans to forty-five thousand five hundred and twenty-two.

By the end of 1858 the drafts and additional regiments embarked from England and the Colonies, amounted to three thousand one hundred and two officers and seventy-eight thousand four hundred and thirty-seven men, and at that period the regiments in India consisted of twelve Cavalry; Royal Artillery, (Horse,) four troops; Foot, nineteen field batteries and six companies garrison. Royal Engineers, four companies. Second battalion Military Train, and seventy-three Infantry regiments. The Cavalry were 1st., 2nd., 3rd., 6th., and 7th. Dragoons Guards; 6th., 7th., 8th., 9th., 12th., 14th., and 17th. Dragoons. The Infantry were 1st.. 3rd., 4th., 5th., 6th., 7th., 8th., 10th., 13th., 18th., 19th., 20th., 23rd., 24th., (first battalions,) 27th., 28th., 29th., 31st., 32nd., 33rd., 34th., 35th., 37th., 38th., 42nd., 43rd , 44th., 46th., 48th., 51st., 52nd., 53rd., 54th., 56th., 57th., 60th., (1st., 2nd., and 3rd. battalions,) 61st., 64th., 66th., 67th., 68th., 69th., 70th., 71st., 72nd., 73rd., 74th., 75th., 77th., 78th., 79th., 80th., 81st., 82nd., 83rd., 84th., 86th., 87th., 88th., 89th., 90th., 91st., 92nd., 93rd., 94th., 95th., 97th., 98th., and 99th. regiments. Rifle Brigade, 2nd. and 3rd., battalions. Medical Staff Corps. A volunteer battalion of German settlers also embarked from the Cape in October, 1858.

but died of cholera at Kurnaul on the 27th. of May. His successor was Major-General Reed, who on the day following quitted Rawul Pindee, and arrived early in June at the camp of Major-General Sir Henry Barnard, K.C.B., at Aleepore, where a numerous force had been collected.

While Brigadier-General Archdale Wilson hastened with a body of troops from Meerut to join the former, the mutineers from Delhi attempted to intercept his march. He was attacked on the 30th. of May at Ghazee-ood-deen-nuggur, when seven hundred British soldiers defeated a disciplined force more than seven-fold their number. This is considered as the commencement of operations before Delhi. On the following day (Whit-Sunday) the attack was renewed, and the enemy was again repulsed, twenty-six guns being captured. The 6th. Dragoon Guards and first battalion 60th. Rifles have reason to be proud of the deeds peformed this day. No further opposition was encountered, and Brigadier-General Wilson joined Sir Henry Barnard at Aleepore. The united forces commenced their march shortly after midnight, and Brigadier-General Reed being unable from sickness to proceed with the army, the command devolved on Major-General Sir Henry Barnard. At dawn on the 8th. of June the British arrived before Badlee-ke-Serai, a fortified position, when the enemy opened fire. Brigadier Hope Grant, C.B., with his column, consisting of portions of the 9th. Lancers, 6th. Dragoon Guards, 75th., first battalion 60th. and 87th. were highly distinguished. On the regimental colour of the 75th. appeared the Royal Tiger, gained in former fields in India, and they added to their well-earned reputation by charging the enemy with the bayonet, who abandoned the whole of his guns. Colonel Chester, of the 23rd. Native Infantry, Adjutant-General of the army, the only officer killed, fell early in the action.*

---

* It appears from that interesting work, "The Chaplain's Narrative of the Siege of Delhi," (the Rev. John Edward Wharton Rotton, M.A.,) that the Adjutant-General actually lived for a few moments after being wounded, and bade Captain Barnard, the son of the General commanding the force at the time, raise his head, that he might catch a glimpse of the wound. Colonel Herbert, of Her Majesty's 75th., tells me, "this was a positive fact; and as soon as Chester saw the nature of the wound which had been inflicted upon him, and was convinced of its being mortal, he coolly, and yet kindly, expressed his convictions to General Barnard's

This entrenched frontier being carried, Sir Henry Barnard divided his army into two columns, one of which proceeded along the main trunk road under Brigadier-General Wilson, while the other marched under his own command to the site of the Delhi cantonments, before they were burnt. Here on an eminence the mutineers were posted, which position was taken by Sir Henry Barnard, the enemy being forced to abandon their guns; while this rapid flank movement to the left had been effected, Brigadier Wilson's column forcing its way through gardens with high walls, compelled the foe to take refuge in Delhi, the two commanders meeting at a place named Hindoo Rao's House. In these actions the Ghoorkas, evinced that gallantry which was so prominent during every subsequent encounter with the enemy.

After these events the British army took up a position before Delhi. The force at this period comprised the following Queen's regiments:— two squadrons of the 6th. Dragoon Guards, (Carabineers,) the 9th. Lancers; head-quarters and six companies of the 60th. Rifles; head-quarters and nine companies of the 75th regiment; in addition to these were three troops of horse artillery; a company of foot artillery, a detachment of sappers and miners, the first Bengal Fusiliers, and the head-quarters and six companies of the second Fusiliers, and the Sirmoor battalion. A strongly-built residence, named Hindoo Rao's House, on the top of a high eminence about half a mile in advance of the camp, offered an excellent position for bombarding the town, and from the three batteries erected thereon a constant fire of shot and shell was kept up. Between Hindoo Rao's House and the Grand Trunk Road the ground was rough and rocky, covered with brushwood and enclosed gardens, over which the Sepoys frequently crept up in skirmishing order, availing themselves of the shelter thus afforded, but they were always repulsed by the guides and riflemen, being at times pursued nearly to the city walls. Every mutineer who was captured was at once shot or bayoneted. The lines of defence were gradually advanced, and the rebels were driven from the Subzee Mundee,

---

son; begging the generous youth, who would stay to minister to his dying moments, to care for himself, and leave him, a dying man, to his fate : he then expired."

formerly used as a market for vegetables, and the Serai, a large building in front of it, which the British strongly fortified, together with the Pagoda opposite the Moree Gate. Early in June cholera appeared in the camp; this added to the trials of the troops; there being in consequence of the small force scarcely any rest by night, as the limited numbers barely admitted of relief, lessened as they were by those required for picket duty. Fighting by day, and being on the alert for a renewal of the conflict by night, occasioned great fatigue, and shewed what British troops can endure; besides which the ammunition supplies were not very plentiful for heavy ordnance.* Another large Serai, near the Ajmeer Gate, was gallantly taken on the 17th. of June, by a body of troops under Major Tombs, of the artillery.

During the evening of the 19th. of June the British were attacked in the Ochterlony Gardens, when Brevet-Lieutenant-Colonel Yule, of the 9th. Lancers, was killed. In consequence of a prophecy that the 23rd. of June, the centenary anniversary of Plassey, was to be fatal to British rule in India, a determined effort was made by the mutineers on that morning, who advanced from the city in large bodies, and attacking the batteries, kept up a sustained and vigorous fire throughout the day. Their prophets proved but false ones, for the enemy was beaten as usual. This victory of the 23rd. of June occasioned much rejoicing in the camp. Frequent skirmishes occurred towards the end of the month, and during July. The besieging force had now been strengthened by a wing of the 8th. Foot and of the 61st. regiment. Early in July Sir Henry Barnard died of cholera, when the command devolved on Major-General Reed, who, although the senior, had relinquished it to him upon the decease of General Anson. Reed, on account also of ill-health, was soon compelled to give over the command to Brigadier-General Wilson. The 8th. and 61st. regiments suffered severely from cholera, attributed to their long march during the height of the rainy season. The former, in four

---

* The following fact is significant of the scarcity of this kind of ammunition:— In one of the field force orders it was notified that two annas would be given for each of the enemy's twenty-four pounder round shot that might be brought into camp, to be again used up. Similar instances occurred during the siege of Sebastopol, and in the Peninsula, as noticed at page 66 of the Crimean section of this work.

months, from July to October, lost one hundred and thirty-three men, and the deaths in the latter during the same period amounted to two hundred and forty-six.

A sortie was made by the enemy on the 9th. of July. During the forenoon of the 14th. another attack occurred, in which Brigadier-General Chamberlain, the Adjutant-General, was severely wounded; Captain Norman, of the 31st. Native Infantry, (frequently thanked in the despatches for his services,) the second in the department, was appointed to carry on the duties of this arduous office. On the 18th. and 23rd. other sorties took place, and the rebels were again repulsed.

Two dense columns of the enemy attempted, on the 31st. of July, to gain the rear of the British camp, but the bridges having been destroyed, they were unable to cross the canal, and after a brisk cannonade the troops returned to the city. An attack, sustained with great determination, occurred on the 1st. of August, the anniversary of the great Mahomedan festival, commemorating Abraham's sacrifice, not of Isaac, but of Ishmael, when the mutineers received a severe punishment. Brigadier Showers, on the 12th. of that month, succeeded in capturing four of the enemy's guns. Four days previously Brigadier-General Nicholson reached the camp in advance of his column, which had been employed in disarming rebellion in the Punjab;* his force, consisting of two thousand five hundred men, Europeans and Sikhs, was a welcome addition to the army before Delhi.

---

* Sir John Lawrence, the able chief commissioner of the Punjab, by his wise and prompt measures secured the tranquility of that portion of India. The necessary steps to disarm the Native regiments were ably carried into effect by the 81st., the only Queen's regiment at Lahore. Putteeala, a powerful Sikh chieftain, also gave zealous aid, not only by sending troops to replace those who had marched from Umballa to join their comrades before Delhi, but also by affording protection to fugitives, and exercising his influence. to keep his countrymen faithful to the British; his relative the Jheend Rajah also proceeded to Delhi with a body of his own troops, and bore an active share in the subsequent operations. The authorities at Peshawur, where fourteen thousand men were stationed, only about one fourth being Europeans, were on the alert; the fort of Attock was at once provisioned for a siege, the 57th. Queen's regiment forming its garrison, and the 64th. Native Infantry were distributed in the frontier forts, the treasure being deposited at Peshawur. The Guides were sent to join the army before Delhi, where they arrived in June, after a march of about six hundred miles, pronounced by Sir Henry Barnard to be without a parallel. Colonel Edwardes, of Punjab fame, also by his appeals caused several bodies of Sikh troops to uphold British rule, and they were found most welcome at Delhi. Above

Brigadier-General Nicholson gained a brilliant victory over the enemy at Nujjuffghur, twenty miles from Delhi, on the 25th. of August, and thus prevented an attack upon the rear of the British camp.

For some time the siege-train from Meerut had been anxiously expected, and on the morning of the 4th. of September it arrived.

A crisis was now fast approaching; fifty-four siege-guns were placed in position in several batteries, and on the 11th. of September an incessant fire was opened, and sustained, upon the line of defence between the Water and Cashmere Gates. The latter was in ruins on the 13th., and shortly after three o'clock on the following morning the assaulting columns prepared to advance. There were four columns of attack; Brigadier-General Nicholson commanded the first; Brigadier-General Jones the second; Brigadier Campbell the third; and Major Reid the fourth. There was also a fifth reserve column under Brigadier Longfield.

It being necessary to blow open the Cashmere Gate, in order that the attacking force might effect an entrance into the city, this desperate duty was performed by Lieutenants Home and Salkeld,* of the Engineers.

---

all, the great object of disarming the suspicions regiments was carried out. Colonel Ellice with three companies of the 24th. regiment, had an affair with the 14th. Native Infantry, at Jhelum on the 7th. of July; and had several casualties, he himself being dangerously wounded; and a flying column, under Brigadier-General Nicholson, encountered the mutineers about noon on the 12th. of July, as they were crossing the Ravee; in this action the 52nd. Light Infantry, under Colonel Campbell, maintained their high character. After another attack on the 16th. of that month, the Brigadier proceeded to several disturbed parts of the country, and eventually joined the troops before Delhi on the 14th. of August.

The column from the Punjab comprised the 52nd. Light Infantry, a wing of the 61st., No. 17 Light Field Battery, 2nd. regiment of Punjab Infantry, a wing of the 7th. Punjab Police Battalion, 4th. Sikh Infantry, two hundred and fifty Mooltanee Horse, with siege guns and ordnance stores. The 52nd. were six hundred and eighty strong, with six sick, but on the 14th. of September, owing to the ravages of fever and cholera, they only mustered two hundred and forty effectives of all ranks.

* In addition to these two officers there were Sergeants John Smith and A. B. Carmichael, and Corporal F. Burgess, alias Joshua Burgess Grierson, of the Sappers and Miners; Bugler Hawthorne, of the 52nd. Light Infantry, and twenty-four Sappers and Miners, viz:—fourteen Native and ten Punjab. Covered by the fire of the 60th. Rifles, this party advanced at the double towards the Cashmere Gate; Lieutenant Home, with Sergeants John Smith and Carmichael, and Havildar Madhoo, all of the Sappers, leading and carrying the powder bags, followed by Lieutenant Salkeld, Corporal Burgess, and a section of the remainder of the party. Sergeant Carmichael was killed

The latter died of his wounds, and the former was shortly afterwards killed by an explosion, whilst blowing up a fort abandoned by the rebels in Boolundshuhur.

Brigadier Nicholson with the first column of attack, consisting of three hundred men of the 75th., two hundred and fifty of the 1st. European Bengal Fusiliers, and five hundred of the 2nd. Punjab Infantry, was ordered to assault the breach in the Cashmere Curtain Gate. A portion escaladed the left face of the bastion at the gate, while the remainder, covered by the fire of the 60th., rushed up the breach made upon their left of the gate. After reaching the Cabool Gate, so destructive a fire was opened by the enemy, that the advancing troops were compelled to desist. Their gallant commander Nicholson, whilst inducing the men to renew the attempt, here fell mortally wounded, and died nine days afterwards. Colonel Herbert, of the 75th., was previously wounded on the glacis, and the command of this portion of the assaulting column devolved on Captain William Brookes, of that regiment.

Brigadier William Jones with the second column, composed of the 8th., 2nd. European Bengal Fusiliers, and 4th. Sikh regiment of infantry, (the storming party consisted of seventy-five men of these corps, and the assault was led by Brevet-Major R. S. Baynes, of the 8th. Foot, who was dangerously wounded,) covered by the fire of the skirmishers of the 60th. Rifles, advanced through the breach in the bastion at the Water Gate, and gained possession of the walls as far as the Cabool Gate without meeting any check. Upon reaching the

whilst laying his powder, and Havildar Madhoo was wounded. Whilst endeavouring to fire the charge Lieutenant Salkeld was shot through the leg and arm, and handed over the slow match to Corporal Burgess, who fell mortally wounded just as he had successfully performed his duty. Havildar Tiluk Singh, of the Sappers and Miners was wounded, and Ram Heth, Sepoy of the same corps, was killed during this part of the operation. The demolition having being most successful, Lieutenant Home then caused the bugle to sound the regimental call of the 52nd. as the signal for the advance of the column; this was repeated three times, as it was feared that amidst the noise of the assault the sound might not be heard. The bugler, Robert Hawthorne, after performing his own dangerous duty, humanely attached himself to Lieutenant Salkeld, and after binding up that officer's wounds under a heavy musketry fire, had him removed without further injury. For this deed, pronounced to be "as noble as any that has ever graced the annals of war," he received the Victoria Cross.

latter the troops turned one of the guns immediately on the Lahore Gate, from which the foe was firing grape and round shot.

Colonel George Campbell, of the 52nd. Light Infantry, proceeded with the third column of assault, consisting of two hundred and forty of the 52nd., five hundred of the 1st. Punjab Infantry, and two hundred and sixty of the Kumaon battalion, and when the Cashmere Gate had been burst open by the explosion, the stormers rushed in, and in a short time the column gained possession of the main guard, where so many murders had occurred at the outbreak of the mutiny, and at once advanced to the attack of the great mosque, the Jumma Musjid, situated about the centre of the city. When almost close to the mosque, it was found that there were no means of gaining an entrance, the force being without powder-bags or artillery; and having to sustain a concentrated musketry fire from the surrounding houses, the column was eventually compelled to withdraw.

Major Reid, of the Sirmoor Battalion, who led the fourth column, (consisting of fifty men, 60th. Rifles, two hundred Sirmoor Battalion, one hundred and sixty 1st. Fusiliers, two hundred Guides, twenty-five Coke's Corps, sixty-five Kumaon Battalion, eighty 61st. Regiment,— seven hundred and eighty in all,) was severely wounded; his fall checked the advance of the Goorkhas; Captain D.D. Muter, of the first battalion of the 60th., succeeded to the command; and the rush of the Rifles and Fusiliers placed them for a moment in possession of the breastwork at the end of the Serai of Kishengunge, but being unsupported, were unable to maintain the position, under the heavy flanking fire to which they became exposed.

Meanwhile the cavalry brigade, (consisting of two hundred of the 9th. Lancers, and four hundred and ten Natives from the Guides, 1st., 2nd., and 5th. Punjab Cavalry, and Hodson's Horse; with three guns of the first Troop Horse Artillery, and four guns of the second, under Major Toombs,) commanded by Brigadier Hope Grant, forming in front of the walls, proceeded to the Cabool Gate, and although exposed to a heavy fire, did excellent service by preventing the mutineers, who came out in great numbers through the gardens, from attacking the British batteries. During the operations on the 14th. of September the casualties amounted to eleven hundred and seventy killed, wounded, and missing.*

Lieutenant-Colonel Deacon, of the 61st., succeeded in capturing the magazine in the city of Delhi, on the 16th. of September. Not a word was spoken, not a trigger pulled, until the stormers and the support had reached the summit of the breach and the magazine yard, when a cheer and a charge were given and made, on which the enemy, taken most completely by surprise, fled precipitately, throwing down the portfires at their guns. Several of them were bayoneted close to the breach, the others were closely pursued by the 61st. and the 4th. Punjab Infantry. A party under Lieutenant-Colonel Rainey, of the former, (under the guidance of Captain H. W. Norman, Assistant-Adjutant-General,) having passed through the magazine, turned to their left, and spiked a gun, which was in position on the eastern wall of the city, and which was pointed at the College Garden Battery: here the enemy fought desperately. Assistant-Surgeon Reade and Colour-Sergeant Mitchell, both of the 61st., also spiked a gun. One hundred and seventy guns, together with stores of all descriptions, were found in the magazine. During the fore and afternoon attacks were made by the rebels, which were repulsed on every occasion by the troops then within the walls, under Lieutenant-Colonel Farquhar, of the Belooch Battalion.

A determined opposition was kept up for a few days in the city, and only slow progress was made; but on the morning

*

	Field Officers	Capt-ains.	Subal-terns	Suba-dars	Jema-dars	Ser-geants	Rank & File
Killed	...	1	6	1	4	22	249
Wounded	8	13	36	10	9	59	742
Missing	...	...	...	...	...	1	9
Total	8	14	42	11	13	82	1000

The force consisted of the following brigades :—CAVALRY BRIGADE—6th. Dragoon Guards, 9th. Lancers, 1st. and 5th. Punjab Cavalry, 4th. Irregular Cavalry, Guide Cavalry, and Hodson's Horse. 1ST. INFANTRY BRIGADE—75th., 2nd. European Bengal Fusiliers, and Kumaon Battalion. 2ND. BRIGADE—52nd. Light Infantry, 60th. Rifles, and Sirmoor Battalion. 3RD. BRIGADE—8th. and 61st. Foot, and 4th. Regiment Sikhs. 4TH. BRIGADE—1st. European Bengal Fusiliers, 1st, 2nd, and 4th. Punjab Infantry. In addition to the foregoing there were artillery,—European and Native, Engineer Brigade, Guide Corps Infantry, and the Belooch Battalion.

of the 20th., possession was secured of the Lahore Gate, and the troops then advanced upon the other bastions and gates, until the entire defences of the city were acquired. The enemy unable to withstand the uninterrupted and vigorous fire from the guns and mortars, from the first entrance of the city by the British, and the steady and persevering advance of the troops, at length took to flight, abandoning their camp, property, and several of their sick and wounded, besides the greater portion of their field artillery; some four or five thousand fled across the bridge of boats into the Doab, or country between the Jumna and the Ganges, and the rest along the right bank of the former river.

After the gate of the palace had been blown in, it was occupied by the troops about noon on Sunday, the 20th. of September, and the head-quarters of Major-General Wilson were established therein the same day. The rapid advance upon the Jumma Musjid by Major Brind, of the artillery, with a detachment of fifty men of the 8th. Foot, and twenty of the 1st. Bengal European Fusiliers, under the command of Captain Bannatyne, of the former regiment, an entrance into which was forced about an hour and a half prior to the assault upon the palace, contributed towards the success of the operations, and the complete occupation of the city. At sunrise on the 21st. a royal salute proclaimed that Delhi was again under British rule; the aged Sovereign, after a trial, was sent a prisoner for life to Rangoon.*

When the capture of Delhi was completed, a flying column,

---

* Well might the Governor-General, in his "Notification," remark, that "Before a single soldier, of the many thousands who are hastening from England to uphold the supremacy of the British power, has set foot on these shores, the rebel force, where it was strongest and most united, and where it had the command of unbounded military appliances, has been destroyed or scattered by an army collected within the limits of the North-western Provinces and the Punjab alone.

"The work has been done before the support of those battalions, which have been collected in Bengal from the forces of the Queen in China, and in Her Majesty's eastern colonies, could reach Major-General Wilson's army; and it is by the courage and endurance of that gallant army alone; by the skill, sound judgment, and steady resolution of its brave commander; and by the aid of some native chiefs, true to their allegiance, that, under the blessing of God, the head of rebellion has been crushed, and the cause of loyalty, humanity, and rightful authority vindicated."

Lord Canning also bore testimony to the invaluable assistance received from Sir John Lawrence, K.C.B., in recruiting and strengthening the army before Delhi.

under the command of Lieutenant-Colonel E.H. Greathed,* consisting of the 9th. Lancers, 8th. and 75th. regiments, the 2nd. and 4th. Punjab Infantry, two hundred of Hodson's Horse, with the 1st., 2nd., and 5th. Punjab Cavalry and Horse Artillery, proceeded on the morning of the 23rd. of September, from Delhi in a south-easterly direction upon Boolundshuhur and Allyghur, with a view of cutting off the mutineers on the right bank of the Jumna, in their endeavour to pass the river into the Doab. At Boolundshuhur, on the 28th. of September, the column defeated a body of the enemy, and afterwards destroyed the fort of Malaghur; here, Lieutenant Home, who shared in the blowing open of the Cashmere Gate at Delhi, met an accidental death by an explosion of gunpowder. While on the march along the Great Trunk road to Allyghur, the rebels were again encountered and scattered.

Pursuing this successful course the troops arrived at Agra, after a night-march from Hattrass; fatigued as they were, and while preparing to encamp, an attack was suddenly made upon them on the 10th. of October, by a numerous body of the enemy. In the action which ensued the 9th. Lancers were specially mentioned. Lieutenant-Colonel Cotton, commanding at Agra, at once repaired to the camp, and assumed the command, but Lieutenant-Colonel Greathed was not aware of his presence for some time. The attack was soon overpowered, and turned into a complete rout, notwithstanding several ineffectual attempts to make a stand, and the pursuit was continued during the rest of the day for a distance of eleven miles, the whole of the enemy's guns, twelve in number, being captured. This was effected under the rays of an Indian sun, and with comparatively small loss,† but the casualties of the enemy were immense.

---

* At one time there were three brothers of this name before Delhi, the 8th. Foot being under the command of Lieutenant-Colonel Greathed at the assault on that city; this was the elder; the other, H. H. Greathed, Esq., Commissioner and Political Agent of the Bengal Civil Service, died of cholera on the 19th. of September, the day previous to its capture; and the youngest, Brevet-Major William Wilberforce Harris Greathed, C.B., of the Bengal Engineers, who was severely wounded in the storming of Delhi, was appointed, in May last, Assistant Military Secretary at Head-Quarters, on Lieutenant-Colonel H. W. Norman, C.B., returning to India to resume the duties of Deputy-Adjutant-General in Bengal.

† Eleven killed and fifty-six wounded; divided amongst the Company's Artillery, 9th. Lancers, 8th. and 75th. Queen's Regiments; 1st., 2nd., and 5th. Punjab Cavalry; Hodson's Horse; 3rd. and 4th. Punjab Infantry; and 3rd. European Regiment.

Lieutenant-Colonel Greathed having crossed the Jumna was joined, on the 14th. of October, by Brigadier Hope Grant,* who, as senior officer, took the command. After dismantling the fort of a rebel Rajah at Mynporee, who did not attempt any resistance, the column put to flight a body of fugitives from Delhi, killing many of them. Possession was gained of the fort of Jhujjur by Brigadier Showers, on the 17th. of October, which is regarded as the close of the operations against Delhi. Brigadier Grant, continuing his march, arrived at Cawnpore on the 28th. of October, and on the 30th. crossed the Ganges, reaching the vicinity of the Alumbagh on the 8th. of the following month.

DEFENCE OF LUCKNOW.
29TH, JUNE TO 25TH, SEPTEMBER, 1857.

Sir Henry Lawrence, having received information in the evening of the 29th. of June, that a body of rebels were about to march upon Lucknow from the village of Chinnahut, distant about eight miles from the town, determined on making a reconnoisance. This was accordingly commenced on the following day. Misled by the reports of wayfarers, who stated that there were few or no men between Lucknow and Chinnahut, the troops proceeded a greater distance than was originally intended, and suddenly fell in with the enemy, who had up to that moment eluded the vigilance of the advanced guard by concealing themselves, in overwhelming numbers, behind a long line of trees.

For some time the foe was held in check by the force, composed of three hundred of the 32nd., and portions of the 13th., 48th., and 71st. Native Infantry, with the howitzer; but the Oude artillerymen and drivers were traitors, and they overturned their six guns into ditches, cut the traces of their horses, and abandoned them, notwithstanding the remonstrances of their own officers, and of

---

* Afterwards promoted Major-General for his eminent services at Delhi, and in that of a division at the relief of Lucknow, and in the subsequent operations in India, his name being frequently mentioned in the despatches.

those on Sir Henry Lawrence's staff, the brigadier himself heading them, and drawing his sword upon the caitiffs. Thus exposed to a vastly superior fire of artillery, and completely outflanked on both sides by the enemy's infantry and cavalry, which actually penetrated to the rear, the British were forced to retire with the loss of three pieces of artillery, and with a sad list of killed and wounded.

By this untoward event the whole available force was so far diminished, that there was not a sufficient number of men remaining to occupy the Residency and the fort named Muchhee Bhowun, an old dilapidated edifice which had been hastily put in repair, although the defences were far from complete, and were moreover commanded by many houses in the city. The brigadier-general therefore, on the 1st. of July,* signalled the garrison of the Muchhee Bhowun to evacuate and blow up that fortress in the course of the night. The orders were ably carried out, and at twelve p.m. the troops marched into the Residency with their guns and treasure, without the loss of a man; and shortly afterwards the explosion of two hundred and forty barrels of gunpowder and six millions of ball cartridges, which were lying in the magazine, announced to Sir Henry Lawrence and his officers—who were anxiously waiting the report—the complete destruction of that post, and all that it contained. If it had not been for this wise and strategic measure, no member of the Lucknow garrison, in all probability, would have survived to tell the tale; for, as the Muchhee Bowun was commanded from other parts of the town, and was moreover indifferently provided with heavy artillery ammunition, while the suffering and loss which the Residency garrison, even with the reinforcements thus obtained, endured in holding the position, proved that if the original intention of holding the two posts had been adhered to, both would have inevitably fallen.

A sad calamity occurred at the outset. On the 1st. of July, an eight-inch shell burst in the room of the Residency

---

* The strength of the Lucknow garrison on the 1st. of July, 1857, consisted of one thousand six hundred and eighteen officers and men, "effective, fit for duty;" the sick and wounded amounted to eighty officers and men.

in which Sir Henry Lawrence was sitting, The missile burst between him and Mr. Couper, close to both, but without injury to either. The whole of his staff implored Sir Henry to take up other quarters, as the place had then become the special target for the round shot and shell of the enemy. This, however, he jestingly declined to do, observing that another shell would certainly never be pitched into that small room. On the very next day however he was mortally wounded by the fragment of another shell which burst exactly in the same spot, and Captain Wilson, Deputy-Assistant Adjutant-General, received a contusion. Sir Henry Lawrence terminated his distinguished career on the morning of the 4th. of July, having previously directed Brigadier-General Inglis to take the command of the troops, and Major Banks to succeed to the office of chief commissioner.

Scarcely had the garrison recovered this shock, when it had to lament the death of Major Banks, who received a bullet through his bead while examining a critical outpost on the 21 st. of July.

When the blockade was commenced only two of the batteries were completed, and the defences were in an unfinished condition, the buildings in the immediate vicinity, which gave cover to the enemy, being only partially cleared away. Indeed the heaviest losses were caused by the fire from the enemy's sharp-shooters, stationed in the adjoining mosques and houses of the native nobility, the necessity of destroying which had been repeatedly pressed on Sir Henry by the staff of engineers, but his invariable reply was, "Spare the holy places, and private property too as far as possible;" and the garrison consequently suffered severely from this tenderness to the religious prejudices, and respect to the rights, of the rebellious citizens and soldiery.

Then ensued a defence as heroic as any in the annals of war. The narrative of Brigadier Inglis, simple and earnest, will never be forgotten by his countrymen. By it the reader will see that not a building within the walls of the Residency was safe;* the wounded were shot while in hospital, and

---

* One of the most remarkable relics of the siege that I have seen was the mess plate of the 32nd. regiment. The spoons were twisted by the effect of the enemy's shot, and the soup

ladies and children met the same fate in houses considered secure. The enemy, while working the guns concealed by the trenches, were shielded from the fire of the garrison, upon whom an incessant cannonade was kept up until the 20th. of July, at ten o'clock on which morning the besiegers, in great numbers, after exploding a mine within the British defences, attempted to storm the Residency, and did not cease their efforts until two o'clock in the afternoon, being driven back by the gallant defenders, who were sustained by the consciousness of the mighty trust committed to their charge.

It was not until the 10th. of August that another assault was attempted, although during the interval the forlorn garrison became exposed to a constant fire, with famine staring it in the face. This second attempt, similar in its features to the first, commencing with the springing of a mine close to the brigade mess, although repeated at various points, met with a like result: in some instances the defenders, acting like grenadiers of a former time, dislodged the foe with hand grenades. On the 18th. of August another mine was sprung in front of the Sikh lines with deadly effect, burying alive eleven men beneath the ruins, whence it was impossible to extricate them, owing to the tremendous fire kept up by the enemy from houses distant less than ten yards in front of the breach. Captain Orr, unattached, and Lieutenants Mecham and Soppitt were blown into the air, but, wonderful to state, received no further injury than a severe shaking. A general assault followed the explosion, which was soon repulsed; but the enemy succeeded in establishing themselves in one of the houses of the British position, from which they were driven in the evening by the bayonets of the 32nd. and 84th. regiments.

Fresh mines were sprung on the 5th. of September, when the last serious assault was made. It was in vain; all these repeated attacks met everywhere with defeat. Thus ended the four great struggles which occurred during the siege. For eighty-seven days and nights officers and men stood or slept under arms.

---

tureen presented a singular appearance, the handles being nearly wrenched off. These battered articles were sent to Windsor Castle for the inspection of Her Majesty.

Notwithstanding all the hardships experienced, the garrison made no less than five sorties, in which two of the enemy's heaviest guns were spiked, and several of the houses, from which a harassing fire was experienced, were blown up. Cholera, small pox, and an unknown, but fatal disease, added to the loss sustained from the enemy's fire. Delicate women, some whilst in their earliest grief for the loss of their husbands, assisted in nursing the sick and wounded. The names of Birch, Polehampton, Barbor, and Gall, will descend to posterity as worthy imitators of Florence Nightingale.

The conduct of the 32nd., (reduced to less than three hundred,) and the detachment of the 84th. was splendid. The loyalty of the native troops, but especially the 13th., was never surpassed. The other regiments were the 48th. and 71st. Native Infantry,* the European and Native Artillery, and the Sikhs of the respective corps.† The number of artillerymen was so reduced, that on the occasion of an attack, the gunners, although aided by men of the 32nd. regiment, and by volunteers of all classes, had to run from one battery to another, wherever the enemy's fire was hottest, there not being nearly sufficient men to serve half the number of guns at the same time. Eventually the number of European gunners was only twenty-four, while, including mortars, there were no less than thirty guns in position. So near too were the heavy guns of the assailants, that their taunts and threats addressed to the native defenders could be easily heard; besides which many of the British military airs, such as "Brighton Camp," "See the Conquering Hero Comes," and the "National Anthem," were, with matchless effrontery, frequently played by the enemy.

In general orders it was announced that "There does not

---

* The native non-commissioned officers and men who formed part of the garrison, received the Indian Order of Merit, and were permitted to count three years of additional service. The 13th., 48th., and 71st. regiments of Native Infantry were afterwards formed into one corps, designated the "Regiment of Lucknow."

† The garrison of Lucknow, from the 30th. of June to the 26th. of September, 1857, had one hundred and forty officers and men, Europeans, killed, and one hundred and ninety wounded; Natives, seventy-two killed and one hundred and thirty-one wounded.

stand recorded in the Annals of War an achievement more truly heroic than the defence of the Residency at Lucknow. The good services of H.M.'s 32nd. regiment throughout this struggle have been remarkable."

Lucknow has been authorized to be borne on the regimental colour and appointments of the 32nd., which, for its gallantry, has been constituted light infantry; and the Queen's officers and men of the garrison were allowed to reckon one year's additional service.

While the force, under Brigadier Inglis, afterwards advanced to the rank of Major-General, and appointed a Knight Commander of the Bath, had been defending the Residency of Lucknow, the eyes of Europe were directed to the efforts made for its relief by Brigadier-General Havelock, who, after his division in Persia had been broken up, proceeded to Bombay, and thence to Calcutta. He was immediately selected to command a moveable column, and hearing that the mutineers were proceeding from Cawnpore* towards Futtehpore, a forced march, under a burning sun, was made upon that place. Major Renaud joined him on the road with about eight hundred troops, the latter having been actively engaged

---

* Cawnpore unfortunately occupies a prominent place in the history of the mutiny. General Sir Hugh Wheeler, seeing the state of the native troops, which composed part of the garrison, formed an entrenched camp round the hospital barracks, and collected a supply of provisions. Owing to the defection of the native corps, some of which at first appeared faithful, the force ultimately consisted of the first company sixth battalion of artillery, sixty-one; 32nd. regiment, eighty-four; 1st. European Fusiliers, fifteen; 84th. regiment, fifty; in all two hundred and ten. To these may be added the officers of the three native infantry regiments, and others, amounting to about one hundred. The non-combatants amounted to five hundred and ninety, one hundred and sixty women and children being included in the latter number, in all nine hundred. Considering the defenceless state of the camp, it was wonderful that the garrison could withstand the enemy for a single day. The Sepoys commenced their attack on the 7th. of June, and continued an almost constant fire on the camp until the 24th. The garrison had only eight guns, while some opposed to them were twenty-four pounders. Frequent attempts were made to carry the enclosure by storm, but they were unsuccessful, the Sepoys being driven back each time. The sufferings of the garrison were so extreme, that on the 25th. of June, arrangements were entered into with Nena Sahib for the evacuation of the place. The result is but too well known. While the unfortunate people were proceeding towards Allahabad, the treacherous mutineers fired upon all in the boats; the one in which General Wheeler (who had been severely wounded) was in they brought back to Cawnpore. Only a few escaped, one of whom, Lieutenant Delafosse, has given a narrative of what he witnessed. All who were not killed in the boats were carried back to Cawnpore; the men being shot, and the females detained prisoners.

in suppressing the mutiny in the neighbourhood. This column consisted of the third company eighth battalion of the royal artillery, seventy-six; 1st. Madras Fusiliers, three hundred and seventy-six; 64th. regiment, four hundred and thirty-five; 78th. Highlanders, two hundred and eighty-four; 84th. regiment, one hundred and ninety; detachment of the Bengal Artillery, twenty-two; Volunteer Cavalry, twenty; total British, one thousand four hundred and three. The native troops:—The Regiment of Ferozepore, four hundred and forty-eight; 13th. Irregular and 3rd. Oude Irregular Cavalry, ninety-five; Galundauze, eighteen; total native troops, five hundred and sixty-one; in all one thousand nine hundred and sixty-four. It is computed that the mutineers numbered three thousand five hundred, and they occupied a strong position at Futtehpore, with twelve guns.

Pushing forward two of their guns, they commenced, on the 12th. of July, a cannonade on the British front, while a body of infantry and cavalry threatened the flanks. The enemy had imagined an easy victory over Major Renaud's force, but they found Brigadier-General Havelock ready to receive them. Astonished by the precision of the fire of the guns under Captain Maude, of the Royal Artillery, and the deadly aim of the Enfield rifles, they fell back upon Futtehpore in disorder, leaving three of their cannon. Here they endeavoured to make a stand, but were compelled to take to flight, abandoning twelve guns. This victory, in Havelock's order of the day, was attributed "to the British Artillery, to the Enfield rifle, to British pluck, and to the blessing of Almighty God."

Brigadier-General Havelock continued his march upon Cawnpore, and on the 15th. of July was twice engaged with the mutineers, first at the village of Aeng, and next at the bridge over the Pandoo Nuddee. Successful in both instances, the column pushed on, having captured the two guns with which it had been intended to defend the bridge. After it had been carried information was received that Nena Sahib occupied a position at Ahirwa; this position was a very strong one, and in order to save the troops from the fire of his heavy guns, the British General made a flank movement, which resulted on the 16th. in a direct charge with the bayonet. The 78th. Highlanders, gallantly led by Colonel Hamilton, supported by the Madras Fusiliers, succeeded in turning the enemy's left flank; while the 64th. and 84th., and the Regiment of Ferozepore, broke the right; the mutineers were driven headlong on Cawnpore, leaving a twenty-four pounder on the field.

The victors bivouacked on the ground, from which the roofless barracks at Cawnpore could be perceived. When Nena Sahib* saw that nothing could withstand the advance of the avenging column, he gave directions on the 17th. for the massacre of the women and children in his power, and with savage barbarity caused their bodies to be thrown into a well.

Early on that morning a heavy explosion was heard, arising from the blowing up, by the enemy, of the magazine at Cawnpore, when Nena Sahib was withdrawing thence upon Bithoor. Cawnpore was at once occupied, and the troops were horrified at the traces which remained of the massacre. The capture of the castellated palace of Nena Sahib at Bithoor, where he was unable to make a stand, was effected without firing a shot, and twenty guns were taken.

Upon Brigadier-General Neill's arrival at Cawnpore, from Benares, he was left in command of the former place, whilst Brigadier-General Havelock commenced his march upon Lucknow. Having passed the Ganges into Oude, the mutineers were next encountered near Unao, on the 29th. of July. The action was commenced by the 78th. Highlanders and the 1st. Fusiliers, with two guns. Afterwards, the 64th., commanded by Colonel Wilson, were ordered up. Patrick Cavanagh, a private of that regiment, was hewn in pieces by the Sepoys whilst exhibiting to his comrades an example of the highest gallantry. This valiant soldier had he survived would have received the Victoria Cross. At the narrow pass between the village and

---

* This miscreant's real name was Doondoo Punt, and he was the adopted son of Bajee Rao, the ex-Peishwah of Poona. After the death of the latter, in 1852, he made claim to the pension which had been allowed to that chief by the treaty of 1818, when he gave himself up to Sir John Malcolm. The refusal of the Indian authorities to recognise his right made him commence his vindictive course. He had been permitted to keep up a retinue of two hundred soldiers, and had a fortified place of residence at Bithoor, ten miles from Cawnpore.

the town of Unao the mutineers were discovered in great force, but, after an obstinate contest they sought safety in flight. Subsequently the troops pushed on towards Busherut Gunge, a walled town, with wet ditches, which was captured by the 1st. Fusiliers, 64th., and 78th. regiments.

Major-General Havelock's* force was not of sufficient strength to continue the advance upon Lucknow, cholera having broken out amongst them; and he fell back on the 2nd. of August, on Munghowar. On the 5th. he again attacked the enemy at Busherat Gunge, driving them; out of the town with great slaughter. Preparations were next commenced for passing over the Ganges to Cawnpore. The baggage had already been forwarded across the river, when he resolved, on the 11th. of August, to attack the mutineers a third time at Busherut Gunge, where they had once more collected in great force, and again defeated them.

Returning to their former position at Munghowar, the troops, on the 12th. and 13th. of August, crossed the Ganges to Cawnpore, where they arrived, nearly worn out by fatigue, sickness, and constant exposure to an Indian sun. Almost immediately, however, they struck another effective blow on the mutineers. A large body of them had collected at Bithoor, and were menacing Brigadier-General Neill at Cawnpore. Major-General Havelock, uniting his force with the former, marched on Bithoor, and gained another victory. During these several encounters forty guns had been taken, and sixty more recovered for the government. Great loss had been inflicted on the enemy, while the British casualties were comparatively small.

The British column afterwards remained at Cawnpore waiting for reinforcements, and on the 16th. of September, Major-General Sir James Outram arrived with the welcome aid; although the senior officer, he nobly relinquished to Major-General Havelock the honour of relieving the Lucknow garrison, and accompanied the column as

---

* Promoted to the rank of Major-General on the 30th. of July, 1857, and was afterwards appointed a Knight Commander of the Bath ; also created a baronet, but dying before the patent was sealed, the dignity was conferred upon his son, now Brevet-Lieutenant-Colonel Sir Henry M. Havelock, Bart., of the 18th. Royal Irish, regiment.

Chief Commissioner of Oude, proffering his military services as a volunteer.

On the 19th. and 20th. of September, the relieving force, amounting to about two thousand five hundred men, and seventeen guns, crossed the Ganges. The 5th. Fusiliers, 84th., detachments of the 64th. and 1st. Madras Fusiliers, composed the first infantry brigade, under Brigadier-General Neill; the 78th. Highlanders, 90th. Light Infantry, and the Sikh Ferozepore regiment, made up the second brigade, under Brigadier Hamilton, of the 78th.; Major Cooper commanded the artillery brigade, consisting of Captains Maude, Oliphant, and Major Eyre's batteries; Captain Borrow commanded the Volunteers and Irregular Cavalry.

Only a feeble resistance was offered by the enemy, who retired upon the old position of Munghowar. Here they were attacked on the morning of the 21st. of September, and after an obstinate contest were routed, two of the four guns captured, being taken in a cavalry charge led by Sir James Outram. Continuing the march on Lucknow, the rebels were discovered on the 23rd., in a strong position, with their left resting on the enclosure of the Alumbagh, an isolated building to the south-east of the city of Lucknow, and about three miles from the Residency, their centre and right being drawn up behind a chain of hillocks. Five guns were taken by the British on this day, but the relieving force was incessantly cannonaded throughout the 24th. The enemy's cavalry, one thousand strong, made a sudden irruption upon the baggage massed in the rear; when the soldiers of the 90th. Light Infantry, forming the baggage-guard, gallantly dispersed the whole body, but not without losing some brave officers and men.

As the troops had been marching for three days under a perfect deluge of rain, irregularly fed, and badly housed in villages, the assault on the city was deferred until the 25th. On that morning the baggage and tents were deposited in the Alumbagh, and the force advanced. The gratifying object of relieving the garrison was the result, but great loss was sustained by the constant fire from the flat-roofed and loopholed houses, the gallant Brigadier-General Neill being shot dead by a bullet; but every obstacle was at length overcome, and the troops established themselves within the enclosure of the Residency.* It was not, however, until the following evening that the remainder of the force, with the sick and wounded, constantly exposed to the attacks of the foe, could be brought in. This succour is regarded, in respect to the medal-clasps, as a continuation of the defence of Lucknow.

RELIEF OF LUCKNOW.
17TH. NOVEMBER, 1857.

Sir Colin Campbell,† who, like Sir Charles Napier, had proceeded at a moment's notice to India, did not find the

---

* Captain William Robert Moorsom, of the 52nd Light Infantry, rendered most important service in guiding Havelock's second column. This young officer had been selected in 1856 to conduct a scientific survey of Lucknow, and having preserved rough copies of it, his knowledge of the city proved of the highest importance, not only on this, but subsequent occasions, his gallantry being repeatedly mentioned in the despatches. Captain Moorsom met a soldier's death at the early age of twenty-four, at the head of a column of attack on the rebel parts of the city of Lucknow, on the 11th. of March, 1858. and the 62nd., feeling that the career of this young officer, who had been engaged in nine pitched battles and numerous skirmishes, having been twice wounded, was an honour to the regiment, erected a monumental tablet to his memory in the cathedral of Rochester. The division of Sir James Outram also erected in Westminster Abbey a memorial window to their youthful Quartermaster-General.

† Captain Oliver J. Jones, R.N., in his "Recollections of a Winter Campaign in India, 1857-8," gives the following amusing anecdote of his first peep at the Commander-in-Chief. The author was wandering through the rooms of a "strongish place" taken from a Rajah.—"In one of them I found a couple of glass candlesticks, not worth sixpence a-piece; but as my establishment only sported an empty porter bottle, I thought they would make a handsome addition, and took them. coming down stairs I met Forster—poor fellow! he is now dead—one of the Chief's aide-de-camps, who said,—'By Jove, old fellow, you'd better not let Sir Colin catch you looting—here he comes!' upon which I dropped them, as Paddy says, like a hot murphy; and in a couple of minutes after saw a Sikh walking off with my elegant candlesticks. Soon afterwards I saw the chief serving out *bamboo backsheesh* to some Sikhs who passed him with loot, with a big stick, and I rejoiced at the warning my friend Forster had given me, else, perhaps, in his wrath, he might have broke my head too."

The promising young officer above referred to, namely, Captain W.F. Godolphin Forger, of the 18th. Royal Irish Regiment, son of Major-General W.F. Forster, K.H, Military Secretary at Head Quarters., died at Lucknow on the 14th. of May, 1858, and up to that date had accompanied Sir Colin Campbell in all his battles and operations against the mutineers.

task completed, as was the case in the Punjab emergency. There was work to be done, and how nobly and successfully it was performed, is now matter of history. Troops constantly arrived from England at Calcutta, and were moved up to Cawnpore as speedily as possible, but owing to the want of transport, only slow progress was made, and Sir Colin was not prepared to proceed therefrom for the final relief of the garrison at Lucknow before the 9th. of November. By a rapid march he joined, on the same day that he quitted Cawnpore, the column under Brigadier-General Grant in camp at Buntara, about six miles from the Alumbagh. Remaining there for reinforcements until the 12th. of November, he advanced on the Alumbagh, which he reached in the evening, after having captured the guns of a body of the enemy who had attacked his vanguard.* As the direct road from the Alumbagh to the Residency was through the heart of the city of Lucknow,† wherein every street was a fortification, the houses being loopholed and filled with desperate men, Sir Colin determined to make a detour to the right, and after forcing his way through the Dilkoosha park and the Martiniere, to cross the canal to the east of Lucknow, and then arrive at the Residency by a circuitous route round the north-east corner of the city.

---

* Although this work is devoted to the deeds of the British Army, it is impossible to pass over the aid afforded to the military operations at Cawnpore and the vicinity, by the Naval Brigade, under their gallant leader, the late Captain (afterwards Sir William) Peel. Along with a small military force of about seven hundred men under Captain Powell, they were engaged on the 1st of November at Kadjwa, twenty-four miles from Futtehpore, and succeeded in routing with severe loss, the mutineers, amounting to four thousand men. On the loss of Captain Powell, who was killed in this encounter, the command fell upon Captain Peel. The duties were very arduous; after this battle, with the exception of a day's rest for the foot-sore men who had marched seventy-two miles in three days, besides gaining the above victory, daily marches had to be made in order to join the column before Lucknow.

† Mr. Thomas Henry Kavanagh, Assistant Commissioner in Oude, when serving under the orders of Lieutenant-General Sir James Outram, in Lucknow, on the 8th. of November, 1857, volunteered on the dangerous duty of proceeding through the city to the camp of the Commander-in-chief, for the purpose of guiding the relieving force to the beleaguered garrison in the Residency,—a task which he performed with chivalrous gallantry and devotion.

A highly interesting work has been written by this gentleman, showing how he won the VICTORIA CROSS, which was conferred upon him under the Royal Warrant of the 13th. of December, 1858; by which this high distinction was accorded to certain non-military persons, who, as Volunteers, bad borne arms against the mutineers in India.

On the 15th. of November, as the troops approached the park, the leading men were met by a long line of musketry fire; the advanced guard was quickly reinforced by a field battery and companies of infantry, when after a running fight of nearly two hours, the rebels were driven across the garden and park at the Martiniere, and far beyond the canal. Both the park and the latter building were at once occupied by the troops, when they sustained an attack in front, and promptly driving back the enemy, pursued them across the canal.

Early on the morning of the 16th. of November, the victorious troops proceeded to attack the Secunder Bagh, (garden or plantation) a high walled enclosure of strong masonry, one hundred and twenty yards square, and carefully loopholed all round. This post was numerously defended. Opposite to it, at a distance of one hundred yards, was a village which was likewise loopholed, and filled with men. As the head of the column advanced along the lane to the left of the Secunder Bagh, a fire was opened on it by the enemy, which was hotly maintained for an hour and a half on both sides. A small breach having been made, it was determined to storm the position, and this was effected by the remainder of the Highlanders and the 53rd. and 4th. Punjab Infantry, supported by a battalion of detachments under Major Barnstos.*

After this brilliant commencement Captain Peel's Royal Naval Siege Train proceeded to the front, and advanced towards the Shah Nujjeef, together with the field battalion and some mortars, the village to the left having been cleared by Brigadier the Honourable Adrian Hope and Lieutenant-Colonel Gordon. This position was resolutely defended against a heavy cannonade of three hours. It was then stormed in the boldest manner by the 93rd. Highlanders, under Brigadier

---

* "There never was a bolder feat of arms, and the loss inflicted on the enemy, after the entrance of the Secunder Bagh was effected was immense: more than two thousand of the enemy were afterwards carried out. The officers who led the regiments were Lieutenant-Colonel L. Hay, H.M.'s 93rd. Highlanders, Lieutenant-Colonel Gordon, H.M.'s 93rd Highlanders; Captain Walton. H.M.'s 53rd. Foot; Lieutenant Paul, 4th. Punjab Infantry (since dead); and Major Barnston, H.M.'s 90th. Foot."— *Sir Colin Campbell's despatch.*

Hope, supported by a battalion of detachments under Major Barnston, who was wounded. Captain Peel gallantly led up his heavy guns within a few yards of the building, to batter the massive stone walls. This concluded the day's operations, and about three o'clock in the afternoon of the 17th. a building named the Mess-house, after being cannonaded by Captain Peel, was stormed by a company of the 90th. under Captain Wolseley, and a picket of the 53rd. under Captain Hopkins, supported by Major Barnston's battalion of detachments under Captain Guise of the 90th., with some of the Punjab Infantry under Lieutenant Powlett. The place was immediately carried, and the troops pushed forward with great vigour, and lined the wall separating the Mess-house from the Motee Mahal. Here a final stand was made, but after an hour's fighting, during which openings had been broken in the wall, the opposition was overcome, and the soldiers pouring through with a body of sappers, accomplished the communications with the Residency. Shortly afterwards Sir Colin had the gratification of greeting Sir James Outram and Sir Henry Havelock, who came out to meet him before the action was terminated.

While the final relief of the besieged garrison had been thus achieved by the indomitable gallantry of the army under Sir Colin Campbell, the garrison within the walls had not been inactive. The mines which had been driven under the outer wall of the garden in advance of the palace, already breached in several places by the enemy, and also under some buildings in its vicinity, were exploded as soon as it was ascertained that the Commander-in-Chief was assailing the Secunder Bagh; at the same time two powerful masked batteries poured shot and shell into the palace. When the advance sounded the effect was electrical; pent up for six weeks, and subjected to constant attacks, the soldiers felt that the hour of retribution had arrived. It was impossible to withstand them, and in a few minutes the whole of the buildings were in their possession, were armed with cannon, and steadily held against all attacks.

It was now Sir Colin Campbell's great object to effect the removal of the non-combatants from the Residency, including the sick and wounded, without subjecting them to the enemy's fire. By a series of masterly arrangements, which may be regarded as a perfect example of such combinations, the desired object was attained. A fire was opened upon the Kaiserbagh on the 20th., and when the foe was led to believe that an immediate assault was contemplated, orders were issued for the garrison to withdraw through the line of pickets at midnight on the 22nd. Brigadier the Honourable Adrian Hope so ably carried out the dispositions to cover the movement, that the mutineers were completely deceived, and instead of following, they commenced firing on the old positions, many hours after they had been quitted by the British. During all these operations from the 16th. of November, the remnant of Brigadier Greathed's brigade closed in the rear, and again formed the rear guard as the troops retired to Dilkoosha, which was reached by the whole force by four o'clock in the afternoon of the 23rd. of November. On the previous day that valued soldier whose name is so identified with Lucknow, the gallant Sir Henry Havelock, died of an attack of dysentery, to the universal regret of the army and of his country.

LUCKNOW.
2ND. TO 21ST. MARCH, 1858.

Sir Colin Campbell, leaving a portion of his army at the Alumbagh under Sir James Outram, commenced his march upon Cawnpore, on the 27th. of November, 1857, and arrived at Bunnee that evening. On the following morning be received intelligence of the attack made upon Major-General Windham,—who had been fiercely engaged with the Gwalior rebels. That officer on the 26th. attacked one of the enemy's divisions eight miles from Cawnpore, routed them, and captured all but one gun. Next morning, being reinforced, they returned to the assault, forced the British within their lines at Nuwabgunge, burning down the camp of three regiments. The Rifle Brigade under Colonel Walpole, supported by the 88th. under Lieutenant-Colonel Maxwell, which suffered very severely, were highly distinguished. On the 28th. the renewed attempts of the enemy were triumphantly defeated.* Then followed the decisive battle of the 6th. of December,† when the Commander-in-chief utterly routed the rebel army, which had been augmented by four regiments from Oude, and the followers of Nena Sahib, estimated at not less than twenty-five thousand men, with about thirty-six guns.

After this action Sir Colin Campbell continued at Cawnpore until the beginning of 1858, employed in restoring order in the stronghold of the mutiny, and in preparing to advance on Lucknow. Several assaults were made by the rebels to dislodge Sir James Outram from his position at the Alumbagh, before he could be aided by Sir Colin Campbell; especially on the 12th. and 16th. of January, and subsequent months, but they were all defeated. The first portion of the army crossed the Ganges at Cawnpore on the 4th. of February. Brigadier Franks, while on his road to Lucknow, on the 19th., defeated two separate bodies of the enemy, at Chanda and Amereepore, and on the 23rd. of that month gained a decisive victory over their united forces, when attempting to capture Badshahgunge, a strong fort near Sultanpore.‡

---

* "The fighting on the 28th. was very severe. On the left advance, Colonel Walpole with the Rifles, supported by Captain Greene's battery, and part of the 82nd. regiment, achieved a complete victory over the enemy, and captured two eighteen-pounder guns.

"The glory of this well-contested fight belongs entirely to the above-named companies and artillery."—*Major-General Windham's despatch.*

† Force employed on the 6th. of December:—Brigadier Greathed's Brigade—8th., 64th., and 2nd. Punjab Infantry. Artillery Brigade—two troops Horse Artillery; three light Field Batteries; guns of the Naval Brigade; heavy Field Battery Royal Artillery. Cavalry Brigade—9th. Lancers; detachments 1st., 2nd. and 5th. Punjab Cavalry, and Hodson's Horse. 4th. Brigade—53rd. Foot; 42nd. and 93rd. Highlanders; 4th. Punjab Rifles. 5th. Infantry Brigade—23rd. Royal Welsh Fusiliers; 32nd. and 82nd. Regiments. 6th. Brigade—second and third battalions Rifle Brigade; detachment 38th. Foot. Engineer Brigade—Royal Engineers, and detachments Bengal and Punjab Sappers and Miners attached to the various brigades of Infantry.

‡ Of this battle, in which twenty-five thousand men were driven from a strong position,—leaving twenty-one guns, nine of siege calibre, with the loss on the enemy's side of one thousand eight hundred, and only eleven on that of the victors,—the Earl of Ellenborough, in the House of Lords, most eloquently remarked that, "When we hear of an electric telegraph passing under the very ground on which the enemy stood, through an unfordable river, to the distance of several miles, and that it was used for the purpose of issuing commands in the midst of a general action, that, I say, was the use of science taken advantage of by real genius. Looking at the manner

Being joined on this day by the siege-train from Agra, and all the requisite arrangements having been completed, Sir Colin Campbell proceeded direct from Cawnpore to the Alumbagh, where the army arrived on the 1st. of March. The divisions under Brigadier-Generals Sir Hope Grant and Walpole, who had been employed watching the mutineers, had meanwhile rejoined, and on the following morning the Dilkoosha palace was seized after a skirmish, in which a gun was captured from the enemy.* This palace was at once occupied as an advanced post on the right, and the Mahomed Bagh on the left, heavy guns being placed at each point to keep down the fire of the rebels. The remainder of the siege-train and additional troops arrived on the next and succeeding days; the right of the British line now rested on Bibiapore and the river Goomtee; the left stretching in the direction of the Alumbagh. Brigadier-General Franks, C.B., joined with his division on the 5th. of March,† after a march of one hundred and thirty miles, during which four actions had been

---

in which the particular battle to which I refer was fought—the battle of Sultanpore, in which the full use of the Enfield rifle and other improvements in modern warfare were developed—not only were they fighting as giants with the force of giants, but they were fighting as giants would fight who had stolen the fire from Heaven."

* Troops employed:—Head-quarters of the division of Artillery and of the Field Artillery brigade under Major-General Sir A. Wilson, K.C.B., and Colonel D. Wood, C.B. Royal Horse Artillery: Lieutenant-Colonel D'Aguilar's troop. Royal Horse Artillery; Lieutenant-Colonel Toombs, C B., and Lieutenant Bishop's troops; Bengal Horse Artillery, under Lieutenant-Colonel Turner; two twenty-four-pounders and two eight-inch howitzers of the "Shannon's" Naval Brigade; two companies Punjab Sappers and Miners. Head-quarters of the Cavalry division, and the 1st. Cavalry Brigade, under Brigadier-General Sir J.H. Grant, K.C.B., and Brigadier Little. 9th. Lancers; 2nd. Punjab Irregular Cavalry; detachment of 5th. Punjab ditto; 1st. Sikh Irregular Cavalry. Second division of Infantry, under Brigadier-General Sir E. Lugard, K.C.B., consisting of third brigade, Brigadier P.M.M. Guy, 34th., 38th., and 53rd. Foot; fourth brigade, Brigadier the Honourable Adrian Hope, 42nd. and 93rd. Highlanders and 4th. Punjab Rifles.

† The force under Brigadier-General Franks consisted of one hundred and forty European and one hundred and seven Native officers, and five thousand six hundred and forty-six men, and was composed of two companies of Royal, one of Bengal, and one of Madras Artillery; detachments of Benares Horse; Lahore Light Horse, Pathan Horse, and third Sikh Irregular Cavalry; Her Majesty's 10th., 20th., and 97th. regiments, and six battalions of Goorkha infantry and artillery.

A dashing cavalry combat occurred at Nyapoorwa, on the 1st. of March, in which Captain Aikman, commanding the 3rd. Sikh cavalry, was greatly distinguished; and on the 4th. of that month, the fort of Dhowrara was captured. This officer received the VICTORIA CROSS, see page 181.

fought, with the small lose of thirty-seven killed and wounded. Thirty-four pieces of ordnance were captured.

Sir James Outram was withdrawn from the Alumbagh, and having crossed to the left bank of the Goomtee* on the 6th. of March, at once pushed on to turn the first line of the works abutting on the river, and on the morning of the 9th. attacked the position, driving the enemy before him at all points, until he was enabled to occupy the Fyzabad road, and plant his batteries so as to enfilade the works on the canal.

Meanwhile a heavy fire was kept up by the British on the Martiniere, from the batteries at the Dilkoosha palace; and in the afternoon of the 9th. of March the former was stormed by the troops under Brigadiers Sir Edward Lugard† and the Honourable Adrian Hope. The regiments were the 42nd., 53rd., and 90th. Next came into operation the second part of the plan of attack against the Kaiser Bagh, which was to use the great blocks of houses and palaces extending from Banks's house to the former as the approach, instead of sapping up towards the front of the second line of works. By these means the Commander-in-chief was able to turn towards his own left, at the same time that the enemy was enfiladed on the right by Sir James Outram's advance. The latter had received orders to plant his guns with a view of raking the position of the rebels, to annoy the Kaiser Bagh with a vertical and direct fire,—also to attack the suburbs in the vicinity of the iron and stone bridges shortly after daybreak, and to command the iron bridge from the left banks.

---

* Force sent across the Goomtee under Sir James Outram:—Lieutenant-Colonel D'Aguilar's troop Royal Horse Artillery; Major Remmington's and Captain Mc.Kinnon's troops Bengal Horse Artillery, under Lieutenant-Colonel F. Turner; Captains Gibbons' and Middleton's Light Field Batteries; Royal Artillery and head quarters Field Artillery Brigade; head-quarters Cavalry Division and of first Cavalry Brigade; 2nd. Dragoon Guards; 9th. Lancers; 2nd. Punjab Cavalry: detachments 1st. and 5th. Punjab Cavalry, under Captains Watson and Sanford; third Infantry Division under Brigadier-General R. Walpole; fifth Brigade, Brigadier Douglas, C.B., 23rd. Royal Welsh Fusiliers, 97th. Highlanders, and 1st. Bengal Fusiliers; sixth Brigade, Brigadier Alfred Horsford, C.B., second and third battalions Rifle Brigade, and 2nd. Punjab Infantry.

† Promoted Major-General for his services on this occasion, and also when in command of the force employed at the relief of Azimghur, in April, 1858.

These instructions were carried out with the most marked success, but the enemy still clung pertinaciously to his own end of the iron bridge, on the right bank, and heavy cannonading ensued from both sides, until the bridge was subsequently taken in reverse. On the 11th. Sir Edward Lugard pressed forward in like manner. As the operation had now become one of an engineering character, the most earnest endeavours were used to save the infantry from being hazarded before due preparation was made. The chief engineer, Brigadier Napier, placed the batteries so as to breach and shell a large block of the palaces designated the Begum Kotee. At four o'clock in the morning the latter were stormed with great gallantry by the 93rd. Highlanders, supported by the 4th. Punjab Rifles and one thousand Ghoorkas, led by Brigadier the Honourable Adrian Hope, under Brigadier-General Sir Edward Lugard's direction. The whole block of buildings was secured by the troops, who inflicted a heavy loss on the enemy, and the attack was pronounced by Sir Colin Campbell to have been "the sternest struggle which occurred during the siege."

The chief engineer pushed forward the approach with the greatest judgement through the enclosures, by the aid of the sappers and heavy guns, the troops immediately occupying the ground as he advanced, and the mortars being moved from one position to another as the ground was won on which they could be placed. The buildings to the right, and the Secunder Bagh, were taken early in the morning of the same day, without opposition, and during the night of the 12th. Sir James Outram was reinforced with a number of heavy guns and mortars, and directed to increase his fire upon the Kaiser Bagh, while the mortars placed in a position at the Begum's house never ceased playing on the Imambarrah, the next large palace it was necessary to storm, between the Begum Kotee and the Kaiser Bagh.

Upon Brigadier-General Franks, C.B., who had relieved Sir Edward Lugard, and the second division with the fourth on the 12th. of March, devolved the duty of attacking the Imambarrah. For this purpose a column of attack was formed on the morning of the 14th., by Brigadier David Russell, who at the second relief of Lucknow had been severely wounded.

The Maharajah Jung Bahadoor too had joined with a force of about nine thousand men and twenty-four field guns, drawn by men, and took up his position in the British line on the 12th., and moved close to the canal on the following day. His Highness passed the canal and attacked the suburbs in his front, and considerably to the left of Banks's house, at the request of the Commander-in-chief; his troops were thus most advantageously employed in covering Sir Colin Campbell's left for several days, during which, from the nature of the operations it was necessary to mass all the available strength of the British force towards the right in the joint attack carried along both banks of the Goomtee.

Early on the 14th. the Imambarrah was carried, and the Sikhs of the Ferozepore Regiment, under Major Brasyer, pressing forward in pursuit, entered the Kaiser Bagh, the third line of defences having been turned without a single gun being fired from them. Supports were quickly thrown in, and all the well-known ground of former defence and attack, the Mess-house, the Tara Kotee, the Motee Mahul, and the Chutter Munzil, were rapidly occupied by the troops, while the engineers devoted their attention to securing the position towards the south and west. The doomed city was now hastily evacuated by the enemy, thousands of fugitives being seen to escape to the north and west. Flying columns were sent after them, and building after building which had been occupied as a defence, was successively taken, until all save the city itself was in the hands of the British.

A combined movement was organized on the 19th. of March. Sir James Outram moved forward directly on the Moosa Bagh, the last position of the foe on the line of the Goomtee; the latter was cannonaded from the left bank by Sir James Hope Grant, whilst Brigadier Campbell, moving round the western side from the Alumbagh, prevented retreat in that direction. The rout was complete, great loss being inflicted on the enemy by all these columns.

Major-General Sir Edward Lugard was directed to attack, on the 21st., a stronghold in the heart of the city, held by Moulvie. This he occupied after a sharp contest, and it then became possible to invite the return of the inhabitants, and to rescue the city from the horrors of this prolonged struggle. Brigadier William Campbell, of the 2nd. Dragoon Guards, attacked the enemy with his cavalry, when retreating from the city in consequence of Sir Edward's advance, occasioning heavy loss, and pursuing the fugitives for six miles.*

CENTRAL INDIA.
JANUARY TO JUNE, 1858.

Major-General Sir Hugh Rose, K.C.B., at the end of January, 1858, captured Rathghur, a strong fort in Central India. For two whole days, the 26th. and 27th. of January, the guns of the British played upon the walls, and when a practicable breach had been effected, the garrison, on the 28th., endeavoured to escape by using ropes to aid them in their descent. Meanwhile an attempt was made by the enemy outside to relieve the fort by an attack on the rear of the camp; this was, however, soon frustrated, and the place was taken.† On the 31st. of January a victory was gained over the insurgents near Barodia.

---

* From the 2nd. to the 21st. of March, 1858, the British had one hundred and twenty-seven officers and men killed, and five hundred and ninety-five wounded, namely:—Artillery and Engineers, including Naval Brigade of the Shannon, Royal Horse and Foot Artillery, Bengal Artillery and Sappers and Miners, Royal Engineers, Punjab Sappers and Delhi Pioneers, thirty-one killed and eighty-nine wounded. Cavalry:—First brigade—9th. Lancers, 2nd. Punjab Cavalry, detachment 5th. ditto, and 1st. Sikh Irregular Cavalry, five killed and thirty-three wounded; second brigade—2nd. Dragoon Guards, 7th. Hussars, Hodson's and Pathan Horse, six killed and twenty wounded. Infantry:—First brigade— 5th. Fusiliers, one killed and four wounded; second brigade—78th. Highlanders, 90th., and Regiment of Ferozepore, eleven killed and seventy-five wounded; third brigade—34th., 38th., and 53rd. regiments, two killed and thirty-two wounded; fourth brigade—42nd. and 93rd. Highlanders, and 4th. Punjab Rifles, twenty-seven killed and one hundred and thirty-five wounded; fifth brigade—23rd. Royal Welsh Fusiliers, 79th. Highlanders, and 1st. European Bengal Fusiliers, nineteen killed and seventy-six wounded; sixth brigade—second and third battalions of the Rifle Brigade and the 2nd. Punjab Infantry, ten killed and fifty-four wounded; seventh brigade—10th., 20th., and 97th. regiments, fifteen killed and seventy-seven wounded.

† The casualties of the second brigade of the Nerbudda Field Force during the siege and attack of Rathghur were three killed and eighteen wounded, and were divided amongst the Bombay Artillery, 14th. Light Dragoons, 3rd. Bombay European Regiment, Bombay and Madras Sappers and Miners, 24th. Native Infantry, and 1st. Cavalry Hyderabad Contingent. At Barodia the casualties were two killed, and twenty-one wounded, shared amongst the Staff, Horse Artillery, 3rd. European Regiment, 3rd. Light Cavalry, and 1st. and 3rd. Cavalry Hyderabad Contingent.

An advance was next made by Sir Hugh Rose upon Saugor, where several Europeans, amongst whom were about a hundred women and children, had been closely besieged since July, 1857. The British general arrived before the fort on the 3rd. of February, 1858, and effected its immediate relief. Meanwhile Major-General Whitlock, commanding the Madras column, had been marching towards Saugor with the same view, and reached Jubbolpore on the 7th. of that month. Thus the Bombay and Madras troops were gradually sweeping the country before them; and compelling the mutinous bands to withdraw towards the line of the Jumna, where at Calpee and Gwalior they mustered strongly.

On the 10th. and 11th. of February the fort of Garakota was captured and demolished, when Sir Hugh Rose withdrew to Saugor, which he quitted on the 27th. of February, and marched upon Jhansi.

The forts of Serai, Marowra, and Thal Behut next fell into the hands of the British. Brigadier C. S. Stuart, with the first brigade, took by assault the fort of Chandairee on the 17th. of March; the impetuous rush of the stormers of the 86th. Foot, and the 25th. Bombay Native Infantry, carried everything before them; the loss before this place amounted only to two killed and twenty-eight wounded, nineteen of these casualties falling on the first-named regiment. The Brigadier having effected a junction with Sir Hugh Rose, was sent on with a body of cavalry and artillery to invest the fortress of Jhansi, a place of great strength both natural and artificial, defended by a garrison of about twelve thousand men, headed by a determined Amazon, the Ranee of Jhansi. Sir Hugh Rose with the rest of the troops arrived before this stronghold on the 21st. of March.

On the 1st. of April the so-called army of the Peishwah advanced across the Betwa to relieve the place, but this attempt was defeated, and the enemy was pursued some distance beyond the river. This was a remarkable action, and was fought by the small force left in camp,* without relaxing

---

* Force employed at the Betwa.—Artillery, three siege guns, sixteen light field guns; 14th. Light Dragoons, two hundred and forty-three rank and file; Hyderabad Cavalry, two hundred and seven sabres; 86th. regiment, two hundred and eight rank and file; 3rd. Bombay European Regiment, two hundred and twenty-six rank and file; 24th. Bombay Native Infantry, two hundred and ninety-eight rank and file; and 25th. Bombay Native Infantry, four hundred rank and file.

in the least the arduous siege and investment of Jhansi. The victory was gained with the small loss of fifteen killed and sixty-six wounded; seven died of wounds. The casualties of the 14th. Light Dragoons were the greatest, namely, five killed and twenty-four wounded. Fifteen hundred of the enemy were killed, and all his artillery stores and ammunition were captured. Captain Need's troop of this regiment was specially commended, and Lieutenant Leith gained the Victoria Cross for having charged alone, and rescued that officer when surrounded by a large number of rebel infantry.

The assault was made on the 3rd. of April, the storming parties being divided into two columns, one of which formed the right, under Lieutenant-Colonel Lowth, of the 86th., and the other the left attack. The latter was led by Major Stuart, of the same regiment, and making its way partly through the breach and partly by escalading a bastion into the city, penetrated to the palace; here it was met by the right column, which had advanced along the streets in the midst of a galling fire from the houses on each side.* The conduct of the 86th. received high commendation. Possession having been gained of a large portion of the city by the 3rd. Europeans and 86th. Foot, these two corps occupied with pickets commanding houses, and several hand-to-hand combats occurred.†

Preparations were being made for the continuance of the attack, when intelligence reached Sir Hugh Rose that the Ranee had during the preceding night fled from the fortress, attended by a small escort; she was seen mounted on a grey horse, and although hotly pursued, was not overtaken; this was succeeded by a general abandonment of the place by the rebels, who proceeded in a north-easterly direction. Jhansi was

---

* Several standards were captured, together with a silk Union Jack which had been given by Lord William Bentinck to the grandfather of the Ranee's husband with permission to have it carried before him as a reward for his fidelity, a privilege accorded to no other Indian Prince. The soldiers who had so bravely won this flag of their country, asked permission to hoist it on the place,—a request to which Sir Hugh Rose at once acceded.

† See Recipients of the Victoria Cross.—Royal Artillery and Engineers, 86th. regiment, and 72nd. Bengal Native Infantry.

taken possession of without further opposition, when nothing could exceed the humanity shewn by the victorious troops.*

In the meantime Awah, in Rajpootana, a strongly-fortified town, had been taken by Colonel Holmes, on the 24th. of January, and Major-General Roberts in March advanced against Kotah, the Rajah of which was friendly to the British, but was coerced by his followers.

Two hundred men of the 83rd., and the Rifle Company of the 13th. Native Infantry, under Brevet-Lieutenant-Colonel Heatly, of the former regiment, were sent by Major-General Roberts, commanding the Rajpootana Field Force, on the 26th. of March, into the portion of the town held by the Maha Rao, who had been assaulted on two successive mornings by the rebels; the service rendered by Lieutenant-Colonel Heatly with this detachment on this occasion, and up to the time of the assault was prominently noticed. Late on the evening of the 28th., the 8th. Hussars, under Lieutenant-Colonel Salis, arrived.

On the 30th. of March the place was carried with the greatest gallantry, the 72nd.† and 95th. regiments leading the way. The first column, under Brigadier Parke, of the 72nd., was composed of two hundred and fifty men from each of the following regiments, namely, the 72nd., under Major Thellusson, 13th. Native Infantry, under Captain Adams, accompanied by a party of Sappers, under Lieutenant Paterson, Royal Engineers. The second column, under Lieutenant-Colonel Holmes, comprised a like number of the 83rd., under Major Steele, and of the 12th. Native Infantry, under Lieutenant Howison; and the third column, under Lieutenant-Colonel Raines, of the 95th., was

---

* Casualties during the siege and storm of Jhansi:—First Brigade;—Artillery, Engineers, 86th. and 25th. Bengal Native Infantry, thirteen killed and ninety-three wounded, including fourteen killed and fifty-four wounded of the 86th. regiment; Second Brigade—Horse Artillery, 14th. Light Dragoons, Madras and Bombay Sappers and Miners, 3rd. Bombay European Regiment, 24th. Native Infantry, twenty-six killed and sixty-eight wounded; Hyderabad Contingent Field Force, fourteen killed and thirty-nine wounded; total two hundred and fifty-three.

† Lieutenant Cameron, of the 72nd., received the Victoria Cross for conspicuous bravery on this day, in having headed a small party of men, and attacked a body of armed fanatic rebels, strongly posted in a loopholed house, with one narrow entrance. He stormed the house, and killed three rebels in single combat. This officer was severely wounded, having lost the half of one hand by a stroke from a tulwar.

similarly made up of the 95th., under Major the Honourable Eyre Massey, of that regiment, and the 10th. Native Infantry, under Lieutenant Roome, each accompanied by a party of Sappers, under an engineer officer. The reserve under Brigadier Macan, consisted of two hundred and fifty of the 83rd., under Lieutenant-Colonel Heatly, and of the 13th. Native Infantry, under Captain Steuart.

By the explosion here of a magazine fired by the rebels, after the capture of the city, Captain Robert Bainbrigge, of the 23rd. Bombay Light Infantry, Brigade-Major of the first brigade of the Rajpootana Field Force, and Captain Evelyn Bazalgette, of the 95th. regiment, were unfortunately killed.

From the 23rd. to the 30th. of March the British casualties amounted to fourteen killed and forty-six wounded—a small loss when compared with the importance of the capture. The cavalry and Colonel Blake's troop of Horse Artillery were sent in pursuit.

Major-General Whitlock, in command of the Madras column, gained a decisive victory at Banda, on the 19th. of April, over the troops of the Nawab of that place. The battle lasted four hours.* The enemy mustered about seven thousand, including one thousand mutinous Sepoys of the Bengal army, and their loss amounted to five hundred men and several guns.† Banda surrendered at once, and the Major-General then moved on towards Calpee to co-operate in the attack intended to be made by Sir Hugh Rose upon that stronghold. The latter, on the 7th. of May, attacked and captured the fort of Koonch. Marching thence to Golowlie on the Jumna, three miles distant from Calpee, a determined attack was there made by the insurgents upon the British, on the 22nd. of May, and the

---

* In addition to four killed and fourteen wounded, the 14th. Light Dragoons had eighteen cases of sunstroke, two proving fatal. The 71st. Highland Light Infantry suffered from the same cause, eight out of the nineteen cases dying from the intense heat; one day in the shade it rose to 130 degrees. Sir Hugh Rose stated in his despatch, that when a wing of the 71st. was prostrated by sun-sickness, the only complaint he heard in the field hospitals from these gallant fellows, was that they could not rise and fight.

† Troops employed in the action at Banda:—Horse Artillery, European and Native; 12th. Lancers, (left wing;) one squadron Hyderabad Cavalry, one hundred and thirty-six; detachments Royal Artillery; Madras Artillery; Sappers and Miners; 3rd. Madras European Regiment; 1st. Regiment of Native Infantry ; Detachment 50th. Native Infantry.

enemy sustained another defeat. On the 23rd. Sir Hugh Rose moved upon Calpee. Seized with a panic, the mutineers, after firing a few shots fled from the town, which was at once occupied; here was discovered a subterraneous magazine, containing five hundred barrels of gunpowder, and vast quantities of ordnance; besides which were four foundries for cannon, several guns used by the enemy having been cast there. Owing to the intense heat, the flying column sent after the rebels to the fort of Sheerghur, whither they had retired, was compelled to relinquish the pursuit; but when overtaking them on the road, they succeeded in killing between five and six hundred.

The work of the gallant Central India Field Force was now considered to be terminated, and it was announced in orders that it was about to be broken up, but there was further employment for the troops. Tantia Topee, the leader of the rebels at Calpee, had given proofs of being the most active and vigorous opponent of the British during the mutiny, being nearly the only rebel leader who had gained anything approaching to a military reputation, having defeated with great adroitness all attempts to capture him. Prior to the capture of Calpee he retired therefrom towards Gwalior, and after his arrival at the capital of Scindiah's territory, endeavoured to gain over the Maharajah's troops. A numerous body of the enemy retreated westward in the direction of Gwalior; Scindiah attacked them at the Morar cantonment near the capital on the 1st. of June, and sustained a complete defeat; his men deserted during the action, and he was obliged to take refuge in the British cantonments at Agra. After this success the rebels placed upon the musnud or throne of Gwalior Rao Sahib, a nephew of Nena Sahib.

Upon receiving this intelligence Major-General Sir Hugh Rose, recalling his detachments, marched to Sassowlee, where he arrived on the 15th. of June. Meanwhile the insurgents at Gwalior, after making themselves masters of the treasure in the capital, commenced deserting in great bodies. Even the Nawab of Banda and Tantia Topee left the place, but the valorous Ranee of Jhansi remained, attired in male costume, to head the Sepoys and the Gwalior Contingent, who alone determined to abide the fortune of war.

On the 16th. of June, Sir Hugh Rose advanced upon Gwalior, and on that day, in the action at Morar, Lieutenant Neave, of the 71st, which regiment well maintained its historical renown, was killed. Brigadiers Smith and Orr, with additional troops, arrived on the 17th. at Kota-ki-Serai, ten miles from Gwalior, where they defeated some of the advanced posts. The charge through the enemy's camp of the 8th. Hussars and the conduct of the 95th., were most highly spoken of. The infantry was commanded by Lieutenant-Colonel Raines of the latter regiment. In a hand-to-hand contest the stout-hearted Ranee of Jhansi was killed, and as her body could not be discovered, it is supposed to have been burnt. Sir Hugh Rose subsequently arrived, and a fierce attack was made on the 19th. by the insurgents, who were repulsed, and after a severe contest on the plain between the town and the heights, were completely defeated.* Gwalior was then occupied, and the Maharajah Scindiah was once more restored to his throne.

After this decisive battle the Central India Field Force was broken up, and was distributed in the garrisons of Gwalior, Jhansi, and other places. Sir Hugh Rose afterwards returned to the Bombay Presidency, prior to which, in general orders, the Commander-in-chief in India thanked him and Major-Generals Roberts and Whitlock for their eminent services.

Such is a brief account of the special services for which clasps have been awarded, which naturally divide into five acts the exciting drama of the Indian Mutiny; there are however several episodes which alone would fill a volume.†

---

* Number killed and wounded of the Central India Field Force during the operations before Gwalior, from 16th. to 19th. of June, 1858:—First brigade—fourth company, second battalion, Artillery; 14th. Light Dragoons; 25th. Bombay Native Infantry; 3rd. Regiment Cavalry Hyderabad Contingent. Second brigade—71st. Highland Light Infantry; Brigadier Smith's brigade; Rajpootana Field Force; 3rd. Troop Horse Artillery; Artillery; 8th. Hussars; 1st. Native Light Cavalry (Lancers) Bombay; 95th. regiment; 10th. Bombay Native Infantry.—Killed twenty-one, wounded sixty-six.

† One of these, the defence of Arrah, is most remarkable. Sixteen Europeans and fifty Sikh soldiers, made a noble stand against three thousand mutineers. The Europeans were Mr. Littledale, judge; Mr. Bombe, collector; Mr. Wake, magistrate; and Mr. Boyle, railway engineer,—all civilians. The first attempt to relieve them failed; on the 27th. of July portions of the 10th. and 37th. regiments, and some Sikhs, about four hundred in all, were sent up the river from Dinapore in two steamers, one of which grounded; this caused a delay, but in the evening of the 29th. the troops were disembarked. Captain Dunbar pushed on until be reached the outskirts of the town,

In this campaign there were many separate columns, which afforded officers greater opportunities of distinguishing themselves than in ordinary cases. So various were the military operations that it is almost impossible to condense them into one connected whole.

Amongst the most determined opponents of the British was the ex-Queen of Oude, commonly known as the Begum, under whom many of the fugitives had rallied. She endeavoured to gain over that active ally Jung Bahadoor, but without success. Moveable columns successfully effected the objects intended. Beni Madho, a powerful chieftain, whilst Lieutenant-Colonel Carmichael was in pursuit, was intercepted and driven across the Goomtee, by Brigadier (now Sir Alfred) Horsford, who, at the head of a separate column, had highly distinguished himself. On the 30th. of December Nena Sahib and his followers were attacked and driven through a jungle which they endeavoured to defend; afterwards across the Raptee, the 7th. Hussars entering that river with the fugitives. The Nena escaped punishment for the time, but although not taken

when the sepoys suddenly opened a destructive fire of musketry from the wood, a great number including himself, being killed, the survivors being hotly pursued to the steamer. Major Vincent Eyre, of the Bengal Horse Artillery, (author of the well-known work on the disasters at Cabool,) who was in command of a flying force, on hearing of this event, advanced from Shawpore, a distance of twenty-eight miles, and on the 2nd. of August encountered the rebels near Goojerajgunge; and although the odds were twenty to one, gallantly defeated them.

Mr. Ross Lowis Mangles, Assistant Magistrate at Patna, and Mr. William Fraser M'Donell, Magistrate of Sarun, both of the Bengal Civil Service, received the Victoria Cross for their services; the—former for volunteering to serve with the above, having, on the morning of the 30th. of July, after Captain Dunbar's death, during the retreat, with signal gallantry and generous self-devotion, and notwithstanding that he had himself been previously wounded, carried for several miles, out of action, a wounded soldier of the 37th. regiment, bore him in safety to the boats, after binding up his wounds under a murderous fire, which killed or wounded almost the whole detachment; and the latter for great coolness and bravery on the same day and occasion, in having climbed under an incessant fire outside the boat, in which he and several soldiers were, up to the rudder, and with considerable difficulty cut through the lashing which secured it to the side of the boat. On this being cut the boat obeyed the helm, and thus thirty-five European soldiers escaped certain death.

In this feat of arms, by which the gallant garrison was relieved, one hundred and fifty-four men of the 5th. Fusiliers, under Captain L'Estrange, maintained the ancient fame of their regiment, and shared with the first company of the fifth battalion of the Bengal Artillery, and the Buxar Gentlemen Volunteers, in this important result; so honourable to them and to their daring commander. Captain Scott, Ensigns Lewis Oldfield, (wounded,) and Mason, and Assistant-Surgeon Thornton, were the other officers of the detachment of the 5th. Fusiliers.

by the British, there is no reason to doubt the certainty of his death. Tantia Topee, in pursuit of whom so many long marches had been made, was ultimately captured and hanged.

Thus may the contest be said to have terminated, and the resistance of one hundred and fifty thousand armed men overcome; in no campaign had greater exertions been displayed, and more honour acquired by the British soldier.

Besides the names of Lieutenant-General Sir James Outram, Major-Generals Sir Henry Havelock, Sir Hugh Rose, Roberts, Whitlock, Sir Archdale Wilson, Sir James Hope Grant, Sir William Rose Mansfield, Sir Thomas Harte Franks, Sir Edward Lugard, Windham, and Sir John Michel, the campaign produced a number of Brigadier-Generals, such as Neill, the Honourable Adrian Hope, Walpole, Sir Robert Napier, Russell, Nicholson, Horsford, Barker, Wetherall, Jones, Parke, Rowcroft, and others, who are intimately associated with the military operations by which an extensive country may be said to have been re-conquered, and peace restored.

Lord Canning, the able Governor-General of India, and the Earl of Elgin, who nobly diverted the troops ordered for China, are inseparably connected with these events; and if difficulty has been experienced in doing justice to individual officers during the mutiny, it is enhanced when attempting to record the deeds of him who, linked with military services extending over half a century, brought this momentous struggle to a successful termination. In other times enemies had to be encountered in India, and great battles had been won, but in this instance the men had been armed and disciplined by their conquerors. No words can be more applicable than those of His Royal Highness the Duke of Cambridge, when the vote of thanks to the Army in India was proposed in the House of Lords, on the 14th. of April, 1859:—"As to Lord Clyde it would be preposterous in me to sing his praises; they are not only patent to every nobleman present, but they are known throughout the length and breadth of this country, of the continent, and in other parts of the world."

THE VICTORIA CROSS.

The Indian Mutiny, like the Crimean War, afforded many opportunities for gaining the Victoria Cross, of which an engraving and description were given in the first section of this work. The following officers and men gained this valued distinction for services performed in India.

SECOND DRAGOON GUARDS. Lieutenant ROBERT BLAIR—A most gallant feat was performed on the 28th. of September, 1857, by this officer, who was ordered to take a party of one sergeant and twelve men, and bring in a deserted ammunition waggon. As his party approached, a body of fifty or sixty of the enemy's horse came down upon him from a village, where they had remained unobserved; without a moment's hesitation he formed up his men, and, regardless of the odds, gallantly led them on, dashing through the rebels. He made good his retreat without losing a man, leaving nine of them dead on the field. Of these he killed four himself; but, after having run a native officer through the body with his sword, he was severely wounded, the joint of his shoulder being nearly severed.

SEVENTH HUSSARS. CORNET WILLIAM GEORGE HAWTREY BANKS.—The decoration of the Victoria Cross was provisionally conferred upon this officer by the Commander-in-chief in India, for conspicuous gallantry, In thrice charging a body of infuriated fanatics, who had rushed on the guns employed in shelling a small mud fort in the vicinity of Moosa-Bagh, Lucknow, on the 19th. of March, 1858—of the wounds received on which occasion he subsequently died. Had he survived his name would have been recommended to Her Majesty for confirmation. Major CHARLES CRAUFURD FRASAR.—For conspicuous and cool gallantry, on the 31st. of December, 1858, in having volunteered, at great personal risk, and under a sharp fire of musketry, to swim to the rescue of Captain Stisted and some men of the 7th. Hussars, who were in imminent danger of being drowned in the River Raptee, while in pursuit of the rebels. Major Fraser succeeded in this gallant service, although at the time partially disabled, not having recovered from a severe wound received while leading a squadron in a charge against some fanatics, in the action at Nawabgunge, on the 13th. of June, 1858.

EIGHTH HUSSARS. Captain CLEMENT WALKER HENEAGE; Sergeant JOSEPH WARD, Farrier GEORGE HOLLIS, and Private JOHN PEARSON.— Were selected for the Victoria Cross by their companions in the gallant charge made by a squadron of the regiment at Gwalior, on the 17th. of June, 1858, when, supported by a division of the Bombay Horse Artillery and Her Majesty's 95th. regiment, they routed the enemy, who were advancing against Brigadier Smith's position, charged through the rebel camp into two batteries, capturing and bringing into camp two of the enemy's guns, under a heavy and converging fire from the fort and town. Troop Sergeant-Major JAMES CHAMPION— At Beejapore on the 8th. of September, 1858, when both the officers attached to the troop were disabled, and himself severely wounded at the commencement of the action by a ball through his body, he continued at his duty forward, throughout the pursuit, and disabled several of the enemy with his pistol. He was also recommended for distinguished conduct at Gwalior.

NINTH LANCERS. Lieutenant ALFRED STOWELL JONES.—The cavalry charged the rebels on the 8th. of June, 1857, and rode through them. Lieutenant Jones, with his squadron, gallantly captured one of their guns, killing the drivers, and, with Lieutenant-Colonel Yule's assistance, turned it upon a village occupied by the rebels, who were quickly dislodged. This was a well-conceived act, gallantly executed.—(Despatch from Major-General James Hope Grant, K.C.B., dated 10th. January, 1858.) Sergeant H. HARTIGAN.—For daring and distinguished gallantry in the following instances:—At the battle of Budle-ke-Serai, near Delhi, on the 8th. of June, 1857, in going to the assistance of Sergeant H. Helstone, who was wounded, dismounted, and surrounded by the enemy, and at the risk of his own life carrying him to the rear. On the 10th. of October, 1857, at Agra, in having run unarmed to the assistance of Sergeant Crews, who was attacked by four rebels. Hartigan caught a tulwar from one of them with his right hand, and with the other hit him on the mouth, disarmed him, and then defended himself against the other three, killing one and wounding two, when he was himself disabled from further service by severe and dangerous wounds. Privates THOMAS HANCOCK and JOHN PURCELL.—The guns, I am happy to say, were saved; but a waggon of Major Scott's battery was blown up. I must not fail to mention the excellent conduct of a Sowar of the 4th. Irregular Cavalry and two men of the 9th. Lancers, Privates Thomas Hancock and John Purcell, who, when my horse was shot down, remained by me throughout. One of these men and the sowar offered me their horses, and I was dragged out by the sowar's horse. Private Hancock was severely wounded, and Private Purcell's horse was killed under him, The Sowar's name is Roopur Khan.—Extract of a letter from Brigadier J.H. Grant, C.B., Commanding Cavalry Brigade of the Field Force, to the Deputy-Assistant Adjutant-General of Division; dated, Camp, Delhi, 22nd. June, 1857. Private J.R. ROBERTS.—For bringing in a comrade, mortally wounded, at Boolundshuhur, on the 28th. of September, 1857, through a street under a heavy musketry fire, in which service he was himself wounded. Lance-Corporal R. KELIS.—For defending, on the same day and place, against a number of the enemy, his commanding officer, Captain Drysdale, who was lying in a street with his collar-bone broken, his horse having been disabled by a shot, and remaining with him until out of danger. Private P. DONOHOE.— For having, on the above occasion, gone to the support of Lieutenant Blair, who had been severely wounded, and with a few other men brought that officer in safety through a large body of the enemy's cavalry. Private J. FREEMAN. —For having gone, on the 10th. of October, 1857, at Agra, to the assistance of Lieutenant Jones, who had been shot, killing the leader of the enemy's cavalry, and for defending this officer against several of the enemy. Troop Sergeant-Major SPENCE.—For conspicuous gallantry on the 17th. of January, 1858, at Shumsabad, in going to the assistance of Private Kidd, who had been wounded, and his horse disabled, and bringing him out of a large number of rebels. Lance-Corporal W. GOAT.—For conspicuous gallantry at Lucknow, on the 6th. of March, 1858, in having dismounted in the presence of a number of the enemy, and taken up the body of Major Smyth, of the 2nd. Dragoon Guards, which he attempted to bring off the field, and after being obliged to relinquish it, being surrounded by the enemy's cavalry, he went a second time under a heavy fire to recover the body. Troop Sergeant-Major RUSHE.—For conspicuous bravery, near Lucknow, on the 19th. of March, 1858, in having, in company with one private of the troop, attacked eight of the enemy, who had posted themselves in a nullah, and killed three of them. Private R. NEWELL.—For going, at Lucknow, on the 19th. of March, 1858, to the assistance of a comrade whose horse had fallen on bad ground, and bringing him away, under a heavy fire of musketry from a large body of the enemy.

FOURTEENTH LIGHT DRAGOONS. Lieutenant JAMES LEITH.—(See page 156.

SEVENTEENTH LIGHT DRAGOONS. Lieutenant HENRY EVELYN WOOD.—For having on 19th. of October, 1858, during the action at Sindwaho, when in command of a troop of the 3rd. Light Cavalry, attacked with much gallantry, almost single-handed, a body of rebels who had made a stand, whom he routed; and also for having subsequently, near Sindhora, gallantly advanced with a Duffader and Sowar of Beatson's Horse, and rescued from a band of robbers a Potail, Chemmum Singh, whom they had captured and carried off to the jungle, where they intended to hang him.

ROYAL ARTILLERY. Captain FRANCIS CORNWALLIS MAUDE, C.B.—This officer steadily and cheerily pushed on with his men, and bore down the desperate opposition of the enemy, though with the loss of one-third of his artillerymen. Sir James Outram reported that this attack appeared to him to indicate no reckless or foolhardy daring, but the calm heroism of a true soldier, who fully appreciated the difficulties and dangers of the task he had undertaken; and that, but for Captain Maude's nerve and coolness on this trying occasion, the army could not have advanced.—Extract from Field Force Orders of Major-General Havelock, 17th. of October, 1857. Bombardier JOSEPH BRENNAN.—For marked gallantry at the assault of Jhansi, on the 3rd. of April, 1858, in bringing up two guns of the Hyderabad Contingent, manned by natives, lying each under a heavy fire from the walls, and directing them so accurately as to compel the enemy to abandon his battery.

ROYAL ENGINEERS. Corporal MICHAEL SLEAVON.—For determined bravery on the attack of the fort of Jhansi, on the 3rd. of April, 1858, in maintaining his position at the head of a sap, and continuing the work under a heavy fire, with a cool and steady determination worthy of the highest praise.

MILITARY TRAIN. Private SAMUEL MORLEY.—On the evacuation of Azimghur by Koer Singh's army, on the 15th. of April, 1858, a squadron of the Military Train and half a troop of Horse Artillery were sent in pursuit. Upon overtaking them and coming into action with their rear guard, a squadron of the 3rd. Sikh Cavalry (also detached in pursuit,) and one troop of the Military Train were ordered to charge, when Lieutenant and Adjutant Hamilton, who commanded the Sikhs, was unhorsed and immediately surrounded by the enemy, who commenced cutting and hacking him whilst on the ground. Private Morley, seeing the predicament that Lieutenant Hamilton was in, although his (Morley's) horse had been shot from under him, immediately and most gallantly rushed up, on foot, to his assistance, and in conjunction with Farrier Murphy, cut down one of the sepoys, and fought over Lieutenant Hamilton's body, until further assistance came up, and thereby was the means of saving that officer from being killed on the spot. Private MICHAEL MURPHY, Farrier.—Received the Victoria Cross for the same act; he cut down several men, and although himself severely wounded, never left Lieutenant Hamilton's side until support arrived.

FIFTH REGIMENT. Sergeant ROBERT GRANT.—For conspicuous devotion at Alumbagh, on the 24th. of September, 1857, In proceeding under a heavy and galling fire to save the life of Private E. Deveney, whose leg had been shot away, and eventually carrying him safe into camp, with the assistance of the late Lieutenant Brown and some comrades. Private PETER M'MANUS.—A party, on the 26th. of September, 1857, was shut up and besieged in a house in the city of Lucknow by the rebel sepoys. Private M'Manus kept outside the house until he himself was wounded, and, under cover of a pillar, kept firing on the sepoys, and prevented their rushing on the house. He also, in conjunction with Private John Ryan, rushed into the street and took Captain Arnold, of the 1st. Madras Fusiliers, out of a dooly, and brought him into the house in spite of a heavy fire, in which that officer was again wounded. Private PATRICK M'HALE.—For conspicuous bravery at Lucknow on the 2nd. of October, 1857, when he was the first man at the capture of one of the guns at the Cawnpore Battery; and again on the 22nd. of December, 1857, when, by a bold rush, he was the first to take possession of one of the enemy's guns, which had sent several rounds of grape through his company, which was skirmishing up to it. On every occasion of attack Private M'Hale was the first to meet the foe, amongst whom be caused such consternation by the boldness of his rush, as to leave little work for those who followed to his support. By his habitual coolness and daring, and sustained bravery in action, his name became a household word for gallantry among his comrades.

TENTH REGIMENT. Private JOHN KIRK.—For daring gallantry at Benares, on the 4th. of June, 1857, on the outbreak of the mutiny of the native troops at that station, in having volunteered to proceed with two non-commissioned officers to rescue Captain Brown, pension paymaster, and his family, who were surrounded by rebels in the compound of their house; and having, at the risk of his own life, succeeded in saving them. Lieutenant HENRY MARSHMAN HAVELOCK.—In the combat at Cawnpore, August, 1857, Lieutenant Havelock was aide-de-camp to his father, Major-General Havelock. The 64th. regiment had been much under artillery fire, from which it had severely suffered. The whole of the infantry were lying down in line, when, perceiving that the enemy had brought out the last reserved gun, a twenty-four-pounder, and were rallying round it, the regiment was ordered up to rise and advance. Without any other word from his father, Lieutenant Havelock placed himself on his horse in front of the centre of the 64th., opposite the muzzle of the gun; Major Stirling, who most nobly and gallantly commanded the regiment, was in front dismounted, his horse having become unrideable from a shell having burst; the lieutenant continued to move steadily on in front of the regiment at a foot pace on his horse. The gun discharged shot until the troops were within a short distance, when they fired grape. In went the corps, led by the lieutenant, who still steered steadily on the gun's muzzle, until it was mastered by a rush of the 64th. Lieutenant-Colonel Stirling was killed in action at Lucknow, on the 28th. of November following. Private DENIS DEMPSEY.—For having, at Lucknow, on the 14th. of March, 1858, carried a powder bag through a burning village with great coolness and gallantry, for the purpose of mining a passage in rear of the enemy's position. This he did, exposed to a very heavy fire from the enemy behind loopholed walls, and to an almost still greater danger from the sparks which flew in every direction from the blazing houses. Also, for having been the first man who entered the village of Jugdispore, on the 12th of August, 1857, under a most galling fire. Private Dempsey was likewise one of those who helped to carry Ensign Erskine, of the 10th. regiment, in the retreat from Arrah, in July, 1857.

THIRTEENTH REGIMENT. Sergeant W. NAPIER.—For conspicuous gallantry near Azimghur, on the 6th. of April, 1858, in having defended, and finally rescued, Private Benjamin Milnes, of the same regiment, when severely wounded on the baggage guard. Sergeant Napier remained with him at the hazard of his life, when surrounded by sepoys, bandaged his wound under fire, and then carried him in safety to the convoy. Private PATRICK CARLIN:—For rescuing, on the 6th. of April, 1858, a wounded Naick, of the 4th. Madras Rifles, in the field of battle, after killing with the Naick's sword a mutineer sepoy, who fired at him while bearing off his wounded comrade on his shoulders.

TWENTY-THIRD REGIMENT. Lieutenant THOMAS BERNARD HACKETT.— For daring gallantry at Secunder Bagh, Lucknow, on the 18th. of November, 1857, in having with others rescued a corporal of the 23rd. regiment, who was lying wounded and exposed to a very heavy fire. Also for conspicious bravery, in having under a heavy fire, ascended the roof and cut down the thatch of a bungalow, to prevent it being set on fire. This was a most important service at the time. Private GEORGE MONGER.—For daring gallantry at Secunder Bagh, Lucknow, on the 18th. of November, 1857, in having volunteered to accompany Lieutenant Hackett, and assisting him in bringing in the corporal above alluded to.

THIRTY-SECOND REGIMENT. Lieutenant SAMUEL HILL LAWRENCE.

—For distinguished bravery in a sortie on the 7th. of July, 1857, made, as reported by Major Wilson, late Deputy-Assistant Adjutant-General of the Lucknow Garrison, "for the purpose of examining a house strongly held by the enemy, in order to discover whether or not a mine was being driven from it." Major Wilson stated that he saw the attack. and was an eye-witness to the great personal gallantry of Lieutenant Lawrence on the occasion, he being the first person to mount the ladder and enter the window of the house, in effecting which he had his pistol knocked out of his hand by one of the enemy. Also for distinguished gallantry in a sortie of the 26th. of September, 1857, in charging, with two of his men, in advance of his company, and capturing a nine-pounder gun. Corporal WILLIAM OXENHAM.—For distinguished gallantry on the 30th. of June, 1857, in saving the life of Mr. Capper, of the Bengal Civil Service, by extricating him from the ruins of a verandah which had fallen on him, Corporal Oxenham being for ten minutes exposed to a heavy fire while doing so. Private WILLIAM DOWLING:—For distinguished gallantry on the 4th. of July, 1857, in going out with two other men, since dead, and; spiking two of the enemy's guns. He killed a Subadar of the enemy by one of the guns. Also for distinguished gallantry on the 9th. of the same month, in going out again with three men, since dead, to spike one of the enemy's guns. He had to retire, the spike being too small, but was exposed to the same danger. Also for distinguished bravery on the 27th. of September, 1857, in spiking an eighteen-pounder gun during a sortie, he being at the same time under a most heavy fire from the enemy.

THIRTY-FOURTH REGIMENT. Private GEORGE RICHARDSON.—For determined courage at Kewanie, Trans-Gogra, on the 27th. of April, 1859, in having, although severely wounded—one arm being disabled—closed with and secured a rebel sepoy armed with a loaded revolver.

FORTY-SECOND REGIMENT. Private WALTER COOK and Private DUNCAN MILLAR.—In the action at Maylah Ghaut, on the 15th. of Jannary, 1858, Brigadier-General Walpole reported that the conduct of Privatoe Cook and Millar deserved to be particularly pointed out. At the time the fight was the severest, and the few men of the 42nd. regiment were skirmishing so close to the enemy, who were in great numbers, that some of the men were wounded by sword cuts, and the only officer with the 42nd. was carried to the rear, severely wounded, and the colour-sergeant was killed, these soldiers went to the front, took a prominent part in directing the company, and displayed a courage, coolness, and discipline which was the admiration of all who witnessed it. Lieutenant FRANCIS EDWARD HENRY FARQUHARSON—For conspicuous bravery when engaged before Lucknow, on the 9th. of March, 1858, in having led a portion of his company, stormed a bastion mounting two guns, and spiked the guns, by which the advanced position held during the night of the 9th. of March was rendered secure from the fire of artillery. This officer was severely wounded while holding an advanced position on the following morning. Quarter-master Sergeant JOHN SIMPSON.—For conspicuous bravery at the attack on the fort of Ruhya, on the 15th. of April, 1858, in having volunteered to go to an exposed point within forty yards of the parapet of the fort under a heavy fire, and brought in first Lieutenant Douglas, and afterwards a private soldier, both of whom were dangerously wounded. Lance-Corporal ALEXANDER THOMPSON.—For daring gallantry on the 15th. of April, 1858, when at the attack on the fort of Ruhya, in having volunteered to assist Captain Cafe, commanding the 4th. Punjab Rifles, in bringing the body of Lieutenant Willoughby, of that corps, from the top of the glacis, in a most exposed situation, under a heavy fire. MEMORANDUM. Private EDWARD SPENCE would have been recommended to Her Majesty for the decoration of the Victoria Cross had he survived. He and Lance-Corporal Thompson of that regiment, volunteered to assist in bringing in the body of Lieutenant Willoughby. Private Spence dauntlessly placed himself in an exposed position, so as to cover the party bearing away the body. He died on the 17th. of the same month, from the effects of the wound which he received on this occasion. Private JAMES DAVIS.—For conspicuous gallantry at the attack on the above-named fort, when with an advanced party to point out the gate of the fort to the engineer officer, this private offered to carry the body of Lieutenant Bramley, who was killed at this point, to the regiment, which duty of danger and affection he performed under the very walls of the fort. Colour-Sergeant WILLIAM GARDNER.—For his conspicuous and gallant conduct on the morning of the 5th. of May, 1858, in having saved the life of Lieutenant-Colonel Cameron, his commanding officer, who, during the action at Bareilly on that day, had been knocked from his horse, when three fanatics rushed upon him. Colour-Sergeant Gardner ran out, and in a moment bayoneted two of them, and was in the act of attacking the third when he was shot down by another soldier of the regiment.

FORTY-THIRD REGIMENT. Private HENRY ADDISON.—For gallant conduct on the 2nd. of January, 1859, near Kurrereah, in defending against a large force and saving the life of Lieutenant Osborn, Political Agent, who had fallen on the ground wounded. Private Addison received two dangerous wounds and lost a leg in this gallant service.

FORTY-FOURTH REGIMENT. Lieutenant ROGERS and Private M' DOUGALL. (See China Campaign, page 189.)

FIFTY-SECOND REGIMENT. Bugler ROBERT HAWTHORNE.—(See page 129). Lance-Corporal HENRY SMITH.—For having most gallantly carried away a wounded comrade, under a heavy fire of grape and musketry, on the Chandnee Chouk, in the city of Delhi, on the morning of the assault on the 14th. of September, 1857.

FIFTY-THIRD REGIMENT. Lieutenant ALFRED KIRKE FRENCH.— For conspicuous bravery on the 16th. of November, 1857, at the taking of the Secunder Bagh, Lucknow, when in command of the grenadier company, being one of the first to enter the building. His conduct was highly praised by the whole company. Elected by the officers of the regiment. Private J. KENNY.—For conspicuous bravery on the above occasion, and for volunteering to bring up ammunition to his company under a very severe cross fire. Private C. IRWIN.—For conspicuous bravery at the assault of the Secunder Bagh on the same day. Although severely wounded through the right shoulder, he was one of the first men of the 53rd. regiment who entered the buildings under a very severe fire. Both were elected by the private soldiers of the regiment. Sergeant-Major CHARLES PYE.—For steadiness and fearless conduct under fire, at Lucknow, on the 17th. of November, 1857, when bringing up ammunition to the mess-house, and on every occasion when the regiment had been engaged. Elected by the officers of the regiment. Afterwards appointed ensign.

SIXTIETH RIFLES. Lieutenant ALFRED SPENCER HEATHCOTE.—For highly gallant and daring conduct at Delhi throughout the siege from June to September, 1857, during which he was wounded. He volunteered for services of extreme danger, especially during the six days of severe fighting in the streets after the assault. Elected by the officers of his regiment. Private SAMUEL TURNER.—For having at Delhi on the night of the 19th. of June, 1857, during a severe conflict with the enemy, who attacked the rear of the camp, carried off on his shoulders, under a heavy fire, a mortally wounded officer, Lieutenant Humphreys, of the Indian service. While so doing, Private Turner was wounded by a sabre cut in the right arm. His gallant conduct saved the above-named officer from the fate of others, whose mangled remains were not recovered until the following day. Colour-Sergeant STEPHEN GARVIN.—For daring and gallant conduct before Delhi on the 23rd. of June, 1857, in volunteering to lead a small party of men, under a heavy fire, to the "Sammy House," for the purpose of dislodging a number of the enemy in position there, who kept up a destructive fire on the advanced battery of heavy guns, in which, after a sharp contest, he succeeded. Also recommended for gallant conduct throughout the operations before Delhi. Private JAMES THOMPSON.—For gallant conduct in saving the life of Captain Wilton, of the 60th., on the 9th. of July, 1857, by dashing forward to his relief, when that officer was surrounded by a party of Ghazees, who made a sudden rush on him from a serai,—and killing two of them before further assistance could reach. Also recommended for conspicuous conduct throughout the siege. Wounded. These three were elected by the privates of the regiment. Private JOHN DIVANE.—For distinguished gallantry in heading a successful charge made by Beeloochee and Sikh troops, on one of the enemy's trenches before Delhi, on the 10th. of September, 1857. He leaped out of the trenches, closely followed by the native troops, and was shot down from the top of the enemy's breastworks. Bugler WILLIAM SUTTON.—For gallant conduct at Delhi, on the 13th. of September, 1857, the night previous to the assault, in volunteering to reconnoitre the breach. His conduct was conspicuous throughout the operations, especially on the 2nd. of August, 1857, on which occasion, during an attack by the enemy in force, he rushed forward over the trenches, and killed one of the enemy's buglers, who was in the act of sounding. Colour-Sergeant GEORGE WALLER.—For conspicuous bravery at Delhi, on the 14th. of September, 1857, in charging and capturing the enemy's guns near the Cabul Gate; and again, on the 18th. of September, 1857, in the repulse of a sudden attack made by the enemy on a gun near the Chandnee Chouk. Elected by the non-commissioned officers of the regiment. Private B. BAMBRICK.— For conspicuous bravery at Bareilly, on the 6th. of May, 1858, when in a serai, he was attacked by three Ghazees, one of whom he cut down. He was wounded twice on this occasion.

SIXTY-FIRST REGIMENT. Surgeon HERBERT TAYLOR READE.—During the siege of Delhi, on the 14th. of September, 1857, while this officer was attending to the wounded at the end of one of the streets of the city, a party of rebels advanced from the direction of the bank, and having established themselves in the houses in the street, commenced firing from the roofs. The wounded were thus in very great danger, and would have fallen into the hands of the enemy, had not Surgeon Reade drawn his sword, and calling upon the few soldiers who were near to follow, succeeded, under a very heavy fire, in dislodging the rebels from their position; his party consisted of about ten in all, of whom two were killed and five or six wounded. Surgeon Reade also accompanied the regiment at the assault of Delhi, and, on the morning of the 16th. of September, 1857, was one of the first up at the breach in the magazine, which was stormed by the 61st. and Belooch Battalion, upon which occasion, he, with a sergeant of his regiment, spiked one of the enemy's guns.

SIXTY-FOURTH REGIMENT. Drummer THOMAS FLINN.—For conspicuous gallantry in the charge on the enemy's guns on the 28th. of November, 1857, when, being himself wounded, he engaged in a hand-to-hand encounter two of the rebel artillerymen.

SIXTY-SEVENTH REGIMENT. Lieutenants LENON and BURSLEM, Ensign CHAPLIN, and Private LANE.—(See China Campaign, page 189.)

SEVENTY-FIRST REGIMENT. Private GEORGE RODGERS.—For daring conduct at Morar, Gwalior, on the 16th. of June, 1858, in attacking by himself a party of seven rebels, one of whom he killed. This was remarked as a valuable service, the party of rebels being well armed and strongly posted in the line of advance of a detachment of the 71st. regiment.

SEVENTY-SECOND REGIMENT. Lieutenant AYLMER SPICER CAMERON.— (See page 157.)

SEVENTY-FIFTH REGIMENT. Ensign RICHARD WADESON.—For conspicuous bravery at Delhi on the 18th. of July, 1857, when the regiment was engaged in the Subjee Mundee, in having saved the life of Private Michael Farrell, when attacked by a sowar of the enemy's cavalry, and killing the sowar. Also, on the same day, for rescuing Private John Barry, of the same regiment, when, wounded and helpless, he was attacked by a cavalry sowar, whom Ensign Wadeson killed. Private PATRICK GREEN.—For having, on the 11th. of September, 1857, when the picket at Koodsia Baugh, at Delhi, was hotly pursued by a large body of the enemy, successfully rescued a comrade who had fallen wounded as a skirmisher.

SEVENTY-EIGHTH REGIMENT. Lieutenant J.P.H. CROWE.—For being the first to enter the redoubt at Bourzekee Chowkee, the entrenched village in front of Busherut-gunge, on the 12th. of August. Lieutenant HERBERT TAYLOR MACPHERSON.—For distinguished conduct at Lucknow, on the 25th. of September, 1857, in setting an example of heroic gallantry to the men of the regiment at the period of the action in which they captured two brass nine-pounders at the point of the bayonet. Assistant-Surgeon VALENTINE M. M'MASTER.—For the intrepidity with which he exposed himself to the fire of the enemy, in bringing in and attending to the wounded on the 25th. of September, at Lucknow. Colour-Sergeant STEWART M'PHERSON.—For daring gallantry in the Lucknow Residency on the 26th. of September, 1857, in having rescued, at great personal risk, a wounded private of his company, who was lying in a most exposed situation under a very heavy fire. Colour-Sergeant M'Pherson was also distinguished on many occasions by his coolness and gallantry in action. Private HENRY WARD.—For his gallant and devoted conduct in having on the night of the 25th. and morning of the 26th. of September, 1857, remained by the dooly of Lieutenant H.M. Havelock, 10th. Foot, Deputy-Assistant Adjutant-General Field Force, who was severely wounded, and on the morning of the 26th. of September, escorted that officer and Private Thomas Pilkington, 78th. Highlanders, who was also wounded, and had taken refuge in the same dooly, through a very heavy cross fire of ordnance and musketry. This soldier remained by the side of the dooly, and by his example and exertions kept the dooly-bearers from dropping their double load throughout the heavy fire, with the same steadiness as if on parade, thus saving the lives of both, and bringing them in safety to the Baillie Guard. Private JAMES HOLLOWELL.—A party, on the 26th. of September, 1857, was shut up and besieged in a house in the city of Lucknow by the rebel sepoys. Private Hollowell, one of the party, behaved throughout the day in the most admirable manner; he directed, encouraged, and led the others, exposing himself fearlessly, and, by his talent in persuading and cheering, prevailed on nine dispirited men to make a successful defence in a burning house with the enemy firing through the windows. Surgeon JOSEPH JEE, C.B.—For most conspicuous gallantry and important services, on the entry of Major-General Havelock's relieving force into Lucknow on the 25th. of September, 1857, in having during action (when the 78th. Highlanders, then in possession of the Char Bagh, captured two nine-pounders at the point of the bayonet,) by great exertion and devoted exposure, attended to the large number of men wounded in the charge, whom he succeeded in getting removed on cots and the backs of their comrades, until he had collected the dooly-bearers, who had fled. Subsequently, on the same day, in endeavouring to reach the Residency with the wounded men, Surgeon Jee became besieged by an overwhelming force in the Mote-Mehal, where he remained during the whole night and following morning, voluntarily and repeatedly exposing himself to a heavy fire in proceeding to dress the wounded men who fell while serving a twenty-four pounder in a most exposed situation. He eventually succeeded in taking many of the wounded, through a cross fire of ordnance and musketry, safely into the Residency, by the river-bank, although repeatedly warned not to make the perilous attempt. Lieutenant ANDREW CATHCART BOGLE.—For conspicuous gallantry on the 29th. of July, 1857, in the attack at Onao, in leading the way into a loopholed house, strongly occupied by the enemy, from which a heavy fire harassed the advance of his regiment. This officer was severely wounded in this important service.

EIGHTY-FOURTH REGIMENT. Captain the Honourable AUGUSTUS

HENRY ARCHIBALD ANSON.—For conspicuous bravery at Boolundshuhur, on the 28th. of September, 1857. The 9th. Light Dragoons had charged through the town, and were re-forming in the serai; the enemy attempted to close the entrance by drawing their carts across it, so as to shut in the cavalry, and form a cover from which to fire upon them. Captain Anson, taking a lance, dashed out of the gateway, and knocked the drivers off their carts. Owing to a wound in his left hand, received at Delhi, he could not stop his horse, and rode into the middle of the enemy, who fired a volley at him, one ball passing through his coat. At Lucknow, at the assault of the Secunder Bagh, on the 16th. of November, 1857, he entered with the storming party on the gates being burst open. He had his horse killed, and was himself slightly wounded. Major-General Sir James Hope Grant, K.C.B., in his despatch stated,—"He had showed the greatest gallantry on every occasion, and has slain many enemies in fight." Sergeant-Major GEORGE LAMBERT, (afterwards Lieutenant and Adjutant of the 84th. Foot.)—For distinguished conduct at Onao, on the 29th. of July; at Bithoor, on the 16th. of August; and at Lucknow, on the 25th. of September, 1857. Lance-Corporal ABRAHAM BOULGER.—For distinguished bravery and forwardness, as a skirmisher, in all the twelve actions fought between the 12th. of July and the 25th. of September, 1857. Private JOEL HOLMES.—For distinguished conduct in volunteering to assist in working a gun of Captain Maude's battery, under a heavy fire, from which gun nearly all the artillerymen had been shot away.—Extract from Major-General Havelock's Field Force Orders, dated 17th. of October, 1857. Lance-Corporal SINNOTT.—For conspicuous gallantry at Lucknow, on the 6th. of October, 1857, in going out with Sergeants Glinn and Mullins, and Private Mullins, to rescue Lieutenant Gibaut, who, in carrying out water to extinguish a fire in the breastwork, had been mortally wounded, and lay outside. They brought in the body under a heavy fire. Lance-Corporal Sinnott was twice wounded. His comrades unanimously elected him for the Victoria Cross, as the most worthy. He had previously repeatedly accompanied Lieutenant Gibaut when he carried out water to extinguish the fire. Private P. MYLOTT.—For being foremost in rushing across a road, under a shower of balls, to take an opposite enclosure; and for gallant conduct at every engagement at which he was present with his regiment, from the 12th. of July, 1857, to the relief of the garrison. Elected by the private soldiers of the regiment.

EIGHTY-SIXTH REGIMENT. Lieutenant and Adjutant HUGH STEWART COCHRANE.—For conspicuous gallantry near Jhansi, on the 1st. of April, 1858, when No. 1 company of the regiment was ordered to take a gun, in dashing forward at a gallop, under a heavy musketry and artillery fire, driving the enemy from the gun, and keeping possession of it till the company came up. Also for conspicuous gallantry in attacking the rear guard of the enemy, when he had three horses shot under him in succession. Captain HENRY JEROME.—For conspicuous gallantry at Jhanai, on the 3rd. of April, 1858, in having with the assistance of Private Byrne, removed, under a very heavy fire, Lieutenant Sewell, of the 86th. regiment, who was severely wounded, at a very exposed point of the attack upon the fort; also, for gallant conduct at the capture of the fort of Chandairee, the storming of Jhansi, and in action with a superior rebel force on the Jumna, on the 28th. of May, 1858, when he was severely wounded. Private JAMES PEARSON.—For having gallantly attacked a number of armed rebels, on the occasion of the storming of Jhansi, on he above day, one of whom he killed, and bayoneted two others. He was himself wounded in the attack. Also for having brought in, at Calpee, under a heavy fire, Private Michael Burns, who afterwards died of his wounds. Private JAMES BYRNE.—For gallant conduct at Jhansi, on the 3rd. of April, 1858, in carrying Lieutenant Sewell, who was lying badly wounded, to a place of safety under a very heavy fire, assisted by Captain Jerome, in the performance of which act he was wounded by a sword cut.

NINETIETH REGIMENT. Lieutenant and Adjutant WILLIAM RENNIE.— For conspicuous gallantry in the advance upon Lucknow, under Major-General Havelock, on the 21st. of September, 1857, in having charged the enemy's guns in advance of the skirmishers of the 90th. Light Infantry, under a heavy musketry fire, and prevented them dragging off one gun, which was consequently captured. For conspicuous gallantry at Lucknow on the 25th. of September, 1857, in having charged in advance of the 90th. column, in the face of a heavy fire of grape, and forced the enemy to abandon his guns. Surgeon ANTHONY DICKSON HOME.— For persevering bravery and admirable conduct in charge of the wounded men left behind the column, when the troops under Major-General Havelock forced their way into the Residency of Lucknow, on the 26th. of September, 1857. The escort left with the wounded, had, by casualties, been reduced to a few stragglers; and being entirely separated from the column, this small party with the wounded were forced into a house, in which they defended themselves till it was set on fire. They then retreated to a shed a few yards from it, and in this place continued to defend themselves for more than twenty-two hours, till relieved. At last only six men and Mr. Home remained to fire. Of four officers who were with the party, all were badly wounded, and three afterwards died. The conduct of the defence during the latter part of the time devolved therefore on Mr. Home; and to his active exertions, previously to being forced into the house, and his good conduct throughout, the safety of any of the wounded, and the successful defence were mainly to be attributed. Dr. Home's account of this defence is most exciting, and at length when escape appeared hopeless he says, "We resigned ourselves completely to our fate. A little after daybreak, we were roused by distant firing. This time it had no effect upon us. It however approached nearer and nearer, when Ryan, suddenly jumping up, shouted, 'Oh boys! them's our chaps!' We then all jumped up, and united in a cheer, and kept shouting to keep on their right. At the same time we fired at the loopholes from which the enemy were firing. In about three minutes we saw Captain Moorsom appear at the entrance-hole of the shed, and, beckoning to him, he entered, and then by his admirable arrangements, we were all brought off safely, and soon after reached the palace, with the rear guard of the 90th." Private John Ryan, the soldier here mentioned, gained the Victoria Cross. (See recipients 1st. Madras Fusiliers, page 184.) Assistant-Surgeon

WILLIAM BRADSHAW.—For intrepidity and good conduct when ordered with Surgeon Home to remove the wounded men left behind the column that forced its way into the Residency of Lucknow, on the 26th. of September, 1857. The bearers had left the doolies, but by great exertions, and notwithstanding the close proximity of the sepoys, Surgeon Home and Assistant-Surgeon Bradshaw got some of the bearers together and the latter, with about twenty doolies, becoming separated from the rest of the party, succeeded in reaching the Residency in safety by the river bank. Major JOHN CHRISTOPHER GUISE.—For conspicuous gallantry in action on the 16th. and 17th. of November, 1857, at Lucknow. Elected by the officers of the regiment. Sergeant S. HILL.—For gallant conduct on the 16th. and 17th. of November, 1857, at the storming of the Secunder Bagh, at Lucknow, In saving the life of Captain Irby, warding off with his firelock a tulwar cut made at his head by a sepoy, and in going out under a heavy fire to help two wounded men. Also for general gallant conduct throughout the operations for the relief of the Lucknow garrison. Private P. GRAHAM.—For bringing in a wounded comrade under a very heavy fire, on the 17th. of November, 1857, at Lucknow. The former was elected by the non-commissioned officers, and the latter by the private soldiers of the regiment.

NINETY-THIRD REGIMENT. Captain WILLIAM GEORGE DRUMMOND STEWART.—For distinguished personal gallantry at Lucknow, on the 16th. of November, 1857, in leading an attack upon and capturing two guns, by which the position of the Mess-house was secured. Elected by the officers of the regiment. Sergeant J. PATON.—For distinguished personal gallantry at Lucknow, on the 16th. of November, 1857, in proceeding alone round the Shah Nujjiff under an extremely heavy fire, discovering a breach on the opposite side, to which he afterwards conducted the regiment, by which means that important position was taken. Elected by the non-commissioned officers of the regiment. Lance-Corporal J. DUNLEY.—For being the first man, now surviving, of the regiment, who, on the 16th. of November, 1857, entered one of the breaches in the Secunder Bagh, at Lucknow, with Captain Burroughs, whom he most gallantly supported against superior numbers. Private D. MACKAY.—For great personal gallantry in capturing an enemy's colour after a most obstinate resistance, at the Secunder Bagh, Lucknow, on the 16th. of November, 1857. He was severely wounded afterwards at the capture of the Shah Nujjiff. Private P. GRANT.—For great personal gallantry, on the 16th. of November, 1857, at the Secunder Bagh, in killing five of the enemy with one of their own swords, who were attempting to follow Lieutenant-Colonel Ewart, when that officer was carrying a colour which he had captured. These three were elected by the private soldiers of the regiment. Lieutenant and Adjutant WILLIAM McBEAN.—For distinguished personal bravery in killing eleven of the enemy with his own hand, in the main breach of the Begum Bagh, at Lucknow, on the 11th. of March, 1858. Colour-Sergeant JAMES MUNRO.—For devoted gallantry, at Secunder Bagh, on the 16th. of November, 1857, in having promptly rushed to the rescue of Captain E. Walsh, of the same corps, when wounded, and in danger of his life, whom he carried to a place of comparative safety, to which the sergeant was brought in, very shortly afterwards, badly wounded.

NINETY-FIFTH REGIMENT. Private BERNARD M'QUIRT.—For gallant conduct on the 6th. of January, 1858, at the capture of the entrenched town of Rowa, when he was severely and dangerously wounded in a hand-to-hand fight with three men, of whom he killed one and wounded another. He received five sabre cuts and a musket-shot in this service.

RIFLE BRIGADE. Captain HENEY WILMOT, Corporal W. NASH, and Private DAVID HAWKES.—For conspicuous gallantry at Lucknow, on the 11th. of March, 1858. Captain Wilmot's company was engaged with a large body of the enemy near the Iron Bridge. That officer found himself at the end of a street with only four of his men, opposed to a considerable body. One of the four was shot through both legs and became utterly helpless; the two men lifted him up, and although Private Hawkes was severely wounded, he carried him for a considerable distance, exposed to the fire of the enemy, Captain Wilmot firing with the men's rifles and covering the retreat of the party. Private SAME SHAW.—An armed rebel had been seen to enter a tope of trees, at Nowabgunge, on the 18th. of June, 1858. Some officers and men ran into the tope in pursuit of him. The man was a Ghazee. Private Shaw drew his short sword, and with that weapon rushed single-handed on the Ghazee. Shaw received a severe tulwar wound, but after a desperate struggle he killed the man.

NAVAL BRIGADE. JOHN HARRISON and Lieutenant NOWELL SALMON.—For conspicuous gallantry at Lucknow, on the 16th. of November, 1857, in climbing up a tree, touching the angle of the Shah Nujjiff, to reply to the fire of the enemy, for which most dangerous service the late Captain Sir William Peel had called for volunteers. EDWARD ROBINSON, A.B.—For conspicuous bravery in having, at Lucknow, on the 18th. of March, 1858, under a heavy musketry fire, within fifty yards, jumped on the sand-bags of a battery, and extinguished a fire among them. He was dangerously wounded in performing this service.

BENGAL HORSE ARTILLERY. Gunner WILLIAM CONOLLY.—This soldier was recommended for the Victoria Cross for his gallantry in action with the enemy at Jhelum, on the 7th. of July, 1857. Lieutenant Cookes, Bengal Horse Artillery, reported that "about daybreak on that day I advanced my half troop at a gallop, and engaged the enemy within easy musket range. The sponge-man of one of my guns having been shot during the advance, Gunner Conolly assumed the duties of second sponge-man, and he had barely assisted in two disharges of his gun, when a musket-ball through the left thigh felled him to the ground. Nothing daunted by pain and loss of blood, he was endeavouring to resume his post, when I ordered a movement in retirement, and though severely wounded, he was mounted on his horse in the gun-team, and rode to the next position which the guns took up, and manfully declined going to the rear when the necessity of his so doing was represented to him. About eleven o'clock a.m., when, the guns were still in action, the same gunner, while sponging, was again knocked down by a musket-ball striking him on the hip, thereby causing great faintness and partial unconsciousness, for the pain appeared excessive, and the blood flowed fast. On seeing this I gave directions for his removal out of action; but this brave man, hearing me, staggered to his feet, and said, 'No, sir, I'll not go there while I can work here;' and shortly afterwards he again resumed his post as sponge-man. Later in the afternoon of the same day my three guns were engaged at one hundred yards from the walls of a village with the defenders, namely, the 14th. Native Infantry, mutineers, amid a storm of bullets, which did great execution. Gunner Conolly, though suffering severely from his two previous wounds, was wielding his sponge with an energy and courage which attracted the admiration of his comrades, and while cheerfully encouraging a wounded man to hasten in bringing up the ammunition, a musket-ball tore through the muscles of his right leg; but with the most undaunted bravery he straggled on; and not till he had loaded six times did this man give way, when through loss of blood he fell in my arms, and I placed him on a waggon, which shortly afterwards bore him in a state of unconsciousness from the fight." Captain GEORGE ALEXANDER RENNY.—Lieutenant-Colonel Farquhar, commanding the 1st. Belooch Regiment, reported that he was in command of the troops stationed in the Delhi Magazine after its capture on the 16th. of September, 1857. Early in the forenoon of that day a vigorous attack was made on the post by the enemy, and was kept up with great violence for some time without the slightest chance of success. Under cover of a heavy cross fire from the high houses on the right flank of the magazine, and from Selinghur and the palace, the enemy advanced to the high wall of the magazine, and endeavoured to sct fire to a thatched roof. The roof was partially set fire to, which was extinguished by a sepoy of the Belooch battalion, a soldier of the 61st. regiment having in vain attempted to do so. The roof having been again set on fire, Captain Renny, with great gallantry, mounted to the top of the wall of the magazine, and flung several shells with lighted fuses into the midst of the enemy, which had an almost immediate effect, as the attack at once became feeble at that point, and soon after ceased there. Sergeant BERNARD DIAMOND and Gunner RICHARD FITZ-GERALD.—For an act of valour performed in action against the rebels and mutineers at Boolundshuhur, on the 28th. of September, 1857, when these two soldiers evinced the most determined bravery in working their gun under a very heavy fire of musketry, whereby they cleared the road of the enemy, after every other man belonging to it had been either killed or disabled by wounds.

BENGAL ARTILLERY. Lieutenant-Colonel HENRY TOMBS, C.B., and Lieutenant JAMES HILLS.—For very gallant conduct on the part of Lieutenant Hills before Delhi, in defending the position assigned to him in case of alarm, and for noble behaviour on the part of Lieutenant-Colonel Tombs in twice coming to his subaltern's rescue, and on each occasion killing his man. This occurred on the 9th. of July, 1857. Captain WILLIAM OLPHERTS, C.B.—For highly-distinguished conduct on the 25th. of September, 1857, when the troops penetrated into the city of Lucknow, in having charged on horseback, with Her Majesty's 90th. regiment, when, gallantly headed by Colonel Campbell, it captured two guns in the face of a heavy fire of grape, and having afterwards returned, under a severe fire of musketry, to bring up limbers and horses to carry off the captured ordnance, which he accomplished. Bombardier J. Thomas.—For distinguished gallantry at Lucknow, on the 27th. of September, 1857, in having brought off on his back, under a heavy fire, under circumstances of considerable difficulty, a wounded soldier of the Madras Fusiliers, when the party to which he was attached was returning to the Residency from a sortie, whereby he saved him from falling into the hands of the enemy. Lieutenant Hastings Edward Harrington, Rough Rider E. Jennings, Gunners J. Park, T. Laughnan, and H. M'Innes.—Elected respectively by the officers and non-commissioned officers generally, and by the private soldiers of each troop or battery, for conspicuous gallantry at the relief of Lucknow, from the 14th. to the 22nd. of November, 1857. Lieutenant Frederick Sleigh Roberts.—Lieutenant Roberts's gallantry was on every occasion most marked. On following up the retreating enemy on the 2nd. of January, 1858, at Khodagunge, he saw in the distance two sepoys going away with a standard. Lieutenant Roberts put spurs to his horse, and overtook them just as they were about to enter a village. They immediately turned round and presented their muskets at him, and one of the men pulled the trigger, but fortunately the cap snapped, and the standard-bearer was cut down by this gallant young officer, and the standard taken possession of by him. He also, on the same day, cut down another sepoy who was standing at bay, with musket and bayonet, keeping off a sowar. Lieutenant Roberts rode to the assistance of the horseman, and rushing at the sepoy, with one blow of his sword cut him across the face, killing him on the spot.

FIRST BENGAL ENGINEERS. Lieutenants Duncan Charles Home and Philip Salkeld, upon whom the Victoria Cross was provisionally conferred by Major-General Sir Archdale Wilson, Bart., K.C.B., for their conspicuous bravery in the performance of the desperate duty of blowing in the Cashmere Gate of the fortress of Delhi, in broad daylight, under a heavy fire of musketry, on the morning of the 14th. of September, 1857, preparatory to the assault, would have been recommended to Her Majesty for confirmation in that distinction had they survived. Lieutenant John James M'Leod Innes.—At the action at Sultanpore, on the 23rd. of February, 1858, Lieutenant Innes, far in advance of the leading skirmishers, was the first to secure a gun which the enemy were abandoning. Retiring from this, they rallied round another gun further back, from which the shot would, in another instant, have ploughed through the advancing columns, when Lieutenant Innes rode up, unsupported, shot the gunner who was about to apply the match, and remaining undaunted at his post, the mark for a hundred matchlock men, who were sheltered in some adjoining huts, kept the artillerymen at bay, until assistance reached him. Sergeant John Smith.—For conspicuous gallantry, in conjunction with Lieutenants Home and Salkeld, in the performance of the desperate duty of blowing in the Cashmere Gate of the fortress of Delhi in broad daylight, under a heavy and destructive fire of musketry, on the morning of the 14th. of September, 1857, preparatory to the assault.

FIRST BENGAL EUROPEAN LIGHT CAVALRY. Lieutenant Hugh

HENRY GOUGH.—Lieutenant Gough, when in command of a party of Hodson's Horse, near the Alumbagh, on the 12th. of November, 1857, particularly distinguished himself by his forward bearing in charging across a swamp, and capturing two guns, although defended by a vastly superior body of the enemy. On this occasion he had his horse wounded in two places, and his turban cut through by sword cuts, whilst engaged in combat with three sepoys. Lieutenant Gough also particularly distinguished himself near Jellalabad, Lucknow, on the 25th. of February, 1858, by shewing a brilliant example to his regiment, when ordered to charge the enemy's guns, and by his gallant and forward conduct he enabled them to effect their object. On this occasion he engaged himself in a series of single combats, until at length he was disabled by a musket-ball through the leg, while charging two sepoys with fixed bayonets. Lieutenant Gough on this day had two horses killed under him, a shot through his helmet, and another through his scabbard, besides being severely wounded.

FIFTH BENGAL EUROPEAN CAVALRY. Major CHARLES JOHN STANLEY GOUGH.—First, for gallantry in an affair at Khurkowdah, near Rhotuck, on the 15th. of August, 1857, in which he saved his brother, who was wounded, and killed two of the enemy. Secondly, for gallantry on the 18th. of August, when he led a troop of the Guide Cavalry in a charge, and cut down two of the enemy's sowars, with one of whom he had a desperate hand-to-hand combat. Thirdly, for gallantry on the 27th. of January, 1858, at Shumshabad; where, in a charge, he attacked one of the enemy's leaders, and pierced him with his sword, which was carried out of his hand in the *melee*. He defended himself with his revolver, and shot two of the enemy. Fourthly, for gallantry on the 23rd. of February, at Meangunge, where he came to the assistance of Brevet-Major O.H. St. George Anson, and killed his opponent, immediately afterwards cutting down another of the enemy in the same gallant manner.

FIRST BENGAL EUROPEAN FUSILIERS. Private JOHN M'GOVERN.—For gallant conduct during the operations before Delhi, but more especially on the 23rd. of June, 1857, when he carried into camp a wounded comrade under a very heavy fire from the enemy's battery, at the risk of his own life. Sergeant J. M'GUIRE and Drummer M. RYAN.—At the assault on Delhi on the 14th. of September, 1857, when the brigade had reached the Cabul Gate, the 1st. Fusiliers and 75th. Foot, and some Sikhs were waiting for orders, and some of the regiments were getting ammunition served out, (three boxes of which exploded from some cause not clearly known, and two others were in a state of ignition,) when Sergeant M'Guire and Drummer Ryan rushed into the burning mass, and, seizing the boxes, threw them, one after another, over the parapet into the water. The confusion consequent on the explosion was very great, and the crowd of soldiers and native followers, who did not know where the danger lay, were rushing into certain destruction, when Sergeant M'Guire and Drummer Ryan, by their coolness and personal daring, saved the lives of many at the risk of their own. Lieutenant FRANCIS DAVID MILLETT BROWN.—For great gallantry at Narrioul, on the 16th. of November, 1857, in having, at the imminent risk of his own life, rushed to the assistance of a wounded soldier of the 1st. European Bengal Fusiliers, whom he carried off under a very fire from the enemy, whose cavalry were within forty or fifty yards of him at the time. Lieutenant THOMAS ADAIR BUTLER.—Date of act of bravery, March 9th., 1858.— "Of which success the skirmishers on the other side of the river were subsequently apprized by Lieutenant Butler, of the Bengal Fusiliers, who swam across the Goomtee, and, climbing the parapet, remained in that position for a considerable time, under a heavy fire of musketry, until the work was occupied."—Extract of Lieutenant-General Sir James Outram's Memorandum of operations carried on under his command at the siege of Lucknow.

LATE SECOND BENGAL NATIVE INFANTRY. Colonel JAMES TRAVERS.— For a daring act of bravery in July, 1857, when the Indore Presidency was suddenly attacked by Holkar's Troops, in having charged the guns with only five men to support him, and driven the gunners from the guns, thereby creating a favourable diversion, which saved the lives of many persons, fugitives to the Residency. It is stated that officers who were present considered that the effect of the charge was to enable many Europeans to escape from actual slaughter, and time was gained which enabled the faithful Bhopal Artillery to man their guns. Colonel Travers's horse was shot in three places, and his accoutrements were shot through in various parts. He commanded the Bhopal Levy.

FOURTH BENGAL NATIVE INFANTRY. Lieutenant FREDERICK ROBERTSON AIKMAN.—This officer, commanding the 3rd. Sikh Cavalry on the advanced picket, with one hundred of his men, having obtained information, just as the force marched on the morning of the 1st. of March, 1858, of the proximity, three miles off the high road, of a body of five hundred rebel infantry, two hundred horse, and two guns, under Moosahib Ali Chuckbdar, attacked and utterly routed them, cutting up more than one hundred men, capturing two guns, and driving the survivors into and over the Goomtee. This feat was performed under every disadvantage of broken ground, and partially under the flanking fire of an adjoining fort. Lieutenant Aikman received a severe sabre cut in the time in a personal encounter with several of the enemy.

ELEVENTH BENGAL NATIVE INFANTRY. Ensign EVERARD ALOYSIUS LISLE PHILLIPS, of this regiment would have been recommended to Her Majesty for the decoration of the Victoria Cross, had he survived, for many gallant deeds which he performed during the siege of Delhi, during which he was wounded three times. At the assault of that city he captured the Water Bastion, with a small party of men, and was finally killed in the streets of Delhi on the 18th. of September.

THIRTEENTH BENGAL NATIVE INFANTRY. Lieutenant WILLIAM GEORGE CUBITT.—For having on the retreat from Chinhut, on the 30th. of June, 1857, saved the lives of three men of the 32nd. regiment at the risk of his own.

TWENTY-SIXTH BENGAL NATIVE INFANTRY. Lieutenant HANSON CHAMBERS TAYLOR JARRETT.—For an act of daring bravery at the village of Baroun, on the 14th. of October, 1858, on an occasion when about seventy sepoys were defending themselves in a brick building, the only approach to which was up a very narrow street, in having called on the men of his regiment to follow him, when, backed by only some four men, he made a dash at the narrow entrance, where, though a shower of balls was poured upon him, he pushed his way up to the wall of the house, and, beating up the bayonets of the rebels with his sword, endeavoured to get in.

THIRTY-SEVENTH BENGAL NATIVE INFANTRY. Sergeant-Major M. ROSAMOND.—This non-commissioned officer volunteered to accompany Lieutenant-Colonel Spottiswoode, commanding the 37th. Regiment of Bengal Native Infantry, to the right of the lines, in order to set them on fire, with the view of driving out the sepoys, on the occasion of the outbreak at Benares on the evening of the 4th. of June, 1857; and also volunteered with Sergeant-Major Gill, of the Loodiana Regiment, to bring off Captain Brown, Pension Paymaster, his wife and infant, and some others, from a detached bungalow into the barracks. His conduct was highly meritorious, and he was afterwards promoted.

LATE FORTY-SIXTH BENGAL NATIVE INFANTRY. Captain (afterwards Lieutenant-Colonel) SAMUEL JAMES BROWNE, C.B.—For having at Seerpoorah, in an engagement with the rebel forces under Khan Alie Khan, on the 31st. of August, 1858, whilst advancing upon the enemy's position at daybreak, pushed on with one orderly sower upon a nine-pounder gun that was commanding one of the approaches to the enemy's position, and attacked the gunners, thereby preventing them from re-loading and firing upon the infantry, who were advancing to the attack. In doing this a personal conflict ensued, in which Captain Browne, Commandant of the 2nd. Punjab Cavalry, received a severe sword-cut wound on the left knee, and shortly afterwards another sword-cut wound, which severed the left arm at the shoulder, not, however, before Captain Browne had succeeded in cutting down one of his assailants. The gun was prevented from being re-loaded, and was eventually captured by the infantry, and the gunner slain.

FIFTY-SIXTH BENGAL NATIVE INFANTRY. Captain WILLIAM MARTIN CAPE.—For bearing away under a heavy fire, with the assistance of Privates Thompson, Crowie, Spence, and Cook, the body of Lieutenant Willoughby, lying near the ditch of the fort of Ruhya, and for running to the rescue of Private Spence, who had been severely wounded in the attempt. (*Vide* 42nd. regiment, page 169.)

SIXTIETH BENGAL NATIVE INFANTRY. Brevet-Captain ROBERT HAYDON SHEBBEARE.—For distinguished gallantry at the head of the guides with the fourth column of assault at Delhi, on the 14th. of September, 1857, when, after twice charging beneath the wall of the loopholed serai, it was found impossible, owing to the murderous fire, to attain the breach. Captain (then Lieutenant) Shebbeare endeavoured to organize the men; but one third of the Europeans having fallen, his efforts to do so failed. He then conducted the rear-guard of the retreat across the canal most successfully. He was miraculously preserved through the affair, but yet left the field with one bullet through his cheek and a had scalp wound along the back of the head from another.

SIXTY-SIXTH (GHOORKHA) BENGAL NATIVE INFANTRY. Lieutenant JOHN ADAM TYTLER.—On the attacking parties approaching the enemy's position under a heavy fire of round shot, grape, and musketry, on the occasion of the action at Choorporah, on the 10th. of February, 1858, Lieutenant Tytler dashed on horseback ahead of all, and alone, up to the enemy's guns, where he remained engaged hand-to-hand, until they were carried by the British, and where he was shot through the left arm, had a spear wound in his chest, and a ball through the right sleeve of his coat.

SEVENTY-SECOND BENGAL NATIVE INFANTRY. Lieutenant HARRY HAMMON LYSTER.—For gallantly charging and breaking, singly, a skirmishing square of the retreating rebel army from Calpee, and killing two or three sepoys in the conflict. Major-General Sir Hugh Rose, G.C.B., reported that this act of bravery was witnessed by himself and by Lieutenant-Colonel Gall, C.B., of the 14th. Light Dragoons.

BENGAL VETERAN ESTABLISHMENT. Captains GEORGE FORREST and WILLIAM RAYNOR.—For gallant conduct in the defence of the magazine at Delhi, on the 11th. of May, 1857. (See page 123.)

COMMISSARIAT DEPARTMENT, (BENGAL ESTABLISHMENT.) Deputy-Assistant Commissary of Ordnance JOHN BUCKLEY.—For gallant conduct in the defence of the magazine at Delhi, on the 11th. of May,1857. (See page 123.)

BENGAL ARMY, (UNATTACHED.) Ensign PATRICK RODDY.—Major-General Sir James Hope Grant, K.C.B., commanding Oude Force, bore testimony to the gallant conduct of this officer on several occasions. One instance was particularly mentioned. On the return from Kuthirga of the Kupperthulla Contingent on the 27th. of September, 1858, Ensign Roddy when engaged with the enemy, charged a rebel (armed with a percussion musket) whom the cavalry were afraid to approach, as each time they attempted to do so the rebel knelt and covered his assailant; this, however, did not deter this officer, who went boldly in, and when within six yards the man fired, killing Ensign Roddy's horse, and before he could get disengaged from the horse the rebel attempted to cut him down. Ensign Roddy seized him until he could get at his sword, when he ran his opponent through the body. He proved to be a subadar of the late 8th. Native Infantry,—a powerful man, and a most determined character.

LOODIANA REGIMENT. Sergeant-Major PETER GILL.—This non-commissioned officer conducted himself with gallantry at Benares, on the night of the 4th. of June, 1857. He volunteered with Sergeant-Major Rosamond, of the 37th. regiment of Bengal Native Infantry, to bring in Captain Brown, Pension Paymaster, and his family from a detached bungalow to the barracks, as already recorded at page 181, and saved the life of the quartermaster-sergeant of the 25th. regiment of Bengal Native Infantry in the early part of the evening, by cutting off the head of the sepoy who had just bayoneted him. Sergeant-Major Gill stated, that on the same night he faced a guard of twenty-seven men, with only a sergeant's sword; and it was also represented that he twice saved the life of Major Barrett, of the 27th. regiment of Bengal Native Infantry, when attacked by sepoys of his own regiment.

FIRST PUNJAB CAVALRY. Lieutenant JOHN WATSON.—Lieutenant Watson, on the 14th. of November, 1857, with his own squadron, and that under Captain (then Lieutenant) Probyn, came upon a body of the rebel cavalry. The ressaldar in command of them,—a fine specimen of the Hindustani Mussulman—and backed up by some half-dozen equally brave men, rode out to the front. Lieutenant Watson singled out this fine-looking fellow, and attacked him. The ressaldar presented his pistol at Lieutenant Watson's breast at a yard's distance, and fired, but most providentially without effect; the ball must, by accident, have previously fallen out. Lieutenant Watson ran the man through with his sword, and dismounted him; but the native officer, nothing daunted, drew his tulwar, and with his sowers renewed his attack upon Lieutenant Watson, who bravely defended himself until his own men joined in the *melee*, and utterly routed the party. In this rencontre Lieutenant Watson received a blow on the head from a tulwar, another on the left arm, which severed his chain gauntlet glove, a tulwar cut on his right arm, which fortunately only divided the sleeve of the jacket, but disabled the arm for some time; a bullet also passed through his coat, and he received a blow on his leg, which lamed him for some days afterwards.

SECOND PUNJAB CAVALRY. Captain DIGHTON MACNAGHTEN PROBYN, C.B.—Was distinguished for gallantry and daring throughout this campaign. At the battle of Agra, when his squadron charged the rebel infantry, he was some time separated from his men, and surrounded by five or six sepoys. He defended himself from the various cuts made at him, and before his own men had joined him, succeeded in cutting down two of his assailants. At another time, in single combat with a sepoy he was wounded in the wrist by the bayonet, and his horse also was slightly wounded; but, though the sepoy fought desperately, he cut him down. The same day he singled out a standard-bearer, and, in presence of a number of the enemy, killed him, and captured the standard. These were stated to be only a few of the gallant deeds of this brave young officer.

BENGAL CIVIL SERVICE. MR. ROSS LOWIS MANGLES, Assistant Magistrate at Patna, MR. THOMAS HENRY KAVANAGH, Assistant Commissioner in Oude, and MR. WILLIAM FRASER M'DONELL, Magistrate of Sarun.(See page 145.)

MADRAS ENGINEERS. Lieutenant HARRY NORTH DALRYMPLE PRENDERGAST. —For conspicuous bravery on the 21st. of November, 1857, at Mundisore, in saving the life of Lieutenant G. Dew, 14th. Light Dragoons, at the risk of his own, by attempting to cut down a Velaitee, who covered him (Lieutenant Dew) with his piece, from only a few paces to the rear. Lieutenant Prendergast was wounded in this affair by the discharge of the piece, and would probably have been cut down had not the rebel been killed by Major Orr. He also distinguished himself by his gallantry in the actions at Rathghur and Betwa, when he was severely wounded. Major-General Sir Hugh Rose, in forwarding his recommendation to this officer, stated:—"Lieutenant Prendergast, Madras Engineers, was specially mentioned by Brigadier, now Sir Charles Stuart, for the gallant act at Mundisore, when he was severely wounded. Secondly, he was 'specially mentioned' by me when acting voluntarily as my aide-de-camp in the action before besieging Rathghur, on the Beena river, for gallant conduct. His horse was killed on that occasion. Thirdly, at the action of 'The Betwa,' he again voluntarily acted as my aide-de-camp, and distinguished himself by his bravery in the charge which I made with Captain Need's Troop, the 14th. Light Dragoons, against the left of the so-called Peishwah's Army, under Tantia Topee. He was severely wounded on that occasion."

FIRST MADRAS FUSILIER.S. Sergeant PATRICK MAHONEY.—For distinguished gallantry, (whilst doing duty with the volunteer cavalry,) in aiding in the capture of the regimental colour of the 1st. Regiment Native Infantry, at Mungulwar, on the 21st. of September, 1857. Private JOHN RYAN.—In addition to the act described at page 168, (5th. Foot,) Private Ryan distinguished himself throughout the day by his intrepidity, and especially devoted himself to rescuing the wounded in the neighbourhood from being massacred. He was most anxious to visit every dooly. Private THOMAS DUFFY.—For his cool intrepidity and daring skill, whereby a twenty-four pounder gun was saved from falling into the hands of the enemy. Private J. SMITH.—For having been one of the first to try and enter the gateway on the north side of the Secunder Bagh. On the gateway being burst open, he was one of the first to enter, and was surrounded by the enemy. He received a sword-cut on the head, a bayonet wound on the left side, and a contusion from the butt end of a musket on the right shoulder, notwithstanding which he fought his way out and continued to perform his duties for the rest of the day. Elected by the private soldiers of the detachment, 1st. Madras Fusiliers.

NINETEENTH MADRAS NATIVE INFANTRY. Captain HERBERT MACKWORTH CLOGSTOUN.—For conspicuous bravery on the 15th. of January, 1859, in charging the rebels into Chichumbah with only eight men of his regiment, (the 2nd. Cavalry Hyderabad Contingent,) compelling them to re-enter the town, and finally to abandon their plunder. He was severely wounded himself, and lost seven out of the eight men who accompanied him.

THIRD BOMBAY EUROPEAN REGIMENT. Private FREDERICK WHIRLPOOL.—For gallantly volunteering on the 3rd. of April, 1858, in the attack of Jhansi, to return and carry away several killed and wounded, which he did twice under a very heavy fire from the wall; also for devoted bravery at the assault of Lohari, on the 2nd. of May, 1858, in rushing to the rescue of Lieutenant Donne, of the regiment, who was dangerously wounded. In this service Private Whirlpool received seventeen desperate wounds, one of which nearly severed his head from his body. The gallant example shown by this man is considered to have greatly contributed to the success of the day.

THIRD BOMBAY LIGHT CAVALRY. Lieutenants MOORE and MALCOLMSON –Introduced in Persian Campaign, page 119.

TWENTIETH BOMBAY NATIVE INFANTRY. Captain J.A. WOOD.— Introduced in Persian Campaign, page 118.

TWENTY-FOURTH BOMBAY NATIVE INFANTRY. Lieutenant WILLIAM ALEXANDER KERR.—On the breaking out of a mutiny in the 27th. Bombay Native Infantry, in July, 1857, a party of the mutineers took up a position in the stronghold, or paga, near the town of Kolapore, and defended themselves to extremity. Lieutenant Kerr, of the Southern Mahratta Irregular Horse, took a prominent share of the attack on the position, on the 10th. of July, 1857, and at the moment when its capture was of great public importance, he made a dash at one of the gateways with some dismounted horsemen, and forced an entrance by breaking down the gate. The attack was completely successful, and the defenders were either killed, wounded, or captured, a result that may with perfect justice be attributed to Lieutenant Kerr's dashing and devoted bravery.

INDIAN MEDICAL ESTABLISHMENT. Hospital Apprentice ARTHUR FITZOIBBON.—(See page 189.)

INDIAN NAVAL BRIGADE. MR. GEORGE BELL CHICKEN.—For great gallantry on the 4th. of September, 1858, at Suhejnee, near Peroo, in having charged into the middle of a considerable number of the rebels, who were preparing to rally and open fire upon the scattered pursuers. They were surrounded on all sides, but, fighting desperately, Mr. Chicken succeeded in killing five before he was out down himself. He would have been cut to pieces had not some of the men of the 1st. Bengal Police and 3rd. Sikh Irregular Cavalry dashed into the crowd to his rescue, and routed it, after killing several of the enemy.

SECOND CHINESE WAR.
1856-1860.

The second war against the Chinese arose from various acts of aggression; amongst which the seizure of the crew of the memorable lorcha named the Arrow, was the most prominent. The operations were at first confined to the navy and marines. Admiral Sir Michael Seymour pursued vigorous measures; he opened fire upon Canton in October, destroyed several Chinese junks on the 5th. of November, 1856, and the Bogue Forts, mounting upwards of four hundred guns, were captured on the 12th. and 13th. of that month. An attack was made on the suburbs of the city of Canton on the 12th. of January, 1857, when a detachment of the 59th., employed in conjunction with the naval forces, sustained a few casualties.

Passing over the expeditions which resulted in the destruction of the Chinese fleet of war-junks in the Canton waters, as belonging to the naval historian, the period approached when the Earl of Elgin arrived at Hong-Kong as the British Plenipotentiary, to negotiate with the Emperor, and if satisfactory terms were not conceded, to carry on the war with vigour. His lordship arrived at Hong-Kong early in July, 1857, and the news of the terrible Indian Mutiny having reached him at Singapore, a portion of the force selected for operations in China was, with a noble patriotism, at once despatched to Calcutta, the Earl following them soon after with additional troops from Hong-gong.

Lieutenant-General the Honourable Thomas Ashburnham, C.B., who had been appointed to the military command of the force destined for China, having left for Calcutta, was succeeded by Major-General (now Sir Charles Thomas) Van Straubenzee. Lord Elgin was not able to act effectively until December, in which month Commissioner Yeh was informed that the British and French governments were united in their determination to proceed against Canton until the demands required were conceded. Operations were eventually prosecuted with increased vigour, in consequence of the evasive replies of the Chinese Commissioners, which resulted in the capture of canton.

CAPTURE OF CANTON.
29TH. DECEMBER, 1857.

A reconnoissance was made on the 22nd. of December, 1857, by a body of British and French troops, to ascertain the exact position and strength of the forts to the north of Canton. A similar step was taken in the course of a day or two, to gain information regarding the eastern side of the city, and a proclamation was subsequently issued, notifying that the place, if not surrendered, would be bombarded and stormed.

After a cannonade, which commenced on the 28th. of December, 1857, the troops were embarked for Kupar Creek, at the south-east of the town, which was deemed the most convenient for landing the attacking force.* This was composed of British and French troops; the former had been formed into two brigades; the first, consisting of the first and second battalions of Royal Marine Light Infantry, was under Colonel

---

* The 59th. regiment, Royal Sappers and Miners, first landed, then the French Naval Brigade, followed by that of the Royal Marines, and later in the day by the British Naval Brigade. The numbers amounted to five thousand six hundred and seventy-nine, namely, eight hundred troops; Royal Marines, two thousand one hundred; Naval Brigade, one thousand eight hundred and twenty-nine; and French Naval Brigade, nine hundred and fifty. The *mot d'ordre*, or parole, throughout the operations was "France and England." Shortly after the landing, Lieutenant Hacket, of the 59th., aide-de-camp to Colonel Graham, whilst carrying an order, was surprised by a party of Chinese, who inhumanly beheaded him, and then made off. Two of them were shot, and a third was afterwards hanged.

Holloway, of that corps; the second, composed of Royal Engineers and Volunteer Company of Sappers, Royal Artillery, and Royal Marine Artillery, Provisional Battalion Royal Marines, the 59th. regiment, and the 38th. Madras Native Infantry, was commanded by Colonel Hope Graham, of the 59th. The artillery was under Colonel Dunlop.

The landing having been effected, the enemy was immediately attacked. The East or Linn Fort was soon gained, the Chinese, after a vigorous fire, having abandoned it and retreated to Gough's Fort. The cannonade continued all day, and throughout the following night, the firing from the ships being continued. On the 29th. the east wall of the city was escaladed by the British and French, and after a considerable resistance, the enemy was driven along it and out of the eastern gate of the city, of which possession was at once taken. On this occasion the 59th., under Major Burmester, advanced as the covering party to the French Naval Brigade and Royal Marines. Major Luard, Brigade-Major to the second brigade, is stated to have been the first on the walls of Canton. The casualties were small; Ensign Bower and Lieutenant Shinkwin, of the 59th., were wounded, the former mortally.

For a week the allies occupied the walls between Magazine Hill and the south-east corner of the city, no descent being made into the streets. All this time everything appeared to be proceeding as usual, the inhabitants pursuing their avocations with the greatest unconcern, no offer of submission being made. This was soon changed; on the morning of the 5th. of January, the troops descended into the streets, when the governor of the city, the Tartar General, and the celebrated Commissioner Yeh were soon captured. The latter was subsequently sent to Calcutta.

After the capture of the Forts at the mouth of the Peiho, on the 20th. of May, 1858, a treaty was signed by the Chinese ministers at Tientsin, on the 26th. of June following, in conformity to the terms proposed by the allies.

CAPTURE OF THE TAKU FORTS.
21ST. AUGUST, 1860.

This treaty the Chinese Government refused to ratify, and the British and French were resolved to obtain that result. In the first instance persuasion and diplomatic efforts were resorted to, but without success. Every attempt at negotiation having proved fruitless, recourse was again had to arms, Major-General Sir James Hope Grant, K.C.B., so distinguished during the Indian Mutiny, being appointed to the command, with the local rank of Lieutenant-General. On the 1st. of August the troops landed at Pehtang, which they quitted on the 12th., and on that morning Major-General Sir Robert Napier commanding the second division, encountered the enemy at Sin-ho. In this action the Armstrong guns were first used in war. The attack of the entrenched fortified camp of Tangku occurred on the 14th. of August, and on the 20th. orders were issued for the attack of the North Taku Forts, by a force composed of British and French troops, about fifteen hundred of each. The 44th., 67th., and Royal Marines, under Sir Robert Napier represented the British quota; there was however a heavy train of field artillery, comprising several eight-inch mortars and two Armstrong batteries. In the evening the gun-boats took up their positions, and the troops having crossed a flat and muddy plain, the night was employed in throwing up trenches and batteries. Such alacrity was shewn by the Chinese for the fight, that early in the morning of the 21st. of August they opened fire upon the troops an hour before the time fixed upon by the Allies; this was followed by a tremendous bombardment in reply, aided by the gun-boats, which pitched shell and rockets into the North Fort. The assault then took place.* The place was defended with great

---

* The storming party consisted of a wing of the 44th., under Lieutenant-Colonel Mac Mahon, and one of the 67th., under Lieutenant-Colonel Thomas, supported by the other wings of those two regiments and the Royal Marines, under Lieutenant-Colonel Gascoigne. A detachment of the latter, under Lieutenant-Colonel Travers, carried a pontoon bridge for crossing the wet ditches, and Major Graham, of the Royal Engineers, conducted the assault. The whole were commanded by Brigadier Reeves, who, although severely wounded in three places, did not quit the field until he had conducted his men into the fort.

determination, although the grand magazine had exploded from the fire of the British artillery. At length the regiments* before named, in conjunction with the French, gained a footing on the walls. Even then the Tartars fought with noble intrepidity, but eventually they endeavoured to take refuge in the next fort about half a mile distant, although few succeeded in the attempt. Their loss was at least three thousand; the British casualties were seventeen killed, and one hundred and fifty-eight wounded; their allies had about thirty killed and upwards of one hundred wounded. Four hundred guns were taken, and the capture of this strong fort caused the Chinese the same afternoon to surrender the others, together with the province of Pecheli, upon a cessation of hostilities being granted.

OCCUPATION OF PEKIN.
13TH. OCTOBER, 1860.

Tientsin was reached by the allies on the 6th. of September, when the Chinese authorities as usual endeavoured to

---

* The following officers and men gained the VICTORIA CROSS for acts of bravery performed on the occasion of the assault and capture of the North Taku Fort :—44th. regiment—Lieutenant ROBERT MONTRESOR ROGERS and Private JOHN M'DOUGALL. 67th. regiment—Lieutenant EDMUND HENRY LENON.—For distinguished gallantry in swimming the ditches, and entering the North Taku Fort by an embrasure during the assault. They were the first of the English established on the walls of the fort, which they entered in the order in which their names are here recorded, each one being assisted by the others to mount the embrasure. 67th. regiment—Lieutenant NATH IEL BURSLEM and Private THOMAS LANE.—For similar gallantry, and for persevering n attempting during the assault, and before the entrance of the fort had been effected by any one, to enlarge an opening in the wall, through which they eventually entered, and, in doing so, were both severely wounded. 67th. regiment—Ensign JOHN WORTHY CHAPLIN— For distinguished gallantry at the North Taku Fort. This officer was carrying the Queen's colour of the regiment, and first planted the colours on the breach made by the storming party, assisted by Private Lane, of the 67th., and subsequently on the cavalier of the fort, which he was the first to mount. In doing this he was severely wounded. Indian Medical Establishment.—Hospital Apprentice ARTHUR FITZGIBRON.—For having behaved with great coolness and courage at the capture of the North Taku Fort; he accompanied a wing of the 67th. regiment, when it took up a position within five hundred yards of the fort, and having quitted cover, he proceeded, under a very heavy fire, to attend to a dooly-bearer, whose wound he had been directed to bind up; and while the regiment was advancing under the enemy's fire, he ran across the open to attend to another wounded man, in doing which he was himself severely wounded.

gain time by negotiation. On arrival at the encamping ground, it was found occupied by a large Chinese army, while batteries had been hastily thrown up; Mr. Parkes, (accompanied by Lieutenant Anderson, of Fane's Irregular Horse, Mr. De Norman, and Mr. Bowlby, the special correspondent of "The Times," whose vigorous reports were of such universal interest, proceeded to Tang-chow to ascertain the reason of this threatening attitude. Mr. Loch, accompanied by Captain Brabazon, Deputy-Assistant Quartermaster-General, were afterwards despatched under a flag of truce to order them to return. Meanwhile the Chinese line opened fire, and an action ensued, when their troops, far superior in numbers, were dispersed, the enemy losing six hundred men, and seventy-five guns. This action was fought on the Chow-Ho on the 18th. of September, and another occurred on the 21st. of September, on which day the 1st. or King's Dragoon Guards performed "very excellent service."* The Chinese entrenched camp was taken, and they were driven back upon Pekin. Nearly six hundred pieces of cannon were captured by the allies during these operations. Continuing the advance on that city, a portion of the French army occupied the famed Summer Palace of the Emperor. On the 7th. of October the Chinese were informed, that if the prisoners were not restored, and one of the gates of Pekin delivered up, the city would be stormed.

---

* The late Lord Herbert, in his first speech in the House of Lords in moving the vote of thanks to the Forces in China, alluded to this service:—"The Tartar cavalry had posted themselves upon an eminence, which had a sudden fall at the foot of it, and in the deepest part they had made a ditch. They evidently thought our cavalry could not pass this ditch, and that they should be able to pick off our men as they came up with the greatest ease with their matchlocks. The spot has been described to me by an eye witness as what would be called, in hunting phraseology, "a very ugly place," one which very many would have looked at twice, and which very few would have gone at. The probability is that the majority of the field would have gone round, and attained their object in some other way. The 1st. Dragoon Guards however rode at it, and so successfully, that they cleared the place without more than one or two men getting out of the ranks. This struck dismay into the Tartars, who had no conception such a feat was possible, and they instantly scattered themselves all over the plain. A Chinese force afterwards attempted to clear the place, as our men had, but they utterly failed, and fell back into the ditch. It is said to have been singular to witness the great respect the enemy always paid to our cavalry, whether regulars or irregulars, but the alarm depicted in their countenances, and their sudden change of tactics whenever our Dragoon Guards afterwards came into the field, was something remarkable."

This was agreed to, and a force of two hundred French and British took peaceable possession of the gate at noon on the 13th. of October. This operation concluded the campaign. The crowning result was that the former treaty was ratified, a large sum of money was paid by the Chinese, and such prisoners as survived were released. Some of them, however, died from the savage treatment they experienced, and amongst them were Mr. De Norman, Lieutenant Anderson, Mr. Bowlby, and Captain Brabazon.*

MEDAL FOR SECOND CHINESE WAR.

On the 6th. of March, 1861, the Queen was pleased to command

---

* Corps employed against Canton, in 1857, and the Taku Forts and Pekin, in 1860. Those present at CANTON, TAKU FORTS, PEKIN, (as shewn by the figure 1,) have been authorised to bear the names of these places on their regimental colours; the 60th. being Rifles, have them on their appointments. The Artillery, Engineers, and Marines have a general motto, and do not receive such distinctions—

Corps.	Canton	Taku Forts.	Pekin.	
Royal Artillery (a)	1	1	1	Two Companies.
Madras Artillery	...	1	...	
Royal Engineers (b)	1	1	1	
Madras Engineers	...	1	...	Two Companies.
1st. King's Dragoon Guards	...	1	1	Two Squadrons.
1st. Sikh Irregular Cavalry,	...	1	1	Head-quarters.
now 11th. Bengal Cavalry				
Fane's Horse	...	1	1	”
now 19th. Bengal Cavalry				
1st, batt. Military Train	...	1	1	”
1st. (Royal) Reg., 2nd. batt	...	1	1	”
2nd. (Queen's) Reg., 1st. batt.	...	1	1	”
3rd. (Buffs) Reg., 1st. batt	...	1	...	”
31st. Regiment	...	1	...	”
44th. Regiment	...	1	...	”
59th. Regiment	1	...	...	”
60th. Regiment 2nd. batt	...	1	1	”
67th Regiment	...	1	1	”
99th. Regiment	...	...	1	”
Royal Marines (c)	1	1	...	”
8th. Punjab Infantry, now 20th	...	1	1	Head-quarters
15th. Punjab Infantry now 22nd	...	1	1	”
88th. Madras Native Infantry (d)	1	...	...	”

a Three batteries at Canton, nine at Taku Forts, five at Pekin.
b Half a Company at Canton, two and a half Companies at Taku and Pekin.
c Three battalions at Canton, one at Taku Forts.
d Detachment of two officers and forty men; being so small a portion of the corps, the word CANTON was not authorised for the regiment.

that a medal should be bestowed upon all the officers and soldiers of Her Majesty's Army and the Indian Forces employed in the foregoing operations. The medal is similar to that granted for the first Chinese War, (page 121,) except that the date 1842, on the reverse, is omitted. The ribbon is the same, namely, scarlet with yellow edges. The clasps are of the same pattern as those for the Mutiny Medal, and are inscribed CANTON, 1857, TARU FORTS, 1860, and PEKIN, 1860.* An additional clasp having thereon CHINA, 1842, was authorized for such of the recipients of the first medal as had been engaged in the second Chinese War.

––––––––

The Chinese Campaign brings the MEDALS OF THE BRITISH ARMY to a conclusion, and although this service cannot be regarded with the same absorbing interest attaching to the Indian Mutiny, yet it forms a glorious addition to the annals of War, being not only remarkable for the first effective employment of Armstrong guns, but also for the success of the sanitary measures adopted to preserve the health of the troops in so distant a quarter of the globe; and above all for the cordial union existing between the allied commanders, Sir Hope Grant and General Montauban. All must trust that the armies of France and England may never be otherwise employed than for the mutual glory of both countries, in the maintenance of one common cause, and in the promotion of the best interests of mankind.

––––––––

* Clasps for FATSHAN, 1857, and TAKU FORTS, 1858, were authorized for the Navy and Marines, but are not specified above, as they were granted expressly for Naval operations.